A Theology of Disagreement

New Testament Ethics for Ecclesial Conflicts

Christopher Landau

scm press

© Christopher Landau 2021
Published in 2021 by SCM Press
Editorial office
3rd Floor, Invicta House,
108–114 Golden Lane,
London EC1Y 0TG, UK
www.scmpress.co.uk

SCM Press is an imprint of Hymns Ancient & Modern Ltd
(a registered charity)

HYMNS Ancient
&Modern

Hymns Ancient & Modern® is a registered trademark of
Hymns Ancient & Modern Ltd
13A Hellesdon Park Road, Norwich,
Norfolk NR6 5DR, UK

British Library Cataloguing in Publication data

A catalogue record for this book is available
from the British Library

978-0-334-06045-1

Typeset by Regent Typesetting
Printed and bound by
CPI Group (UK) Ltd

Contents

Acknowledgements

I begin with a perhaps curious debt of gratitude: to disagreeing Christians. Had it not been for my years as a BBC correspondent, I would not have known first-hand of so many instances where neighbour-love was strikingly absent from ecclesial disagreements. Years of conversations and interviews had a cumulative impact, prompting me to ask this book's foundational questions about how Christians approach their inevitable disagreements.

Personal thanks must go above all to Carolyn, my wife. When this project began, we were a youngish couple at theological college; in the years since the completion of the DPhil that underpins this book, we have grown to a noisy family of five. (Plus our faithful cat, Benedictus, who has witnessed it all.)

Re-engaging with the academic study of theology after an eight-year gap was challenging, but the process was aided in particular by my gracious and ever-insightful supervisor, the Revd Professor Nigel Biggar. I also wish to acknowledge the various bodies that funded my doctoral study: the Church of England Research Degrees Panel; the University of Oxford Squire and Marriott Fund; the Lady Peel Charitable Trust; and the St Luke's College Foundation.

It might sound pious, finally, to thank God. But for this journalist-turned-priest, the way my faith came alive during my twenties was both unexpected and thrilling. My intention was always to engage in theological study that helps build up the church; I hope and pray that *A Theology of Disagreement* can encourage the pursuit of loving unity – even with my Christian neighbours with whom I disagree.

The Revd Dr Christopher Landau
Oxford, Lent 2021

Introduction

When any movement abandons a commitment that is foundational to its very self, profound problems follow.

It is the contention of this book that disagreeing Christians too easily overlook the call to loving unity within the Body of Christ, found consistently within the pages of the New Testament.

But it is not as if Christians are alone in abandoning foundational narratives. In October 1998, little more than a year after the Labour Party had won a landslide general election victory after 18 years in opposition, the Secretary of State for Trade and Industry, Peter Mandelson, was on a visit to California's 'Silicon Valley'. He told a group of computer executives that he was 'intensely relaxed about people getting filthy rich – as long as they pay their taxes'.[1]

That short phrase, 'intensely relaxed', has haunted Mr, now Lord, Mandelson,[2] for it seemed to encapsulate the way in which Britain's socialist political party had strayed far from its founding narrative. As the then historian, and future Labour MP, Tristram Hunt noted in a newspaper column, 'Downing Street advances something called "grown-up liberalism" in place of paternalist socialism.'[3]

Peter Mandelson's phrase offers a telling example of a movement losing sight of a core living element of its historic purpose. Whatever one's political affiliations, it is clear that there is nothing particularly resonant with socialism in the words of a politician who is 'intensely relaxed about people getting filthy rich'.

This book suggests that the Labour Party was not alone in veering away from its founding narrative. To borrow Mandelson's phrase, the church has also become 'intensely relaxed' about abandoning attempts to sustain the love by which, as Jesus tells his followers, others 'will know that you are my disciples'.[4]

Even the most casual contemporary observer of Christianity can easily recognize that this notion of Christian community being identifiable through the mutual love of its members – exactly Jesus' assertion in John 13.35 – is difficult to reconcile with the schismatic reality of current ecclesial life, dominated in the public sphere by divisive debates on matters such as gender or sexuality.

In his first public words having been appointed as Archbishop of Canterbury in 2012, reflecting on the Church of England's damaging divisions over the ordination of women to the episcopate, Justin Welby said that he wanted the church to be 'a place where we can disagree in love'.[5] That is no small ambition. The scale of strained relationships among the world's Christians might easily lead us to infer that 'love your neighbour' no longer applies within the church – particularly if that neighbour is a fellow Christian with whom you disagree, and you have the opportunity to disagree in public. The central contention of this book is that the church is yet to find a coherent theology of disagreement, which might enable it to face its inevitable disagreements in a way that is reflective of the love that it claims to have at its very foundations.

This book follows, and critiques, the methodological approach of Richard Hays in *The Moral Vision of the New Testament*[6] in order to establish how New Testament texts might inform a theological ethic of disagreement. My approach centres on a frank recognition that many, if not most, Christian disagreements find their roots in divergent approaches to the Bible. In the sense that this book wishes to demonstrate, as well as articulate, its theological approach, it is logical to assume a biblical focus. If Christian disagreement is often based on the Bible, it seems self-evident that an effective theology of disagreement will need to grow out of a robust engagement with Scripture, providing some sort of basis upon which disagreeing Christians might (however reluctantly) agree as to how the issue of disagreement might be faced.

Chapters 1–5 examine instances of disagreement and texts of relevance to disagreement within the New Testament, following Hays' 'descriptive' task. Part 2 begins by evaluating Hays' methodology, and then proposes a theology of disagreement arising from the New Testament text. Part 3 undertakes what Hays describes as the 'pragmatic task' of living the text – so I relate a theology of disagreement to illustrative examples of the church's public theological witness, its understanding of pneumatology, and its liturgy. I thus affirm the role of tradition, reason and experience in the construction and shaping of a Christian ethic – a role given insufficient attention by Hays. In so doing, I demonstrate the ways in which sources of authority beyond the Bible, and the lived experience of the church, contribute to the formulation of Christian ethics. I will argue, in particular, that pneumatological concerns deserve greater prominence in moral theological discourse. But first we need to consider our principal context, of Christian engagement with the New Testament in pursuit of moral wisdom, not least as the arena in which Richard Hays' work has made such a defining contribution.

The authority of the Bible in Christian moral theology

The Moral Vision of the New Testament has had such a considerable impact, attracting superlative plaudits,[7] because it maintains a confidence in scripturally rooted ethics that had otherwise been widely waning within Christian ethics in preceding years. Although it is beyond the scope of this book to offer a full account of this context into which Richard Hays wrote, it is worth noting some of the key themes within theological ethics that prompted Hays' intervention. In particular, James Gustafson's seminal essay, 'The Place of Scripture in Christian Ethics: A Methodological Study' – which influenced Hays' approach[8] – offers a key insight into some of the methodological questions being faced about the place of Scripture in moral theological reflection. This then leads into a discussion concerning the relationship between Christian ethics and the church; finally, Kathryn Tanner's observations about the 'plain sense' of Scripture offer a theoretical underpinning to the basic approach to appraising the narrative of the New Testament as made by Richard Hays and followed here.

Writing in 1970, James Gustafson's consideration of the place of Scripture in Christian ethics usefully demonstrates the sorts of problems we confront as we prepare to analyse Richard Hays' confident claim that moral coherence can be found as a result of reading the New Testament. Gustafson outlined two key factors requiring further reflection: questions concerning the self-understanding of 'Christian ethics', and the ways that Scripture is approached by that discipline's practitioners. Gustafson encouraged a broadening of perspective beyond a restrictive focus on the morality of specific acts: if 'one includes in ethics a concern for the formation of the moral agent, then Scripture will be used in a quite different way'.[9] This move – anticipating a renewed scholarly interest in virtue ethics – broadens the gaze of a reader of Scripture in search of texts that might prompt moral reflection. It is an approach that demonstrates why texts that are not themselves laden with ethical specificities (not least, in our case, the Gospel of John) are nonetheless valuable.

Ethics is rightly seen, then, as considering the formation of Christian disciples and the exploration of the factors that inform the moral decisions made by those disciples – and it would be absurd to suggest that the only relevant texts for such studies are those dealing with specific moral cases, even though such cases remain an important element of Christian ethical reflection. On this point, Gustafson resonates with the sort of appeal we shall examine from Hays in relation to the power and potential of allegory and metaphor. But Gustafson's approach, in practice, becomes fraught with difficulties.[10] Crucially, for Gustafson, 'Scripture *alone* is never the final court of appeal for Christian Ethics', but it 'deeply informs' the judgements of 'finite moral agents responsible to God'.[11] These final remarks encapsulate the nature of our problem. Gustafson does not wish to abandon the moral relevance of Scripture such that it has no role at all to play in moral formation; but his scheme creates space for everything from biblical literalism to the most tentative Christian nominalism – and little guidance is offered when it comes to determining which critical approach should be used in any specific instance.

In our own context of the consideration of a theology of disagreement, Gustafson's approach is particularly limiting – for it provides no basis upon which the adjudication of a Christian disagreement might be proposed with regard to Scripture, or any precise terms upon which the Bible might be read in search of principles to apply to questions of ecclesial disagreement or disunity. This gives rise to questions about the confidence that scholars might have in Christian ethics as a discipline that can provide a robust framework within which a biblical text may be analysed for the purposes of moral reflection: the scale and continuing prominence of ecclesial disagreement throughout the history of the church might simply lead to a conclusion that there is no single approach to the Bible that can have the realistic aim of resourcing the discussion on mutually agreed terms. Gustafson does at least affirm that the church as ecclesial community should be recognized as the principal location for biblical reflection – but he does little to suggest the parameters within which the church might undertake its engagement with Scripture.

The implications of this are worth considering. Stephen Mott points out that 'objections to using the New Testament for contemporary social ethics come from both ends of the theological spectrum', but in the face of theologians' caution, he poses this question: 'Great numbers of Christians who have been active for social change and social service consider the New Testament to be foundational to their efforts. Great Christian social movements have drawn upon it. Have they been deceived about what has guided their behaviour and in the process misused the biblical documents?'[12] It is an extremely important question, for it raises the implications of a situation where the study of theology is too often perceived as being divorced from the life of the church. Whether or not this is seen as a problem is itself contested, but Christian ethicists should be reminded that while they dispute among themselves the status of biblical texts, church communities continue to use those texts to inform ethical decision-making – with varying levels of sophistication.

There is a basic and problematic contrast between the way that the New Testament is approached in scholarly and ecclesial contexts. And although generalization in this regard can be unhelpful, Lisa Sowle Cahill makes the straightforward and important point that 'it is within the church as faith community that the Scriptures assume authority; the church is the community defined by its allegiance to the Scriptures or as shaped by scriptural witness'.[13] She contrasts this ongoing authority afforded to the Bible within the worshipping community with the approach of contemporary ethicists, who 'still have not reached precision about the ways in which the biblical literature functions as an authority for that community'.[14] She suggests that Gustafson's contribution was to affirm 'a more communal and practical understanding both of biblical authority and of the interworking of biblical and other sources in forming the Christian moral perspective'.[15]

This book will later demonstrate that a key weakness in Richard Hays' approach is his relative lack of interest in sources of wisdom beyond the Bible. But such an observation should not undermine his defence of the task of discerning Christian ethics rooted in the New Testament. He assumes such a clear biblical focus partly in response to the inconsistencies of approach to the Bible he identifies among contemporary ethicists, theologians, and church leaders, and partly out of determination to show that theological ethics can, and should, be grounded in the texts at the heart of Christian life.[16] Similar concerns prompted Stanley Hauerwas to write a gospel commentary; he is emphatic about the importance of specifically *theological* engagement with Scripture, undertaken to build up the life of the church: 'We are dying – and I mean quite literally we are dying – for examples of what reading Scripture theologically might look like. Scripture, vivified by the Holy Spirit, is at the heart of the Church. Without a heart we cannot live.'[17]

In the preface to the Brazos Theological Commentary on the Bible, of which Hauerwas' volume on the Gospel of Matthew is part, R. R. Reno is explicit about the impact of a separation between academic theology and the life of the church in Western contexts:

> Biblical scholars turn out monographs. Church leaders have meetings. But each dimension of a formerly unified Christian practice now tends to function independently. It is as if a weakened army had been fragmented, and various corps had retreated to isolated fortresses in order to survive.[18]

Reno points out that he deliberately appointed dogmatic theologians, rather than specifically biblical scholars, as authors. For Hauerwas, this approach liberated him to write with a confident confessionalism that might raise an eyebrow in contemporary biblical scholarship:

Matthew's gospel is meant to train us to be disciples of Jesus. I should like to think that learning to read Matthew's gospel through the commentary I have written might be a small aid in helping Matthew's gospel to do the work it was written to do.[19]

It is fair to say that these are not the sort of sentiments found prominently in the introductory remarks of most scholarly biblical commentaries. Markus Bockmuehl is one biblical scholar who has highlighted some substantial exegetical limitations in Hauerwas' project, while also noting that the commentary presents to biblical specialists 'a welcome challenge to take with utmost intellectual and existential seriousness the theological concern of the subject matter, a challenge we seem professionally conditioned to wriggle out of'.[20]

Richard Hays' *Moral Vision of the New Testament* as a methodological basis

Richard Hays cannot be accused of such wriggling. In the area of study before us, where Christian moral reflection is rooted in the reading of Scripture, his influence is inescapable. *The Moral Vision of the New Testament* represents the most serious recent attempt to create a method whereby theological ethics can draw on the wisdom of Scripture.[21] One of his key concerns is to demonstrate that the insights of historical criticism need not lead those engaging with the Bible in the light of such insights to conclude, as Jack T. Sanders memorably did, that 'we are now at least relieved of the need or temptation to begin with Jesus, or the early church, or the New Testament, if we wish to develop coherent ethical positions'.[22] For Hays, 'normative Christian ethics is fundamentally a hermeneutical enterprise: it must begin and end in the interpretation and application of Scripture for the life of the community of faith'.[23] Hays claims that the real question for the Christian concerned with serious moral reflection is not *whether* the New Testament has a normative status in moral reflection, but *how* it is seen to authorize or shape the life of the church.

He begins his consideration of the task of New Testament ethics with a bold claim: that the church faces a 'hermeneutical crisis'[24] that is nowhere more 'embarrassing' than in relation to ethical questions. The crisis is revealed in the seemingly limitless array of responses that 'appeals to Scripture' can generate in relation to the same moral questions, thereby undermining any notion of scriptural coherence. Yet coherence is, for Hays, something worth searching for within the New Testament. His claim is that it is only through the adoption of a fourfold approach to engagement with the text – descriptive, synthetic, hermeneutical and pragmatic – that the church can learn to read Scripture in such a way that can usefully and coherently inform Christian ethical practice. Central to this approach is his desire to allow each text within the scriptural canon to be heard with its own authentic voice.

These four strands to Hays' approach require careful scrutiny. The first task, of description, is primarily one of exegesis. Careful reading of the text, and observation of the moral teaching found within it, happens at this stage in a way that does not seek to discriminate between particular approaches to a given moral question. Indeed, differences in emphasis in one text should not be softened by a corrective from another; so, for example, Luke's exhortation for Jesus' followers to give up all their possessions should not simply be moderated by an appeal to the example of members of the Corinthian church giving 'according to their means' (2 Cor. 8.3). Instead, Hays regards the first responsibility of the contemporary reader as being to hear the voice of each biblical witness. Only once the nature and concerns of those voices have been established can the reader move from the 'descriptive' task to the act of synthesis, then hermeneutics, and finally, the 'pragmatic task – living the text'.[25]

As we consider instances of disagreement within the New Testament in the five chapters that follow, we will recognize that an engagement with Hays' methodological approach equals the prioritizing of theological interpretation – in a way that itself critiques some of the approach of mainstream biblical scholarship:

> Our primary interpretative interest lies not in the hypothetical prehistory of the texts but in their final form and subsequent interpretation. The reconstructive historical task is valid and interesting – perhaps even necessary – but it is subsidiary to the concerns of New Testament ethics as a theological discipline.[26]

It is worth stating that any notion of 'final form' of the biblical text is hard to sustain given constant developments in translation practice. But Hays' broader point, that the Christian ethicist should be content to engage with the narrative as they receive it, rather than having to deconstruct it before any moral observation is made, is significant – and shapes our approach to the New Testament text.

As Hays himself argues, this is not to be naive to textual complexity or to deny potentially rich insights from biblical criticism; rather, it is an approach that helps marshal the diverse voices of the New Testament, 'to clarify how the church can read Scripture in a faithful and disciplined manner so that Scripture might come to shape the life of the church'.[27] In this regard, Kathryn Tanner's arguments concerning a 'plain sense'[28] reading of Scripture are instructive:

> When the plain sense of canonical texts is identified as a narrative – the sense of canonical texts focused in particular in the Christian case around the narrative depiction of a God made man – the very use of these texts to shape and nurture community life becomes open-ended … A creative display of exegetical ingenuity is necessary, then, to answer even the most basic question of establishing Christian identity through appeals to canonical texts.[29]

Engaging with the plain sense of Scripture does not avoid exegetical challenges or provide neat answers to the shaping of Christian communal life. But it does affirm an approach to reading the Bible that acknowledges the received text as authoritative – in that it is canonical – and worthy of engagement within the terms established by its own narrative. And this 'plain sense' reading is crucial in community formation:

> As the sense of a text functioning as scripture, the plain sense is the sense of the text that establishes group identity: Christians are those who assume that sense as basic in their use of the text to shape and reform their lives as Christians. Because it is scripture's, the plain sense, in the process of serving as a standard sense vis-à-vis other interpretative or applied senses, works as a standard for the community's continuing self-identity.[30]

Our interest in disagreement, and its persistent presence in the life of the church, makes straightforwardly clear that any appeal to the 'plain sense' of Scripture does not instantaneously generate a uniform response to the text; and even when it does operate 'as a standard for the community's continuing self-identity', it must be acknowledged that varied Christian groups will routinely arrive at differing interpretations of biblical texts. But the existence of varied interpretative responses does not, of itself, undermine the value of seeking a plain-sense reading of Scripture – particularly if it helps to highlight situations where the church has become complacent about certain moral demands expressed clearly in these foundational accounts of the practices of early Christian communities. The argument of this book is that a careful reading of the diverse narratives of the New Testament demonstrates that even while varied responses to the fact of disagreement remain, the texts' repeated and consistent call for the maintenance and development of loving unity among Christians is a moral dimension to discipleship which is too easily overlooked by members of the church as they disagree one with another. As we prepare to analyse Richard Hays' core argument that the New Testament contains sufficient moral coherence that it can and should still shape the self-identity of Christian communities, we now turn to disagreement itself – considering both its definition and its place within moral theological study.

Preliminary definitions for a theology of disagreement

It is important that we recognize that the specific question of disagreement among Christians is a neglected one. Notwithstanding the many ways that disagreements have affected the church throughout its history, it is striking that theological discourse in this area too often articulates extremes, either enjoying the lofty uplands of theological idealism, where loving unity apparently prevails, or coping with territory where conflict has become entrenched, and where resources are made available to face schism and seek reconciliation. Moments of initial disagreement, where difference is articulated but where a conflict is yet to begin, have been given very little specific thought within theological ethics.

A clear definition of 'disagreement' is essential, not least because a distinction between *disagreement* and two other commonly used terms in this area, *conflict* and *dispute*, will prove significant. The primary definition of the *Oxford English Dictionary* is that a disagreement constitutes 'want of agreement or harmony; difference; discordancy, diversity, discrepancy'.[31] We should note that this definition does not imply that a disagreement is necessarily damaging. Difference, diversity and discrepancy are all indications of a lack of unanimity, but not in a way that is inherently harmful. Contrast this with the definition of 'conflict' as primarily 'an encounter with arms, a fight, a battle'. Subsequently, conflict is defined as 'a prolonged struggle ... the clashing or variance of opposed principles, statements, arguments, etc.', with its 'chief sense' now being 'to come into collision, to clash; to be at variance, be incompatible'. It is clearly a more aggressive term than disagreement, however much the words are sometimes used interchangeably in discussions of debates within the church. Finally, the definition of 'dispute' is also worth noting: 'the act of disputing or arguing against; active verbal contention, controversy, debate'. Tellingly, a dispute can be defined as 'a difference of opinion', but only 'in weakened sense'; whereas 'frequently' it is defined 'with the added notion of vehemence, a heated contention, a quarrel'.

Although a disagreement can, in the dictionary's fourth definition, also constitute 'quarrel, dissension, variance, strife', the point for our purposes is that although there is some overlap between 'disagreement' and 'conflict' or 'dispute', there is also a clear distinction to be made. A disagreement is not inherently hostile when compared with a conflict or a dispute. It does demonstrate a lack of harmony, but a conflict or dispute indicates a greater degree of separation between two parties. A disagreement can, very quickly, make a downward descent into *becoming* a dispute or a conflict, but this book is concerned with the initial space, sometimes experienced only fleetingly, where a disagreement has emerged – but has yet to become toxic. For a faith with the pursuit of peace and loving unity at its heart, it is worthwhile to consider what ethical apparatus might be available to promote effective disagreement that, in turn, might reduce the scale and frequency of damaging disputes and conflicts.

We should not forget that disagreements, disputes and conflicts all have to start somewhere. Our particular concern is with disagreements that emerge within the mutually acknowledged boundaries of the community of faith. This might relate to ethical questions, such as how a church that has previously been tacitly united in its understanding of marriage responds to the advent of equal civil marriage. But it might also relate to the everyday questions of church life, such as whether pews should be removed or a liturgy updated. These are instances where the airing of diverse opinions might well lead to disagreement. The question is how Christians are equipped to face such differences of opinion without subsequent conversations inevitably turning sour. A theology of disagreement seeks to resource the church to consider how the *manner* in which disagreements are faced can helpfully assist processes whereby the matter under consideration is addressed fruitfully.

Following this definition of disagreement, it should be noted that an act of verbal or physical aggression by one party towards another, if described with precision, necessarily constitutes something more intense than a disagreement. A disagreement can be morally neutral in its initial stages, whereas an act of aggression is not, and may well prompt conflict or dispute. It is one thing for the churchwarden and verger to discuss their different views about pews and realize that a disagreement is emerging; it is quite another if the verger decides to take an axe to some of those same pews and then expects the conversation with the churchwarden to proceed as if nothing had happened. Questions concerning how a Christian might respond to an act of aggression – and what kind of response is justified – are therefore closely related to the scope of this book, but *not* part of its consideration of disagreement when understood as the emergence of difference or the lack of harmony between two or more parties.

It is also worth noting that our concern here is for disagreements that emerge *within the church*, and how they might be faced. Broader questions about the way the church disagrees in public with other parties may well be informed by our observations, but are not within the primary scope of our concern. When the churchwarden enlists the support of the town's atheist mayor in a campaign to preserve Victorian woodwork, the language she uses and the terms of reference upon which she draws may well need not to assume a theological foundation. Churches as institutions, and individual Christians, face such challenges as they seek to communicate effectively in a plural context. But this book is concerned with initial disagreements within the church, especially when they are played out in public (perhaps by the churchwarden writing to the local paper lamenting the pews' threatened future). Our interest is what ethic informs public speech in the midst of disagreement, when both parties are speaking from within the church and claim to be seeking its well-being.

Christians from all perspectives within a particular debate, however it began and however public its context, play their own part in the process whereby it does or does not move from being the sort of loving disagreement Justin Welby longs to see, to the damaging spectacle that any observer of Christian public discourse – whether historical or contemporary – knows only too well. Questions about the ethics that might underpin how these disagreements are approached too easily get eclipsed by a mutual clamour to claim the solid ground of truth, regardless of the impact on opponents. Meanwhile, scant regard is given to whether that emerging conflict was, of itself, undertaken in a recognizably Christian way – or, in other words, whether there existed a theology of disagreement that could model something authentically Christian, without naively assuming that all disagreement can be avoided.

The question here is whether we are content simply to accept a normative discourse which routinely fails even to attempt an approach to ecclesial disagreement that might model a recognizable dimension of Christian love – not a vague, slippery understanding of love, but a robust articulation of the quality of relationship within the triune God that should also be manifest in the church as the Body of Christ. For a Christian ethicist, the questions that present themselves are ones concerning whether, in its manifestly unloving disagreements, the church has become detached from some of the moral principles that should be foundational for its inner life and public witness. If such a disparity is identified, then the task of the Christian ethicist is to articulate the problem and propose solutions that are authentic iterations of Christian morality. Much of our challenge will be in returning time and again to root causes and initial stages of disagreement, when opportunities for more loving discourse remain possible to achieve.

Disagreement in theological and philosophical context

In the second chapter of *After Virtue*, entitled 'The Nature of Moral Disagreement Today and the Claims of Emotivism', Alasdair MacIntyre writes: 'The most striking feature of contemporary moral utterance is that so much of it is used to express disagreements; and the most striking feature of the debates in which these disagreements are expressed is their interminable character.'[32] Few observers of the life of the church would fail to recognize that such a description applies as well to public ecclesial disagreements as it does to any debates undertaken without reference to religion. And while a sustained engagement with MacIntyre is beyond the scope of our discussion, we should at least recall that by the end of the book he pleads for 'the construction of local forms of community within which civility and the intellectual moral life can be sustained through the new dark ages that are already upon us'.[33] MacIntyre's call for 'another St Benedict' represents a tacit admission that the church has within it the capacity to function as a community that sustains a commitment to serious moral formation, not fatally undermined by its disagreements.

In an essay first delivered as a speech to fellow bishops from around the Anglican Communion at the 1998 Lambeth Conference, Rowan Williams seeks to show that the church can indeed undertake this sort of intellectual engagement in the face of disagreement, urging his colleagues to consider their ethical divergence in relation to their understanding of the Body of Christ. In so doing he demonstrates that the fact of disagreement has both cognitive and affective implications. Disagreement is not merely about intellectual truth and the pursuit of the right reading of Scripture; Williams suggests that, if that were so, disagreements might more easily be resolved. But for him, ethical concerns about approaches to disagreement are equally significant, and associated questions about whether love is visibly operating within the Body require attention. He views this complex, multifaceted nature of ecclesial disagreement as the reason why difference is experienced so keenly and positions are defended so staunchly.

> Being in the Body means that we are touched by one another's commitments and thus by one another's failures. If another Christian comes to a different conclusion and decides in different ways from myself, and if I can still recognise their discipline and practice as sufficiently like mine to sustain a conversation, this leaves my own decisions to some extent under question. I cannot have absolute subjective certainty that this is the only imaginable reading of the tradition; I need to keep my reflections under critical review.[34]

Williams demonstrates that disagreement is so potentially damaging because it brings together the church's ongoing search for truth with the emotive passion associated with the defence of the truth as a particular individual understands it.[35] Disagreeing Christians might, suggests Williams, be assisted by a renewed perspective on their shared status as flawed and yet baptized humans seeking to live as faithful disciples: 'If I conclude that my Christian brother or sister is deeply and damagingly mistaken in their decision, I accept for myself the brokenness in the Body that this entails. These are my wounds; just as the one who disagrees with me is wounded by what they consider my failure or even betrayal.'[36]

In these observations, Williams succeeds in capturing the way in which disagreement wounds the church, not only because its presence forces a recognition that ultimate truth remains elusive, but also because the fracturing of relationships within the Body is generally a painful experience for all parties. But examples of theological engagement with the fact and impact of disagreement remain rare.[37] A theology of disagreement can resource theological reflection on the place of disagreement in the life of the church; I will consider its potential role in enabling the facing of disagreement in a way that remains consonant with the Christian call to love God, self and neighbour. For now, it is worth us noting one particular example of a deliberately generous scholarly engagement across disciplinary divides, which models something of a Christian ethic in its very approach to engagement with an academic opponent. Charles Camosy's interaction with Peter Singer offers us an example of a charitable disposition in action, notwithstanding the irony that it may yet seem easier for a Christian ethicist to engage politely – 'Beyond Polarization' – with an atheist who condones infanticide, than it is for many disagreeing Christians to engage with similar fruitfulness with one another.

At best, one might argue, a charitable Christian theological world view has, for Camosy, opened up new possibilities for intellectual dialogue and discovery. He writes that his 'basic thesis is that if Christians and those who take Peter Singer's approach engage each other in the spirit of intellectual solidarity, rather than defining by opposition, we will find (1) that our disagreements are actually quite narrow and interesting, and (2) that we can work together on many important issues of ethics and public policy'.[38] It is this identification of 'narrow and interesting' areas of disagreement that is worth noting. Deliberately careful work, combined with a charitable disposition, leads to the possibility that discussion will proceed to focus in the areas of actual rather than perceived difference. It is an approach that I will later consider in relation to formal ecumenical dialogues between Anglicans and Roman Catholics.[39]

In considering the foundations for such engagement, Camosy considers the *Compendium of the Social Doctrine of the Church*, issued by the Pontifical Council for Justice and Peace, where he notes that 'being in solidarity with our fellow human beings means that we are to seek "points of possible agreement where attitudes of separation and fragmentation prevail"'.[40] In fact, it is worth also quoting from the sentence in the *Compendium* that follows: 'It translates into the willingness to give oneself for the good of one's neighbour, beyond any individual or particular interest.'[41] We might well ask how often it is that we witness the act of disagreement itself being considered in relation to the self-sacrificing neighbour-regard at the heart of Christian faith. Too easily, ethical reflection happens apparently divorced from the wider moral landscape of Christian discipleship, and similarly distant from any particular sense of reliance on God in the midst of ethical disagreement. As such, it is fascinating that Camosy teases out the way in which Singer's utilitarianism comes close to needing theism for the intellectual credibility of its own arguments: 'something like God's providence and grace are necessary to jump the "moral gap" that exists between what many like Singer claim we ought to do and what we actually can do in light of our finite and flawed human nature.'[42]

If Camosy's engagement with Singer demonstrates a rare example of theological discourse giving specific attention to the fact of disagreement, a final preliminary observation is required about the contrasting situation in contemporary philosophy – where there is widespread and detailed engagement with the fact of disagreement and its epistemology. Bryan Frances, in what claims to be 'the first full-length textbook on this philosophical topic',[43] suggests that there are two central questions to ask about disagreement: epistemological and ethical. The former considers how parties should respond to the realization that disagreement occurs between them; the latter, how then they should behave. This former question has faced rigorous philosophical examination, with recent studies emphasizing the emergence of a spectrum labelled with terminology that may provoke a wry smile in a theological reader, for the discussion proceeds between 'conformist' and 'non-conformist' approaches. Conformists, in this sense, are those who argue that opinions should be revised in the course of a disagreement; non-conformists affirm the continued holding of divergent views. Part of this discussion involves philosophers reflecting on an agent's discovery that she holds views deemed disagreeable by others, and the extent to which this knowledge may affect her actions.[44] In this scenario, the Christian ethicist can at least celebrate that within a theological framework certain questions about other-regard and the possibility of neighbour-love may be assumed, rather than seen as a novel discovery – but this is just one example of how Christian ethics differs from secular philosophy in relation to the conceptual framework within which foundational questions concerning the epistemology of disagreement are approached.

Another telling example involves a discussion of how it might be determined that two parties had the right to participate in a given disagreement. Have they both had equal access to information that might inform an accurate judgement on a given topic? Do they approach the discussion as intellectual equals? How does their cultural context inform their approach? Are they – in the philosophers' term – 'epistemic peers'?[45] The danger here is that philosophical reflection on disagreement is substantially reduced in scope, only to scenarios where 'epistemic peers' can engage in debate, as if such neatly matching intellectual biographies can conveniently be found. My later consideration of Jesus' engagement with the Syrophoenician woman will offer a telling kingdom-shaped contrast with this secular philosophical approach; it would be hard to find someone less obviously an epistemic peer of Jesus, and yet it was she who dared to challenge him, and Jesus' unexpected response was to engage.[46]

Christopher McMahon's championing of 'reasonable disagreement', seemingly as the best and limited hope for a multicultural, multifaith, liberal society, offers a further telling example of a secular philosophical approach that seeks to civilize debate but without any ultimate hope or expectation of either agreement or reconciliation: 'Shared deliberation conducted in good faith can be expected to eliminate mistakes in reasoning and thus winnow out the unreasonable views. But different reasonable views will remain.'[47] There is a helpful reminder here that too often, whether in the church or wider society, disagreements short-circuit due to a lack of patience or appropriate process among those engaged in debate. McMahon's exploration of reasonable disagreement is helpful as a reminder of the qualities one might hope to find in a functioning disagreement – but the Christian theological tradition must surely always want to encourage the pursuit of an ultimate truth that, however seemingly unclear, remains the goal of discipleship. Reasonable disagreement could only ever be a staging post on that journey.

From the perspective of a theological world view, we can recognize that philosophy has already begun to ask questions that, if translated for our context, can be of real value to the church in assisting a more effective engagement with the inevitability of difference and disagreement. Where philosophy struggles to determine the value of prior commitments, the church values tradition and uses reason to discern how that tradition lives afresh in each generation; philosophy's discussion of 'epistemic peers' is overturned by a kingdom perspective where the last shall be first and the least are of inestimable value; a philosopher's weary resignation to 'reasonable disagreement' as the best outcome to hope for seems to exhibit a poverty of ambition when compared with the Christian who trusts that they are being led into all truth. But, as Alasdair MacIntyre's observations at the beginning of this section remind us, the church can well identify with the prevalence of interminable disagreement. And while we may be confident that theology has the resources to offer more constructive answers to the questions being considered in contemporary philosophy, we must also concede that these considerations of the epistemic nature of disagreement have barely begun within theological ethics. The questions being faced unflinchingly by philosophers need to be addressed by theologians.

Our final preliminary observation concerns the title of this book. As we shall see in Part 3, the presence of silos in academic theology means that, too often, potentially helpful insights from moral theology fail to be heard in other sub-disciplines. In part, this can be because liturgists or biblical scholars assume that ethics has little to do with their disciplines (and, I fear, ethicists may often assume the same in reverse). By writing deliberately of a *theology* of disagreement, this work aims to show that this aspect of the church's moral life has been neglected in a way that has had an impact not merely within theological ethics but across a wider landscape of theological reflection. Although I will proceed to offer a detailed critique of Richard Hays' specific methodology, I will not argue with his determination to assert the place of the New Testament as the primary source for the discernment of Christian ethics. But an affirmation of the foundational status of Scripture should not lead us to ignore how the insights of tradition, reason and experience inform our reflection on disagreement. As we shall see, consideration of theological perspectives from, for example, the fields of pneumatology and liturgy in Part 3 will add considerably to the New Testament foundations for a theology of disagreement established by the end of Part 2.

Of course, the scope of this book is such that it can only hope to offer *a* theology of disagreement, but such moral reflection – rooted in Scripture and also shaped by tradition, reason and experience – is surely a task that can happen confidently under a 'theological' banner. This book thus bears a title that attempts to move beyond the compartmentalizing of Christian ethical reflection within academic discourse. Part of this approach involves dialogue with theological disciplines beyond biblical studies in a way not undertaken by Richard Hays; but first, our task is to engage with the plain narrative sense of the New Testament as we have received it. This book is unique in analysing instances of disagreement, and discussion of disagreement, across the whole New Testament, in pursuit of a coherent theological ethic that can resource the church in its inevitable disagreements. It is to this 'descriptive task' of the careful reading of Scripture that we now turn.

Notes

1 Shiv Malik, 2012, 'Peter Mandelson gets nervous about people getting "filthy rich"', *The Guardian*, www.guardian.co.uk/politics/2012/jan/26/mandelson-people-getting-filthy-rich (accessed 12 May 2012).

2 Following the global financial crisis, on 26 January 2012 Mandelson told Evan Davis in a BBC Radio 4 *Today* programme interview, 'I don't think I would say that now'. See http://news.bbc.co.uk/today/hi/today/newsid_9687000/9687064. stm (accessed 15 March 2012).

3 Tristram Hunt, 'Fight the good fight: With its proposed changes in drink and gambling legislation, Labour exposes the loss of its Puritan roots', *The Observer*, 20 November 2005, p. 31.

4 John 13.35. All biblical quotations, unless otherwise indicated, are from the New Revised Standard Version.

5 Press conference marking his appointment as Archbishop of Canterbury, 9 November 2012. See www.archbishopofcanterbury.org/articles.php/5003/bishop-justin-welbys-opening-statement#transcript (accessed 20 January 2013). The need for a clear definition of 'love' in relation to disagreement is explored in Chapter 6, p. 118.

6 Richard B. Hays, 1996, *The Moral Vision of the New Testament*, New York: HarperCollins.

7 Consider some of the comments to be found on the back cover, praising Hays' achievement: 'This is without question the best book available in the area of New Testament ethics and should transform the way this discipline is viewed by both church and academy' (William Klassen); 'Hays' passionately written book, with its bold agenda, has neither peer nor rival' (Leander Keck); 'This book isn't just a breath of fresh air. It's a hurricane, blowing away the fog of half-understood pseudo-morality and fashionable compromise, and revealing instead the early Christian vision of true humanness and genuine holiness. If this isn't a book for our time, I don't know what is' (Tom Wright). See Hays, *Moral Vision*, back cover.

8 Hays notes that his 'modes of appeal to Scripture' – rules, principles, paradigms and symbolic world – follow Gustafson's own categories (Hays, *Moral Vision*, p. 213, n. 3).

9 James Gustafson, 1970, 'The Place of Scripture in Christian Ethics: A Methodological Study', *Interpretation* 24,4, p. 432.

10 He outlines four main possible approaches – which increase in their levels of flexibility – to the examination of what he terms the 'revealed morality' of Scripture: revealed morality as moral law with clear and unambiguous injunctions for the believer to follow; revealed morality as outlining moral ideals (accompanied by a recognition that compromises, or approximations will follow as an inevitable consequence of human failure to live up to such ideals); revealed morality as offering analogies that can inform contemporary moral action; and revealed morality as simply offering one component in moral deliberation, but never being self-sufficient in its authority.

11 Gustafson, 'Scripture', p. 455. See the discussion of the role of extra-biblical sources that follows in Chapter 6, p. 113.

12 Stephen Charles Mott, 1987, 'The Use of the New Testament for Social Ethics', *Journal of Religious Ethics* 15,2, p. 225.

13 Lisa Sowle Cahill, 1990, 'The New Testament and Ethics: Communities of Social Change', *Interpretation* 44,4, pp. 384–5.

14 Sowle Cahill, 'New Testament', p. 388.

15 Sowle Cahill, 'New Testament', p. 383.

16 Hays summarizes the problem in this way: 'we see Christians distributed across the various ethical spectrums – from Oliver North to Daniel Berrigan, from Phyllis Schlafly to Elisabeth Schüssler Fiorenza, from Jerry Falwell to Bishop John Shelby Spong – all insisting that the Bible somehow informs their understanding of God's purposes.' Hays, *Moral Vision*, p. 2.

17 Stanley Hauerwas, 2011, *Learning to Speak Christian*, London: SCM Press, p. 112.

18 R. R. Reno, 2006, 'Series Preface' in Stanley Hauerwas, *Matthew*, London: SCM Press, p. 13.

19 Hauerwas, 'Introduction' in *Matthew*, p. 18.

20 Markus Bockmuehl, 2008, 'Ruminative Overlay: Matthew's Hauerwas', *Pro Ecclesia* 17,1, p. 20.

21 Significant examples that preceded Hays include Alan Verhey, 1984, *The Great Reversal: Ethics and the New Testament*, Grand Rapids: Eerdmans; Wayne Meeks, 1986, *The Moral World of the First Christians*, London: SPCK; Eduard Lohse, 1991, *Theological Ethics of the New Testament*, Minneapolis: Fortress Press; and Stephen E. Fowl and L. Gregory Jones, 1991, *Reading in Communion: Scripture and Ethics in Christian Life*, London: SPCK.

22 Jack T. Sanders, 1975, *Ethics in the New Testament*, London: SCM Press, p. 130.

23 Hays, *Moral Vision*, p. 10.

24 Hays, *Moral Vision*, p. 1.

25 See Hays, *Moral Vision*, pp. 3–7, for his initial outline of 'the fourfold task of New Testament ethics'.

26 Hays, *Moral Vision*, p. 14.

27 Hays, *Moral Vision*, p. 3.

28 'To call a text scripture is to say, in a Christian context, that the text is to be used ... to shape, nurture, and reform the continuing self-identity of the church.' Kathryn Tanner, 1987, 'Theology and the plain sense' in Garrett Green, ed., *Scriptural Authority and Narrative Interpretation*, Philadelphia: Fortress Press, p. 62.

29 Tanner, 'Theology', p. 74.

30 Tanner, 'Theology', p. 63.

31 'Disagreement, Noun' in J. A. Simpson and E. S. C. Weiner, eds, 1989, *The Oxford English Dictionary*, 2nd edn, Oxford: Clarendon Press. All subsequent definitions also taken from the *OED*.

32 Alasdair MacIntyre, 1981, *After Virtue: A Study in Moral Theory*, 3rd edn, London: Gerald Duckworth & Co., p. 6.

33 MacIntyre, *After Virtue*, p. 263.

34 Rowan Williams, 2000, 'Making Moral Decisions' in Robin Gill, ed., *The Cambridge Companion to Christian Ethics*, Cambridge: Cambridge University Press, p. 11.

35 Oliver O'Donovan asserts the importance of this orientation towards truth when he writes, 'If we cannot envisage a community of agreement, our thought cannot have any end in view, either.' Oliver O'Donovan, 2013, *Self, World and Time: Ethics as Theology*, vol. 1, Grand Rapids: Eerdmans, p. 46. The task of theology is always orientated towards the pursuit of some sort of truth – even when postmodern approaches expect multiple truths to coexist. But this cognitive pursuit of truth is itself subject to occasions of intense disagreement over what constitutes the truth (or truths) in view. One might suggest that a cognitive, truth-directed impasse in disagreement need not necessarily be accompanied by an affective impasse, where processes of effective disagreement and dialogue have stalled. This book is primarily concerned with the affective question of how disagreements might appropriately be faced in a way that is consonant with Christian ethics rooted in the New Testament. As O'Donovan cautions, such a process is fruitless without an end in view – but the core interest of a theology of disagreement is the Christian ethical insights that might inform how disagreeing Christians might engage one another in ways that build up loving unity in the Body of Christ.

36 Williams, 'Making Moral Decisions', pp. 11–12.

37 An exception to this observation is Andrew Atherstone and Andrew Goddard, eds, 2015, *Good Disagreement? Grace and Truth in a Divided Church*, Oxford: Lion Hudson. With particular attention paid to the context of the Anglican Communion, it offers a variety of perspectives on disagreement but does not address specifically the core concern of this book, namely the ethical approach that might be taken when disagreements inevitably arise. It also devotes little attention to the pneumatological concerns expressed in Chapter 9 of this study. Tom Wright's contribution, 'Pastoral Theology for Perplexing Topics: Paul and *Adiaphora*' (pp. 63–82), is particularly insightful; for a discussion of his treatment of *adiaphora*, and its potential to act as a distraction for a theology of disagreement, see the section on Romans 14 in Chapter 4, p. 75.

38 Charles C. Camosy, 2012, *Peter Singer and Christian Ethics: Beyond Polarization*, Cambridge: Cambridge University Press, p. 7.

39 See Chapter 8, 'Ecumenical disagreement and the myth of unity'.

40 Camosy, *Singer*, p. 8.

41 Pontifical Council for Justice and Peace, *Compendium of the Social Doctrine of the Church*, www.vatican.va/roman_curia/pontifical_councils/justpeace/documents/rc_pc_justpeace_doc_20060526_compendio-dott-soc_en.html (accessed 6 July 2015).

42 Camosy, *Singer*, p. 242.

43 Bryan Frances, 2014, *Disagreement*, Cambridge: Polity Press, back cover.

44 Frances, *Disagreement*, p. 2.

45 'Introduction' in David Christensen and Jennifer Lackey, eds, 2013, *The Epistemology of Disagreement: New Essays*, Oxford: Oxford University Press, p. 2.

46 See Chapter 1, p. 7.

47 Christopher McMahon, 2009, *Reasonable Disagreement: A Theory of Political Morality*, Cambridge: Cambridge University Press, p. 92.

PART I

Disagreement in the New Testament

The Paradox of Jesus: Both Biographical Paradigm and Moral Teacher

The biographical accounts of the life and ministry of Jesus, found within the Synoptic Gospels, offer a logical location for the beginnings of our search for examples of disagreement from the New Testament that can resource an emerging theology of disagreement. In our particular context, this also means applying Richard Hays' methodology for ethicists using Scripture to our reading of the Synoptic Gospels. Following Hays, we will mostly be responding to the narrative concerns of the text itself; the primary focus of this chapter and those that follow in Part 1 is a *descriptive* consideration of instances where disagreement occurs or is discussed within the texts of the New Testament.

Given our focus on internal disagreement within the church, there is a significant distinction to be made from the outset, between the legacy of Jesus' example – his own engagement with others as recorded biographically by Gospel writers – and his teaching. We will consider how Jesus promotes an ethic of loving unity within the kingdom, and therefore within the church, while rigorously and sometimes vituperatively challenging morality and other practices that stand in contradiction with the kingdom. There is a tension here, with inescapable implications for the formulation of a Christian ethic that responds to the fact of disagreement within the church. In Richard Hays' terms, we might describe this distinction as a tension that, having been identified, needs to be allowed to stand – for now at least – in the context of this initial, *descriptive* task.

In the sections that follow, it is a distinction that prompts theological reflection on how contemporary discipleship may best be understood in the context of the facing of disagreement within the church, and whether to be a faithful disciple means following Christ's teaching, his example or both. The seemingly uncontroversial Christian call to Christlikeness is one that is particularly complex, and potentially ambiguous, for disagreeing Christians. The use of anger in contemporary ecclesial disagreement is sometimes justified with reference to Jesus' angry engagement with his religious opponents; my concern will be to show that a distinction should be made between Jesus' words and actions when defining the kingdom in debate with those who stand beyond it, and the ethic of mutual loving relationship that he both models and commends among those who have chosen to follow him. The extent to which Christians might appropriately use anger in disagreement with those *outside* the church, perhaps appealing to Jesus' engagement with the Pharisees as justification, is beyond the scope of our discussion: our focus is on the moral theology that can be discerned from the New Testament to resource approaches to disagreement within the church.

As we shall see, many of the virtuous attributes that might ordinarily be associated with Christian discipleship are not necessarily found in the person and attitudes of Jesus – but crucially, his anger and rancour tend to be visible on occasions where the way of the kingdom is being articulated or defended. Part of my discussion will involve a consideration of what place anger, insult and provocation may have within recognizably Christian discourse, while acknowledging that my focus is those disagreements that happen within the bounds of Christian community.

As will become evident with particular clarity in our subsequent consideration of John's Gospel, the biblical scholar pursuing hermeneutics, and the ethicist with a concern for moral theology, may well not both find material of interest in the same biblical verses. In my exploration of disagreement as an ethical theme within the Synoptic Gospels, my task is to discern examples where instances of disagreement can help resource a theology of disagreement – and this process is carried out within the biblical narrative as we have received it. This is not to be naive to the complexities of the biblical text; but it is to underline the essentially interpretative, theological role that the Christian ethicist has in mind as they approach the Bible, drawing on the fruits of specifically textual scholarship as necessary.

The conclusion of this chapter includes some preliminary reflections on the possibility of a theological synthesis regarding disagreement in the Synoptic Gospels, though this 'synthetic' work, and Hays' 'hermeneutical task', will largely be undertaken in Part 2, with all the relevant New Testament texts before us. The fourth 'pragmatic task' in Hays' scheme, 'Living the Text', concerns applied ecclesiological questions, which are addressed in relation to disagreement in Part 3. In this chapter, we can be confident to focus our Synoptic consideration on the words and deeds of Jesus, relating other instances of disagreement to his own example. But this needs to be done having carefully distinguished between different sorts of encounter between Jesus and others within the Gospel texts: it is to such instances that we now turn.

Jesus as paradigm

Jesus' disagreements with those who oppose him or do not follow him

The disagreements between Jesus and those he encounters in an oppositional way in the course of his public ministry often follow a strikingly similar narrative pattern: Jesus hears criticism, is provocative in response and may out-wit or out-manoeuvre his interlocutors rather than answer their questions directly. A series of three encounters with different groups in Matthew 9 is instructive. In response to the scribes, who accuse him of blasphemy, Jesus questions his critics: 'Why do you think evil in your hearts? For which is easier, to say, "Your sins are forgiven", or to say, "Stand up and walk"?' (vv. 4b–5). Following this exchange, the Pharisees' questioning of the dubious company kept by Jesus is met with a response that might easily be characterized as blunt: 'Those who are well have no need of a physician, but those who are sick … I have come to call not the righteous but sinners' (vv. 12–13). Finally, in this chapter, a question about fasting is put to Jesus by the 'disciples of John'. Again, Jesus responds obliquely, with a series of metaphorical questions and observations that do not engage with the specific question of fasting, but which do underline that his life and ministry inaugurate a new and distinctive approach to religious observance (see Matt. 9.14–17).

When faced with disagreement with figures in religious authority, Jesus regularly speaks in ways that hardly seem designed to appease or ingratiate. The account of his speaking in the synagogue in Nazareth in Luke 4 offers a particularly striking example of his inflammatory approach to public speech. The rage of his Jewish hearers following his account of historical examples of favour shown towards Gentiles (Luke 4.24–27) leads to a moment of dramatic impending violence resolved only by Jesus' apparently miraculous passage through the midst of the furious crowd. Later in the same Gospel, the indignation of the leader of another synagogue following a Sabbath healing is met with an accusation of hypocrisy by Jesus. Luke records the impact of Jesus contrasting a willingness to give water to animals on the Sabbath with a refusal to heal humans on the same day: 'When he said this, all his opponents were put to shame; and the entire crowd was rejoicing at all the wonderful things that he was doing' (Luke 13.17).

Here we witness that Jesus' strident approach to disagreement is central to the communication of his message: the humiliation of opponents enabled the crowds' clear understanding of the substantial change in religious attitudes that he was promoting. So disagreement, in such cases – of which there are many – *enables* Jesus to distinguish his own ministry

from inherited Jewish practices. The account of the healing of the paralysed man in Mark 2 adds a further dimension to our understanding
of Jesus' approach to disagreement, when scribes present 'were sitting
there, questioning in their hearts' (v. 6). Here, Jesus uses his own spiritual
insight to perceive the scribes' disagreement with him. Without their
actually uttering a word, Jesus questions them with characteristic forth-
rightness, and then proceeds to command the paralysed man to stand up
and walk. In this instance, Jesus' engagement with his opponents does
not involve a verbalized disagreement, but highlights his readiness to confront thoughts as well as actions that represent opposition to his ministry.

A sequence of encounters between Jesus and opponents in Mark 12
further underlines the willingness of Jesus to engage in strident disputes
– but here, crucially for our purposes, this antagonistic approach to disagreement is found in the closest possible proximity to Jesus' articulation
of the double love command. After some Pharisees and Herodians have
challenged him on a question regarding taxation, and he has responded
bluntly, some Sadducees' question about marriage in the resurrection
draws a scathing response: 'Is not this the reason you are wrong, that you
know neither the scriptures nor the power of God?' (v. 24). Jesus ends by
telling them that they are 'quite wrong' – disagreeing emphatically. The
verses that follow in Mark's account are of primary interest as we consider a theology of disagreement. When, in verse 28, 'One of the scribes
came near and heard them disputing with one another', disagreement is
clearly established as the context for what follows. Amid the rancour and
arguments concerning the questions being put to him by those in religious
authority, Jesus gives primary importance to the commands to love God
and neighbour – and the scribe responds, 'You are right, Teacher' (v. 32).
In the space of a few moments, dispute has been replaced by affirmation,
and Jesus comments that the scribe is not far from the kingdom of God.
As William Lane notes, 'The love which determines the whole disposition of one's life and places one's whole personality in the service of God
reflects a commitment to God which springs from divine sonship.'[1]

In Part 2 I will consider the ethical significance of the double love
command as a potential methodological foundation for Christian ethical
reflection. Importantly at this stage, we need to recognize the narrative
weight of these two commands and the extent to which they can offer a
robust basis for scripturally grounded theological reflection. It is, after all,
hardly controversial to suggest that Jesus makes clear his ethical priorities
when he states that 'there is no other commandment greater than these'
(Mark 12.31). But what is often lacking in theological ethical discourse
is an attempt to use this as a starting point from which to approach
particular questions in moral theology. In the context of a theology of

disagreement, the immediate scriptural context is tantalizing, for it is in the midst of an angry and combative disagreement with opponents that Jesus outlines some of the key ethical teachings of his earthly ministry. His appeal to the centrality of love – an appeal too often made with bland generality in contemporary church disputes – comes in the midst of his own argumentative exchanges, which can hardly be described as straightforwardly loving in their approach towards the other with whom Jesus disagrees.

There is a need to distinguish between the recorded words and actions of Jesus as he confronts opposition to the kingdom, and his theological teaching as he establishes how the kingdom on earth becomes visible, including what sort of moral practices are compatible with its inauguration. In relation to the former, his approach can be combative and dismissive of opponents, but crucially such instances refer to critique of the current situation rather than a description of life in the kingdom he proclaims. Tom Wright points out that Jesus' anger and controversy was ultimately concerned with kingdom matters: 'It was precisely Jesus' eschatological programme which led him into opposition with a good many of his contemporaries, and which finally steered him towards the actions which provoked his death.'[2] But Jesus' approach in such instances does not offer a straightforward paradigm for the subsequent facing of disagreement *within* the church as an expression of the kingdom. The invitation to kingdom life points to a new beginning for human relationships, grounded in the priority given to unity among disciples. In Mark 3, the scribes who came down from Jerusalem accuse Jesus of demonic activity. He responds, 'If a kingdom is divided against itself, that kingdom cannot stand. And if a house is divided against itself, that house will not be able to stand' (vv. 24–25). In these words, rebutting the scribes' suggestion that he uses demonic power to cast out demons, Jesus indicates that any kingdom derives its strength from its unity. As we shall go on to see, unity among believers as an expression of the presence of the kingdom of God is a key New Testament theme that has its own bearing on how disagreeing Christians might choose to approach occasions of disunity.

Our discussion thus far, considering Jesus' engagement with those with whom he disagrees publicly, has focused on his interaction with figures from the religious establishment that he sought to criticize. His encounter with the Syrophoenician woman is, however, an important final example of a disagreement involving Jesus, noteworthy on several counts, and unique in that it represents an example of Jesus' mind being changed as a result of a moment of disagreement. In Mark's Gospel, immediately after an exchange with the disciples where he tells them that dietary laws are to be overturned – food not being responsible for the generation of evil intentions – Jesus fails to enter a house without being noticed and is confronted by 'a Gentile, of Syrophoenician origin. She begged him to cast the demon out of her daughter' (Mark 7.26). The subsequent exchange between the woman and Jesus deserves sustained reflection as we explore instances of disagreement within the Synoptic Gospel accounts of Jesus' life.

Morna Hooker suggests that the key challenge presented by this narrative is

> its presentation of Jesus as almost churlish in his reluctance to help the Gentile woman, and erratic in the way in which he then changed his mind. Most readers of the gospel feel that this is out of character with what they would otherwise know of Jesus. Yet it seems unlikely that such a story would have been invented.[3]

Viewed in the context of Jesus' mission to the Jews, this episode constitutes a crucial indication that Gentiles too are welcome at the heavenly banquet, even though Jesus' own ministry is focused on Israel. Nonetheless, the offensive nature of 'dogs' as a Jewish term for Gentiles is inescapable. As R. T. France notes, 'It is the sort of language a Gentile might expect from a Jew, but to find it in a saying of Jesus is shocking.'[4] Alongside this uncompromising language is the culturally unexpected phenomenon of a Gentile woman challenging a male Jewish teacher. The reader is left in little doubt that it is as a result of her retort, 'Sir, even the dogs under the table eat the children's crumbs' (7.28), that Jesus chose to heal her daughter.

The woman's clearly expressed faith in Jesus' ability to heal is coupled with her willingness to challenge Jesus at the point that they disagree. Moreover, it is through the act of disagreement that the way is opened for healing to occur – and this after Jesus has first sought to dismiss her. Craig Evans points out that the account of the same incident in Matthew's Gospel intensifies the unexpected nature of Jesus' engagement with a Gentile. In verse 24 Jesus affirms that he 'was sent only to the lost sheep of the house of Israel', making this interaction beyond the Jewish people all the more significant. Evans notes that the exchange should not be read in a way that implies parity between Jew and Gentile at this point in the New Testament: the woman 'is not attempting to put herself on an equal footing with the people of Israel. Implicit in her reply is the conviction that God's grace is so great that there is more than enough to go around, even while it is being extended to Israel first.'[5]

This incident in the life of Jesus is particularly striking in two ways: it highlights the caustic nature of the language used by Jesus in the context of verbal disagreement, and it offers one crucial instance where Jesus' course of action changed as a result of such disagreement. Finally, we should not overlook the fact that this episode is primarily one concerning healing, where the miraculous nature of Jesus' public ministry is presented. Unusually, here Jesus heals at a distance, without any physical interaction with the woman's daughter. Jesus is presented as someone not beyond challenge in the context of his earthly ministry, and as one who responds positively to a stranger in a context that could have been seen, for him, as humiliating. Disagreement, in this instance, is not to be viewed as something unconstructive or wholly unhelpful; rather, here it represents a challenge to Jesus to which he responds positively and in a way that then further demonstrates the nature and scale of his mission.

There is one key way in which we can distinguish between the many examples of Jesus engaging with those who oppose him from a standpoint of existing religious authority, and the opposition of the Syrophoenician woman: in the many former cases, no faith in Jesus is expressed, whereas in this one lonely example, disagreement expressed within the context of faith in Christ's ability to heal leads to disagreement being transformed, followed by an act of miraculous healing. The woman's oppositional language, expressed in the context of faith, leads to something fruitful: here we witness Jesus enlarging the scope of his healing ministry, to include Gentiles, as a result of an initial moment of disagreement. Whereas the scribes, Pharisees and others merely sought to criticize or undermine Jesus, the woman's expressed opposition to him also involved the revealing of her faith in his potential ability to heal her sick daughter. We can, then, observe that in this example, faith in Christ offers a context where disagreement can be fruitful and prompt signs of the kingdom. Disagreement can be open and frank; but questions remain about how the words and actions of Jesus himself might influence an emerging theology of disagreement.

Jesus' disagreement with his disciples

Our focus now turns to the disagreements witnessed between Jesus and his disciples. But before we consider specific instances of such disagreement, it is worth noting the Synoptic accounts of the initial call of the disciples, which offer important narrative context for our understanding of subsequent disagreement both among the disciples and in the wider church. In the Gospels of both Matthew and Mark, a striking feature of Jesus' call to the two pairs of brother Galilean fishermen is the swift nature of their response to him: 'Immediately they left their nets and followed him' (Matt. 4.20); 'Immediately they left the boat and their father, and followed him' (v. 22). R. T. France notes that here we see emphasized 'the extraordinary readiness of these working men to abandon all that was familiar and secure for the sake of a charismatic stranger.'⁶ Responding to Jesus' call of discipleship is presented as the radical *and unquestioning* abandonment of all that is familiar, in faith and trust. These men did not hesitate. They certainly did not stop to challenge Jesus or to disagree with him about the necessity of an instant response. The attractiveness of Jesus and his invitation was irresistible, and so livelihood and family were left behind in support of Jesus' teaching and healing ministry.

There is, of course, a grave danger in placing too much emphasis on arguments based upon what does not happen in a particular biblical narrative. But here I am not seeking to emphasize the lack of disagreement so much as to point out that the key feature of the initial call of the disciples was their unhesitatingly positive response to Jesus' call. The description of these events in the Gospel of Luke provides a further insight into the nature of the disciples' response to Jesus' invitation to serve. When Jesus sees Simon fishing in the lake of Gennesaret, he tells him to put out into deep water and let down his nets for a catch. 'Simon answered, "Master, we have worked hard all night long but have caught nothing. Yet if you say so, I will let down the nets"' (Luke 5.5). Here Simon outlines why he might consider disagreeing with Jesus – he's been fishing without success for hours already – but instead, because it is Jesus asking, he cooperates with the request. The irresistible nature of Jesus' call is underlined once again, and the abundance of fish then caught further demonstrates to Simon the extraordinary nature of the man calling him: 'When they had brought their boats to shore, they left everything and followed him' (v. 11).

This theme of instantaneous response to Jesus' call is further demonstrated in Luke 9, when unnamed men claim to want to follow Jesus – though first, one wants to bury his father. Jesus' response, notoriously blunt, provides another example of his desire for an immediate and wholehearted response from those who choose to follow him: 'Let the dead bury their own dead, but you go and proclaim the kingdom of God' (Luke 9.60). Another man simply wants to say goodbye to his family before he begins life as a disciple, but Jesus tells him, 'No one who puts a hand to the plough and looks back is fit for service in the kingdom of God' (v. 62, NIV). Unafraid to disagree with or challenge those who seek to follow him, Jesus reiterates the scale of the sacrifice that service in the kingdom demands. And, crucially, it is service undertaken without quibble or question: those who follow do so in trust. Now this is not to suggest that discipleship is to be always marked by a lack of questioning – as the Gospel accounts make clear – but in our context it remains significant that these initial responses to Jesus are marked not by prolonged questioning or disagreement but by surprisingly unhesitating responses to this unexpected call.

The account of the feeding of the five thousand in Matthew's Gospel offers a rare example of a resolved disagreement between Jesus and his disciples. Having withdrawn from the disciples after hearing of John the Baptist's death, Jesus was pursued by crowds, and 'had compassion for them and cured their sick' (Matt. 14.14). Afterwards, the disciples propose sending the crowds away. Their reasoning is practical and eminently sensible: the place is deserted, the hour is late, so it follows that the people should go to nearby villages to buy food. Jesus disagrees. By insisting that the disciples bring the crowds to him, along with their very limited provisions, Jesus shows his ability to overcome the apparent earthly impossibility of a given situation – in this case, famously, the provision of sufficient food for so many. The wider theological resonances of this incident are widely explored, including analysis of eucharistic resonances and the significance of 12 baskets remaining, but the immediate narrative context of Jesus' actions can be overlooked. Here, a disagreement has forced the disciples to reconsider the scale of their leader's capabilities. Human pragmatism is displaced by the miraculous; through disagreeing with his disciples, Jesus has opened their eyes to abundance in his kingdom.

It is in the aftermath of the second mass feeding, of four thousand people, that Mark's Gospel highlights the degree of frustration and indignation felt by Jesus as he recognizes the disciples' inability to grasp the kingdom significance of his actions. In the boat sailing towards Bethsaida, the disciples worry that they only have one loaf of bread with them. They attribute Jesus' irritation to this. But Jesus' exasperation is at their inability to comprehend: 'Why are you talking about having no bread? Do you still not perceive or understand? Are your hearts hardened?' (Mark 8.17). As he reminds them of the two feeding miracles, he points towards their apparent inability to recognize the theological significance of the miraculous events that have happened in their midst. In particular, they seem unable to take evidence from one miraculous occurrence and use it to build their faith that Jesus may also be able to act miraculously in another context. For his part, Jesus does not hesitate to challenge or provoke his disciples. Disagreement and contestation are seemingly necessary if he is to communicate effectively to them the full potential of his ministry.

In the second half of Matthew's Gospel, two incidents further illustrate this emerging theme of disagreement sharpening the disciples' focus and developing their appreciation of Jesus' ministry. When, in chapter 16, Jesus begins to explain the events in Jerusalem that will lead to his death, Peter takes him to one side and rebukes him. Jesus' response is dramatic: 'he turned and said to Peter, "Get behind me, Satan! You are a stumbling-block to me; for you are setting your mind not on divine things but on human things"' (v. 23). Here Jesus articulates the point that was implicit in his criticism of the disciples as they worried about their lack of bread after the feeding of the four thousand; their default response is to focus on the human rather than on the divine, thus limiting what they deem may be possible in the context of their life of discipleship. We might identify something reassuring in Peter's mistake. As Davies and Allison observe, 'the apostle serves as a warning that privilege and even divine election will not keep one from evil mischief.'[7] Peter, upon whose shoulders so much would later be entrusted, sharply disagreed with Jesus' view of his future – but was neither sidelined nor excluded in the aftermath. Indeed, in the very next chapter, Peter is trusted to be one of the three witnesses of the transfiguration.

A brief mention in Matthew 19 of Jesus' engagement with children further illustrates how a disagreement can lead to deeper understanding: as Davies and Allison observe pithily concerning the disciples, 'their error affords Jesus the opportunity to clarify'.[8] We might, charitably, suggest that the disciples had good reasons for being protective of their master, but in this instance Jesus flatly contradicts his followers' restriction, instead inviting the children to come to him, 'for it is to such as these that the kingdom of heaven belongs' (Matt. 19.14). John's questioning of Jesus in Mark 9 follows a similar pattern: the disciples are concerned by someone casting out demons in Jesus' name, and try to stop him. 'But Jesus said, "Do not stop him; for no one who does a deed of power in my name will be able soon afterwards to speak evil of me. Whoever is not against us is for us"' (Mark 9.39–40). As we have seen before, a protectionist desire on the part of the disciples is met with a strongly negative response from Jesus, who is concerned to see the growth of the kingdom – and unafraid that disagreement and challenge will form part of the refining process.

Disagreement among Jesus' followers

When James and John ask to sit at Jesus' right and left hand, in his glory, the response of the other ten disciples offers a telling insight into the potential for rivalry and enmity among the closest of Jesus' followers. The 'anger' of the ten is a rare example of vivid emotion being described among the disciples. Jesus counters it by calling the whole group together, teaching that 'whoever wishes to become great among you must be your servant, and whoever wishes to be first among you must be slave of all' (Mark 10.43–44). Unlike several of the examples of Jesus' disagreement with his disciples that we have already explored, where Jesus is swift to challenge, here he responds with more sensitivity. The challenge of servant leadership is outlined, but without the rancour that we have witnessed in Jesus' speech elsewhere. We might speculate as to whether Jesus reasoned that the anger of the disciples would only have increased had his tone been harsh in this instance; what we can conclude is that once more, a potential occasion of friction is transformed into an opportunity for the clarification of Jesus' purpose.

Two disputes about who among the disciples is the greatest, recorded in Luke's Gospel, offer further evidence for the sometimes fractious interaction between the disciples. In chapter 9, Luke reminds his readers of the depth of knowledge and spiritual insight found in Jesus, who, 'aware of their inner thoughts, took a little child and put it by his side, and said to them, "Whoever welcomes this child in my name welcomes me, and whoever welcomes me welcomes the one who sent me; for the least among all of you is the greatest"' (vv. 47–48). Before focusing on the use of a child to illustrate how greatness should be perceived in the kingdom, it is worth noting this restatement of Jesus' ability to know even the innermost thoughts of his disciples. As we consider how Christians approach their inevitable disagreements, we should not lose sight of the fact that in all ecclesial arguments, God knows our thoughts as well as the words we choose to speak. In this instance, as also in Luke 22.24–27, Jesus challenges his disciples to accept the radical implications of servant leadership, learning from children and those who serve at table in order to appreciate the social priorities of the life of the kingdom.

Our consideration of disagreement within the Synoptic Gospels has, thus far, focused on the narrative accounts of the life of Jesus and his disciples, exploring occasions of disagreement, and beginning to point to some of the theological and ethical observations that can be made in response. We can conclude that Jesus was entirely unafraid of facing disagreement, both with opponents and among his followers. We have also noted that the presence of disagreement can point towards a human rather than divine focus: disagreement can lead to a concentration on the humanly possible, while Jesus seeks to point towards the miraculous potential of life in God's kingdom. But this is not to say that disagreement should be regarded wholly negatively. Jesus himself demonstrates a refusal to avoid it, and repeatedly we then observe its potential to stimulate fresh perspectives and deeper understanding of God's purpose. So while disagreement can be humanly limiting, it can also have a refining quality that invites those who are willing to understand more fully the nature of Christian discipleship. Repeatedly, we have seen that faith in Jesus Christ is the context that alters whether disagreement is ultimately fruitful. Without sincere faith, it degenerates into pharisaical point-scoring; but as the Syrophoenician woman learnt, a disagreement even with Jesus himself was worthwhile.

Jesus as teacher

Having considered these examples of disagreement witnessed within the life and ministry of Jesus, we now move to a thematic consideration of the different approaches to disagreement that we find outlined in his teaching within the Synoptic Gospels. We will consider how a theological ethic of disagreement can begin to be discerned among the ethical priorities and concerns of Jesus, and how these might relate to a broader set of ethical aspirations in Christian life; in particular, how the place of disagreement might best be understood when considered alongside familiar Christian appeals to the importance of loving unity, forgiveness and reconciliation within the life of the church.

On the good of an absence of disagreement

If we are to make sense, theologically, of the place of disagreement within Christian life, we need to be clear about the ethical context within which disagreement might be approached effectively – even Christianly. But within the Synoptic Gospel accounts of the teaching ministry of Jesus, we cannot ignore the significant occasions when the promotion of loving unity among the disciples of Christ commends a vision of unified fellowship rather than protracted disagreement. As we shall go on to explore, the call to Christian unity need not and should not lead to the avoidance or suppression of disagreement at all costs, but neither should an exploration of the place of disagreement in the life of the church imply that its presence is necessarily desirable.

Several themes outlined in the Sermon on the Mount encourage Jesus' followers to recognize that their embrace of unity and reconciliation will set them apart from the wider world. In the Beatitudes, peacemakers are blessed as children of God (Matt. 5.9), and an expectation of criticism and even persecution is outlined:

> Blessed are you when people revile you and persecute you and utter all kinds of evil against you falsely on my account. Rejoice and be glad, for your reward is great in heaven, for in the same way they persecuted the prophets who were before you. (vv. 11–12)

We should note that Jesus implies a pre-existing level of unity among those who follow him; it is those external to the community who will revile and persecute. Part of our challenge as we read these words of Jesus is to acknowledge their intent while facing the divided reality of the contemporary church. There is plenty of revilement *within* the church, let alone attacks from outside it. Appeals to the promotion of unity will not alone enable the church to mend its divisions, but part of the development of an effective theology of disagreement will include a determination to strive towards the unity outlined by Jesus, even when the gap between his aspiration and contemporary reality seems vast.

In such a context, Jesus' own teaching within the Sermon on the Mount on the facing and resolution of tensions carries particular significance – and we shall later consider, in Chapter 10, how Christian liturgy embodies moral theology in the context of worship. Anger with a brother or sister means one is liable to judgement; insulting a brother or sister means one is liable to the council; 'And anyone who says, "You fool!" will be in danger of the fire of hell' (Matt 5.22, NIV). Thus Jesus outlines his wish that tensions should be resolved before gifts are offered at the altar: reconciliation should be sought before such offerings are made. This picture of Jesus' followers as those whose mutual anger is addressed through an act of reconciliation does, in its simplicity, remind us how far from this vision stands the life of the church – both historically and in our own times. The notion that Christian disputes should be settled before they reach court is lamentably absent from, for example, property disputes in the fracturing Episcopalian Church in the United States.[9] A theology of disagreement attempts to enable Christians to move beyond a binary situation where either an idealized unity is articulated or a sorry disunity is experienced with weary inevitability. Effective disagreement could lead to a more mature approach to inevitable Christian disagreement, so that tensions can be tolerated even if not all may be resolved.

Part of the theological rationale for such an approach is articulated in Jesus' later appeal to replace the hatred of enemies with love: '"You have heard that it was said, 'You shall love your neighbour and hate your enemy.' But I say to you, Love your enemies and pray for those who persecute you, so that you may be children of your Father in heaven' (Matt. 5.43–45a). We have already commented on how the disciples' misunderstanding of Jesus' desired relationship with children acts as an example of resolved disagreement in Matthew 19; here, earlier in that Gospel, those listening to Jesus are reminded of their need to acknowledge their status as children of their heavenly Father, and this is achieved, at least in part, through love and prayer for enemies. An important implication of this call, seldom explored, is the impact this command of Jesus has on relationships *within* the church, especially when fellow Christians become mutually hostile. We well know that it is no exaggeration to point out that there are plenty of Christians who would identify clear enemies within the boundaries of the Body of Christ (having manifestly failed to resolve differences 'when offering gifts at the altar' in the way analogous to that outlined by Jesus only moments before in Matthew's Gospel). One of the challenges that we seek to face is how Christians learn to love and pray for those enemies with whom they break bread or share a common baptism.

Jesus' calls for peace among his followers, including his words, 'Have salt in yourselves, and be at peace with one another' (Mark 9.50b), have a cumulative weight to them: the Christian cannot but recognize how disunity within the church represents a fundamental breach with the vision Jesus outlines for the corporate life of his followers. Within the Sermon on the Mount, the relationship between that call to peace and a life of non-violence is stated explicitly: 'if anyone strikes you on the right cheek, turn the other also' (Matt. 5.39b). Here, too, we must engage in this tension between the (perhaps impossibly) high ethical demands that Jesus outlines and the limited sense in which the church ever fulfils them. Our task is to consider how a call to love enemies and turn the other cheek might influence our approach to moments of disagreement. If these are, at the very least, important principles to strive to live by, then a Christian engaged in disagreement will seek to engage positively with even their bitterest opponent, trying not even to retaliate in the face of unwarranted aggression. That few within (or beyond) the church ever attempt to approach moments of disagreement in such a way points to how relaxed we have become about debilitating disagreement in the life of the church and wider society.

The question is whether apparently impossible ethical demands are worth bothering with; Jesus' answer is a repeated and emphatic yes, though the promise of grace and sins forgiven offers a broader context where human failure can be faced and redeemed. But we cannot dodge the scale of the challenge before us. As Jesus' final observation in this chapter makes clear, the ethical call of Christianity is uncompromising: 'Be perfect, therefore, as your heavenly Father is perfect' (Matt. 5.48). A theology of disagreement needs to hold together an honest recognition of human imperfection with a vision of the kingdom that encourages followers of Christ to make his presence visible through lives of counter-cultural sacrifice and denial. Too often, Christian participation in disagreements that descend into protracted conflict has been marked by a refusal even to consider how some of these teachings from the Sermon on the Mount might influence Christian conduct in the contemporary church. It may be that loving enemies within the church is the very hardest context within which Jesus' commandment can wholeheartedly be followed.

The place of forgiveness within a theological ethic of disagreement must also be emphasized. Jesus' followers are not merely encouraged to turn the other cheek, or love their enemies, or become childlike; crucially, the call is to engage in an active ministry of forgiveness: 'For if you forgive others their trespasses, your heavenly Father will also forgive you' (Matt. 6.14; also Luke 11.4). In the sense that some disagreements fester as a result of unforgiveness, the relevance of this may be self-evident. But seen alongside clear appeals to an honest awareness about the impact of words spoken – 'it is what comes out of the mouth that defiles' (Matt. 15.11b) – we are reminded that Jesus calls his followers to speak with care and forgive others with generosity. How we speak is reflective of our very self: 'The good person out of the good treasure of the heart produces good, and the evil person out of evil treasure produces evil; for it is out of the abundance of the heart that the mouth speaks' (Luke 6.45). Such words of Jesus have a sobering bearing on how disagreements might be approached. An instance of harsh words flowing rather too easily may be tellingly indicative of the less than perfect state of the speaker's heart; it may just be that an enemy is being hated too easily, and Jesus' costly call quietly ignored.

A telling example of human intemperance standing in the way of kingdom values is found in the parable of the prodigal son. The older brother's response to news of the return of his feckless sibling brims with indignation as he confronts his father:

> 'Listen! For all these years I have been working like a slave for you, and I have never disobeyed your command; yet you have never given me even a young goat so that I might celebrate with my friends. But when this son of yours came back, who has devoured your property with prostitutes, you killed the fatted calf for him!' (Luke 15.29–30)

It is hard not to be sympathetic to these sentiments, but the father's insistence that the other son's return should be celebrated generously offers a helpful insight into Jesus' concern that a charitable welcome should be extended towards those whose prior faults we might otherwise seek to highlight, often for our own benefit. Within the parable itself, disagreement between father and son is resolved by the father's wise words; in telling this story, Jesus offers his hearers a compelling example of the danger of resentment – it leads too easily to a bitterness that prevents the realization of gospel reconciliation. The call to Christians is to see the best in others, and to delight in any growth in their relationship with the Father. Often, this will mean that expressions of Christian life will, at best, be occasions without disagreement. That said, we should not be much surprised by the rarity of such glimpses of the realized kingdom. And, as we shall now see, the open discussion of difference can have a useful place in the life of the church.

On not avoiding disagreement

Jesus' teaching on judgement at the start of Matthew 7 is a good place from which to begin to develop a more nuanced account of the place of disagreement within Christian life. Too often, I suggest, it is a text whose interpretation focuses disproportionately on the bold command of the first verse – 'Do not judge, so that you may not be judged' (Matt. 7.1) – without taking seriously the implications of the fifth: 'You hypocrite, first take the log out of your own eye, and then you will see clearly to take the speck out of your neighbour's eye' (v. 5). We may correctly assume that taking the log out of our own eye is no easily achieved task, but the narrative does not remove the possibility that we might be able to do just that. And then, at this point, sufficient clarity has been achieved such that a judgement concerning the speck in the neighbour's eye can be undertaken. In our consideration of a theology of disagreement, this text does not offer a blueprint for how disagreements might be approached, but it does endorse the notion that within Christian life, judgement of another is permissible in very specific circumstances. An occasion for judgements being made by one of another might well also be an occasion of disagreement: the Christian who is confident that they have removed the log from their own eye is then permitted to address the speck in the eye of their neighbour.

At the very least, this teaching narrows the range of circumstances where a Christian might confidently launch into challenge or judgement of another's affairs, without excluding the possibility of disagreement altogether; and it is worth noting that only a few verses later, the Golden Rule is articulated: 'In everything do to others as you would have them do to you; for this is the law and the prophets' (Matt. 7.12). A culture of mutual respect and reciprocity is desired as a hallmark of life within the kingdom, and this has the potential to enable fruitful disagreement. Later in Matthew's Gospel, Jesus offers concrete expression of how difference should be faced within the ecclesial community: 'If another member of the church sins against you, go and point out the fault when the two of you are alone. If the member listens to you, you have regained that one' (Matt. 18.15). Notwithstanding the assumption within this example that it is clear who is in the wrong, it offers evidence that Jesus does envisage debate and disagreement among his followers – though with the hope that this disciplinary process will lead to the restoration of unity. More surprising, perhaps, is the fate of those who fail to be persuaded individually, by a small group, or before the whole church: 'if the offender refuses to listen even to the church, let such a one be to you as a Gentile and a tax collector' (v. 17).

This scenario illustrates that Jesus himself envisaged the possibility that disagreement can lead to a fracture within the life of the church. In this instance, attempts at resolution have been made, but the sinful party refuses to alter their conduct, and thus experiences some degree of exclusion as a result. That this should mean treatment akin to that of a Gentile emphasizes, for Craig Evans, the 'Jewish orientation' of Matthew's Gospel: 'The Jesus who conferred upon his disciples the authority to preach and heal in his name has also conferred upon his disciples authority in all matters of teaching and discipline.'[10] So the church emerges as an institution that is expected to regulate its affairs and articulate the boundaries of what constitutes acceptable behaviour for members of the Body. Within such a group, disagreement is inevitable, and though unity is highly prized, that does not mean a limitless flexibility in the face of conflict. Indeed, in Luke's Gospel, Jesus is explicit about the need to rebuke those who cause others to stumble, while at the same time urging forgiveness of those who repent of their sins (Luke 17.1–4).

In the context of mission, Jesus is emphatic about the inevitability that disagreements and opposition will be faced in the course of the itinerant ministry of his disciples. And just as a time comes when disagreements within the church can lead appropriately to some degree of separation, so here Jesus tells his disciples, 'If anyone will not welcome you or listen to your words, shake off the dust from your feet as you leave that house or town' (Matt. 10.14). As with the other instances of disagreement noted in this section, it has to be recognized that Jesus' advice to his disciples is predicated on the assumption that they are right and those they encounter are wrong. There is no particular expectation of reasoned argument among equals – and in that sense, it is in our subsequent consideration of the Acts of the Apostles, in chapter 3, that we will encounter New Testament texts that inform theological disagreement on contemporary matters where faithful Christians are in mutual opposition concerning a particular issue. That said, these instances from the Synoptic Gospels help demonstrate that within the teaching of Jesus himself, unity within the church is not anticipated as something that can be achieved perfectly; nor should it be striven for at all costs. These Synoptic fragments help us to construct a theology of disagreement that accepts the frailty of the church, while still aiming to respond to the call to loving unity at the heart of Jesus' mandate to his followers.

At the end of a discussion about divorce in Matthew's Gospel, involving Jesus in discussion with both Pharisees and his disciples, we encounter a perplexing passage that is of significant value as we continue to define the contexts within which disagreement can appropriately be expressed in the life of the church. Having been challenged by the Pharisees about acceptable causes for divorce, Jesus then responds to his disciples' assertion that there are circumstances where it is better not to marry:

> But he said to them, 'Not everyone can accept this teaching, but only those to whom it is given. For there are eunuchs who have been so from birth, and there are eunuchs who have been made eunuchs by others, and there are eunuchs for the sake of the kingdom of heaven. Let anyone accept this who can.' (Matt. 19.11–12)

These are words of Jesus that, for our purposes, demand careful attention. Jesus' initial words of response to the disciples are striking: they indicate his awareness that a piece of teaching, however correct or appropriate, may not be accepted by everyone. Divergence of response is to be expected.

That this observation is then followed by an indication of the three classes of 'eunuch' further underlines the way in which this moment of discussion with the disciples represents a recognition on Jesus' part of the presence of apparently unreconciled diversity in certain situations. Crucially, he concedes that not everyone will accept this state of affairs, but he hopes that anyone who can, will. Jesus thus highlights human complexity to his disciples, affirming the place of those who by virtue of their lack of marriage risked marginalization. Here, the presence of disagreement is acknowledged, as is the lack of any foreseeable resolution to it. The disciples are made aware, by Jesus, of this example of divergent responses to the presence of eunuchs, and the fact that disagreement exists as a result. For the reader of Matthew's Gospel, it can hardly escape attention that this discussion is followed immediately by another example of Jesus encouraging children to come to him, and reminding his disciples that it is to them that the kingdom belongs. Human complexity has been outlined, but is then immediately followed by a reminder that it is in the innocence of childhood that the most appropriate response to Jesus' call is found. Disagreement can be acknowledged and held in tension, but the example of little children running to Jesus in faith remains paradigmatic in its simplicity and wholeheartedness.

One final observation in this section reminds us that however much Jesus exhorts loving unity among his disciples, and the embrace of a childlike faith, he also speaks with candour concerning the potential for hostility engendered as a result of his ministry and legacy: 'Do you think that I have come to bring peace to the earth? No, I tell you, but rather division!' (Luke 12.51). However deliberate the exaggeration in these words, no reader can fail to recognize that the divisive implications that can follow from faithful discipleship are being rigorously explored. In verse 57, Jesus asks, 'And why do you not judge for yourselves what is right?', suggesting that if only this were the case, the use of judges and the threat of prison could be avoided; appropriate discrimination should be encouraged. While these verses do not offer any kind of straightforward blueprint for the life of the church, they do show the equivocal nature of Jesus' teaching when it comes to matters of disagreement. As we seek to develop a theology of disagreement using a modified version of Richard Hays' approach to the reading of New Testament texts, these verses that allow for – and even endorse – the place of disagreement within the life of faith will need careful consideration if a fruitful theological synthesis is to be achieved, without ignoring biblical complexity.

On discerned disagreement in the context of faithful discipleship

Earlier in this chapter we considered some of Jesus' words in Luke 6, specifically his call to generous love and careful speech. It is worth also considering the final section of these sayings, where he challenges his disciples to put their faith into action. He introduces the parable of the wise and foolish builders with words that offer an encapsulation of Christian discipleship: 'I will show you what someone is like who comes to me, hears my words, and acts on them' (Luke 6.47). This threefold call – to come to Jesus, to hear and to act – offers an important reminder of the context within which Jesus envisages the possibility of fruitful disagreement. It is those who trust in him and seek to act in faithful response that he seeks to commend as disciples; indeed, his frustration at the opposite reality is evident in the preceding verse: 'Why do you call me "Lord, Lord", and do not do what I tell you?' (v. 46). His priority is that his disciples should find faith and then live it out. Jesus' frustration towards his disciples is most evident in those situations where they fail to follow his instructions – falling asleep in Gethsemane as recorded at Mark 14.32–42, for example – but this sort of frustration should be seen as indicative of the priority Jesus gives to those who follow him doing so wholeheartedly.

The Great Commission contains similar sentiments: baptism should be seen alongside a commitment to encourage faithful discipleship, and Jesus commands the Eleven to make disciples of all nations, not only baptizing, but 'teaching them to obey everything that I have commanded you' (Matt. 28.20a). This is not a call to obedience that excludes the potential for disagreement, but it does place at the heart of discipleship a commitment to obey, and this in turn has to have implications for how the place of disagreement might be viewed within the life of the church. Mary's yes to God in Luke 1.38 similarly emphasizes the iconic quality of faithful submission in Christian life: 'Here am I, the servant of the Lord; let it be with me according to your word.' Just as Jesus could not avoid drinking the cup offered by his father, so Mary commits in faith to trusting in the Lord who calls. An important question in all disagreements is whether it is one being faced in faith and with the possibility of ultimately building up the church in its mission.

The parable of the sower provides a further prompt for theological reflection on the importance of a deep-rooted faith that leads to fruitfulness. Some seeds fall on the path and are taken away immediately; others grow with little root and soon fall away after initial growth; others are seduced by other desires; and then, finally, 'these are the ones sown on the good soil: they hear the word and accept it and bear fruit, thirty and sixty and a hundredfold' (Mark 4.20). Now this is not to suggest that the presence of disagreement, of itself, renders a seed liable to poor germination, but we cannot overlook the fact that *acceptance* of the word is seen as a prerequisite to fruitfulness. A danger, at least implied, is that endless disagreement about what constitutes the word – rather than an acceptance of it – undermines fruitfulness. We may well then point out that if only what constitutes the word were more clearly defined, the church might be able to live out its mission with fewer distracting disagreements. But we also must recognize that a particular challenge for the church, both historically and in its current life, is the facing of disagreement among opposed Christians who all claim to accept the word that leads to life. A theology of disagreement needs to be able to offer to the church tools of discernment that enable disagreements to be faced without fundamentally undermining a commitment to faithful obedience, such that ecclesial debates do not inevitably undermine the church's mission and witness.

As we shall see in Part 3, a deeper appreciation of the place of the Holy Spirit in Christian disagreement is crucial. For now, it is important to note within the Synoptic Gospels the confidence with which Jesus outlines his conviction that the Holy Spirit will speak in and through his disciples, even as they face opposition and violence from religious authorities in the course of their mission: 'When they hand you over [to councils], do not worry about how you are to speak or what you are to say; for what you are to say will be given to you at that time; for it is not you who speak, but the Spirit of your Father speaking through you' (Matt. 10.19–20).

This comment comes shortly after Jesus has told his disciples to leave houses or towns where their words are not welcomed (vv. 12–14), seemingly suggesting that it is better for his disciples to move on than stay and attempt to be heard by those who exhibit a degree of hostility towards them. Instead, they are to be encouraged by the way in which the Spirit will guide their speech in moments of challenge or danger, 'for the Holy Spirit will teach you at that very hour what you ought to say' (Luke 12.12). It is this sense of assurance in the ability of the Spirit to inspire appropriate speech that leads me to suggest that one quality of authentic Christian disagreement can be identified as *discerned disagreement in the context of faithful discipleship*. It is not disagreement that is entered into intemperately or casually, and without care for its impact on the church; rather, it is engaged in following discernment, seeking to be carried out within a framework of faithful response to God's call.

Conclusion

It is only with all relevant texts from across the New Testament having been considered that the 'synthetic' task proposed by Richard Hays can be attempted by the Christian ethicist seeking to find a coherent response to a particular moral issue amid the canon's diverse voices. At this point, having considered texts from the Synoptic Gospels, it is possible to make some initial reflections on how instances from the ministry of Jesus as recounted by Matthew, Mark and Luke might inform an emerging theology of disagreement rooted in a reading of the New Testament.

I have already highlighted that a distinction can be made between Jesus' actions in articulating and defending the kingdom, and his teaching to those who choose to follow him. He battles with authority figures, speaking provocatively and combatively, but in pursuit of a theology that affirms loving unity within the church. In the fraught context of contemporary ecclesial disagreement, it is instructive to consider how this distinction may inform contemporary debates. The Christian who regards Jesus as an angry anti-establishment figure, and then understands such characteristics as paradigmatic for their own engagement in ecclesial disagreement, risks prioritizing the biographical imitation of Jesus over the following of his commands; Jesus' approach to disagreement with the Pharisees is never proposed as an example of how to approach debate or disagreement within the church.

This does not mean that Jesus himself is beyond challenge in disagreement, as the Syrophoenician woman demonstrates. The Christian call is to love God, including with one's mind, and that has to include the creation of opportunities within the church where vigorous debate and disagreement can occur. But is such disagreement always held *in faith* in a way that might seem consistent with the priority Jesus places on the disciples' fidelity to his call? Or might ecclesial disagreement more often be experienced as a wilderness place within the church, where sustaining faith seems to have been replaced by secularized politicking? It is in such a climate that an appeal to the place and work of the Holy Spirit may be most important, guiding and leading the church even in the midst of its arguments.

Such tentative conclusions cannot be pressed further before we have engaged in our broader descriptive task of instances and examples of disagreement from across the New Testament. But in our consideration of the Synoptic Gospels, the beginnings of a theology of disagreement can be seen to emerge. It is when the disciples are faithful to their call that the kingdom grows as Jesus wishes; the presence of disagreement can be indicative of a focus on human possibility rather than divine potential; judging others is possible, but planks in our own eyes must first be removed. Disagreement is neither overwhelmingly condemned nor casually condoned. As our focus moves to the Gospel and Epistles of John, these emerging themes will be given a clearer theological basis, as we seek to consider how the church can be faithful to its calling while facing and working through its inevitable disagreements.

Notes

1 William L. Lane, 1974, *The Gospel According to Mark*, London: Marshall, Morgan & Scott, p. 433.

2 Tom Wright, 1996, *Jesus and the Victory of God*, London: SPCK, p. 383.

3 Morna Hooker, 1991, *The Gospel According to Mark*, London: Continuum, p. 182. See also the extended discussion in Kelly Iverson, 2007, *Gentiles in the Gospel of Mark*, London: T&T Clark, pp. 44–57.

4 R. T. France, 2002, *The Gospel of Mark: A Commentary on the Greek Text*, Grand Rapids: Eerdmans, p. 299. Francis J. Moloney also notes that Jesus' response 'establishes a rhetorical effect that throws into sharp relief the Gentile woman's recognition of her nothingness' – her disagreement with Jesus provides the context within which her daughter's healing follows. See Francis J. Moloney, 2002, *The Gospel of Mark: A Commentary*, Grand Rapids: Baker Academic, p. 148.

5 Craig Evans, 2012, *Matthew*, Cambridge: Cambridge University Press, p. 304.

6 R. T. France, 2007, *The Gospel of Matthew*, Grand Rapids: Eerdmans, p. 148.

7 W. D. Davies and Dale C. Allison, 2004, *Matthew: A Shorter Commentary*, London: T&T Clark, p. 274.

8 Davies and Allison, *Matthew*, p. 319.

9 See also Luke 12.57–59.

10 Evans, *Matthew*, p. 335.

2

Johannine Perspectives
on Loving Unity

At first glance, the Gospel and Epistles of John might seem to be an unlikely source of rich pickings to resource a theology of disagreement. These are texts short on ethical specificities; but as we shall see, the theological framework offered, particularly in the Gospel's Farewell Discourse, can offer foundations for our study as a whole.[1] Specifically, John 13.35 receives sustained attention in this chapter as a verse that articulates the priority of mutual love within the Christian community, and the centrality of this love to the recognizability of that community by outsiders. My contention is that legitimate scholarly concern for questions about sectarianism within the Johannine literature has risked eclipsing the recognition of an ethical norm for Christian life that is outlined within both the Gospel and the Epistles of John as a whole, and summarized in 13.35. An initial focus on this particular verse thus opens up a wider discussion of the Gospel of John. Later, I will consider the two themes of love and unity in greater detail, both in the Gospel and the Johannine Epistles, before a final consideration of the image of the vine and Jesus washing his disciples' feet, as embodied examples of the ethical norms being proposed within a theology of disagreement.

John 13.35 as a foundational text for an ethic of Christian relating

A core contention of this book is that Christian disagreement is damaging to the church, but the fact of such disagreement is seldom considered in relation to missionary effectiveness. And yet, in John 13.35, the quality of internal church relationships is unambiguously linked by Jesus to the way in which the Christian community is noticeable and attractive to those who are beyond it: 'By this everyone will know that you are my disciples, if you have love for one another' (John 13.35). That mission and ethics are brought together in these words of Jesus is hardly controversial, and yet it is striking how little attention is given to the impact that visibly unloving public Christian discourse might have on the mission of the church. Conversely, we will later consider how loving disagreement could model something deeply attractive to a world routinely unable to disagree well. Such an approach reminds us that a call to be loving need not equal a call to bland niceness where wrongdoing is ignored; our question concerns the importance of a Christian determination to sustain mutual love, even in the midst of disagreement. We hardly need note that this arduous work of maintaining loving unity with fellow Christians with whom one disagrees represents an option all too easily dismissed in contemporary Christian discourse.

Part of our challenge, perhaps surprisingly, is the very clarity and simplicity of Jesus' words in John 13.35, which has meant they have been of intriguingly limited interest to some biblical scholars: the text *itself* is relatively unremarkable, however important its theological claim. Such an observation exposes the potential within biblical scholarship for a disproportionate focus on historical and literary analysis, to the detriment of theological exploration. In our case, a verse of clear theological significance for the self-understanding of the Christian community is repeatedly overlooked by biblical scholars. John 13.35 receives no specific mention in John Ashton's 500-page work on the Gospel,[2] and is entirely ignored in Ashton's edited volume, *The Interpretation of John*.[3] Stephen Smalley merely cites the verse in two footnotes, and then only in relation to 13.34;[4] and C. H. Dodd gives the verse only the briefest of mentions in *The Interpretation of the Fourth Gospel* and not at all in *Historical Tradition in the Fourth Gospel*.[5] This overlooking is not universal, but we should at least note that in some key works that analyse the Gospel of John, its rendering of the command to love, and the implications that follow, are seen as being of peripheral interest.

It is also important to consider how this verse is seen within broader scholarly discussion of the self-understanding of the oft-cited 'Johannine community'. Raymond E. Brown underlines the fact that Johannine Christians' concern for their reputation with outsiders was not merely a missionary strategy designed to grow their community; instead, this command to mutual love was rooted in clear christological convictions, which were no abstract theological claim, but something that demanded to be lived out in practice. It is the love of Jesus that inspires the disciples to seek to demonstrate love for one another. Brown quotes 13.35 when he notes that 'such an understanding of God and of Jesus demands that the Johannine Christian, who is a child of God, behave in a way worthy of his Father and of Jesus his Brother'.[6] In reconstructing the 'Community of the Beloved Disciple', Brown has joined other scholars in emphasizing the precarious position of the Johannine community in relation to the synagogue and Jewish authorities. An emphasis on the familial qualities of internal relationships within the community can be read as further evidence for a growing sense of separation from the wider world. But Brown regards this as an inappropriate emphasis: 'The Gospel is not an in-group manifesto meant as a triumph over outsiders; its goal is to challenge the Johannine community itself to understand Jesus more deeply.'[7]

The challenge for the Christian ethicist engaging with such discussions is that, for all their important insights, they can risk missing a more fundamental and lasting point to emerge from the verse. Given the context in which contemporary Christians engage with Scripture – seeing at least some value in the text not merely in order to understand a historical Johannine community, but in order to inform moral decision-making in their own lives – we should be alert to questions about the status of these words of Jesus not merely in relation to his own 12 disciples, but in relation to all those subsequently who follow him. This book claims that a scholarly focus on dualistic opposition to the world within the Johannine community has resulted in a loss of focus on questions about the importance of the recognizable love evident between members of the Christian community. However strongly or weakly defined the church is against the world, reflection on the internal relationships within the ecclesial community is worthwhile, particularly for the ethicist with an eye to the levels of current ecclesial disunity wherever one looks in the global church. Ethicists engaging with Scripture need to help ensure that appropriate concerns for historical and textual questions do not risk the masking of crucial ethical questions.

Here again we recognize a sometimes stark difference in perspective between the biblical scholar's internal textual concerns and the ethicist's questions concerning how these texts may impact on the moral shape of the life of the church. John 13.35 advocates an internal unity that tends to be conspicuous by its absence in current Christian public discourse – especially on controversial ethical issues. So for the Christian ethicist, concerned primarily with how the contemporary church engages with John, received as it is as part of canonical Scripture, an analysis of 13.35 inescapably includes consideration of how this appeal to mutual love then informs Christian engagement with the world, not merely in the Johannine community but in today's church. Such a leap needs to be made with care, armed with insights from biblical scholarship and a good deal of cultural awareness – but it is a leap that should not be resisted, however cautiously it should be attempted. In the context of 13.35, it is a leap with inescapable resonances for contemporary understanding of Christian mission: if the recognizability of mutual love is an enduring quality of Christian discipleship, then a Western church that is both riven with disputes and in numerical decline might consider asking itself whether the nature of its internal relationships has any bearing on the vitality of the Christian community itself.

Crucially, we should not overlook a simple question about why John's Gospel was written, and what hopes for the Christian community inspired that process. Neither should we forget how significant a gap of theological intent exists between some biblical scholarship and the approach to Scripture that may be found in churches that routinely read and honour the Gospel in worship. An illustration of this tension can be found towards the end of a review of scholarly responses to the Gospel: in a study focused on questions of authorship, composition and sources, Ruth Edwards maintains an air of critical suspicion when she appears reluctant to admit that the Gospel's 'primary purpose *seems* to have been theological and evangelistic rather than historical'.[8] It is a revealing comment, for it demonstrates how it is possible for a textually focused account to lose sight of the theological qualities of the text, and indeed, potentially, its very reason for existing at all. Our question is not so much *whether* John's Gospel is theological or evangelistic, but rather *how* those qualities may be translated into and inform the life of the contemporary church. Having considered the contested status of John 13.35 as a foundational expression of an ethic that inspires mutual love and unity among Johannine Christians, we now consider the themes of love and unity in greater detail, considering as we do so to what extent the Johannine understanding of these concepts usefully informs moral decision-making in the contemporary church.

Johannine love and Christian disagreement

Part of the inescapable challenge facing any appeal to the importance of love is the sheer breadth of sentiment – or ethical intent – that 'loving' might encapsulate. In this section, then, it is necessary to try and discern how love, as a theme of clear narrative significance, might best be understood within these Johannine writings. Only then, if there is clarity about what is meant when we appeal to the importance of love, not least in John 13.35, can one explore how this understanding might then inform ethical approaches to disagreement within the church. First, I analyse the role of narrative and story in the establishment of a Johannine love ethic, with particular reference to the Samaritan woman; I then consider the place of faith and eschatological hope in forming an understanding of love; finally, I examine the appeal to acts as well as emotion – to deeds as well as words – found in 1 John.

It is worth beginning by noting that the Gospel of John is an example of a text where ethical norms *are* outlined, but (perhaps inconveniently) in the form of principles to live by rather than specific rules to follow. Tom Wright usefully suggests that the very narrative form of much scriptural writing is designed to remind God's people that to live the life to which they are called means entering into the story begun in the pages of the Bible:

> Story authority, as Jesus knew only too well, is the authority that really works. Throw a rule book at people's heads, or offer them a list of doctrines, and they can duck or avoid it, or simply disagree and go away. Tell them a story, though, and you invite them to come into a different world; you invite them to share a world-view or better still a 'God-view'.[9]

Quoting Wright, Hans Boersma argues that it is on this basis that the Gospel of John becomes worthy of ethical exploration, for it engages its readers through storytelling, forming part of God's larger narrative where love is foundational: 'rather than being morally bankrupt, the fourth gospel opens up a worldview that invites us to enter into the story of Israel and Jesus, and so into the new age where love is the basic ground rule.'[10] That both writers speak of a 'world view' is worth noting: my claim is that within the Johannine literature, foundational, 'world view'-forming principles about authentic Christian love can be found.

Jesus and the Samaritan woman: John 4

This love can be witnessed in unexpected places in the narrative – but we should be cautious about how easily this process of identifying a prevailing world view, rooted in love, might proceed. A consideration of Jesus' encounter with the woman of Samaria in the fourth chapter of the Gospel is instructive, not for its specific verbal content about Christian love but for the way that Jesus engages with the woman, revealing much about himself and his priorities (John 4.1–29). Here, after all, is an episode that does not contain within it specific moral teaching but which may usefully tell us something significant about the fullness of life to which Jesus calls his followers. Richard Hays calls the Jesus of John's Gospel 'a relentless revealer of a single metaphysical secret',[11] and it is this disclosure of his identity as Messiah that gives the meeting with the Samaritan woman its narrative force. But this is, of course, a theological response to the text. And we must recognize that the scholarship which might usefully inform that theological understanding is not necessarily willing, of itself, to sit within the sort of theological framework inhabited by an ethicist and biblical scholar like Richard Hays.

In relation to the woman of Samaria, we should at least note that Jesus does not choose to highlight her moral failings but instead encourages her recognition of who he is. To be on a journey of discipleship at all is prioritized over an examination of her own morality. Given that Christian churches today still struggle to handle disagreement and other moral questions, it is at the very least worth noting Jesus' strategy to recognize, but not dwell on, the woman's sinful past. Jesus' love is seen here to be generous and compassionate in its approach: it is an example that the contemporary church might well bear in mind as it struggles to determine how to engage with questions of contested personal morality. If the encouragement of discipleship becomes the priority, as it was for Jesus on this occasion, questions of personal morality might then be seen in a broader context – that of the life of a church made up of sinners journeying towards holiness.

It is all too easy to ignore the way that Jesus does not pass judgement on the woman's serial monogamy; or to fail to ask how the episode is, of itself, reflective of the love that the Father shows through the life, death and resurrection of his Son. Considering the question of whether John intends to affirm only that love held among Christians, we might note that here we see a Samaritan being made aware of the eschatological reality of Jesus – the convictions expressed in 3.16 are demonstrated in person through dialogue as Jesus' messiahship is articulated. Critics of Johannine ethics have repeatedly contrasted the internalizing sectarianism of John with the neighbour-love epitomized by Luke's good Samaritan, but here in 4.1–29 it is a *Samaritan* woman who receives this gift of knowledge of the Messiah. This is, surely, an incident that demonstrates some of Jesus' loving characteristics – and that aids our understanding of 'love' in the Fourth Gospel. But it does so through its theological weight, containing within it ethical insights – and in the earlier sections of the Gospel, prior to the Farewell Discourse, it is in instances such as this that important ethical observations can be made.

Love as eschatological sign: John 3; 1 John 3

The signs associated with Jesus in these earlier chapters of John's Gospel point to the miraculous intervention of the Messiah in the world of unsuspecting Jews. Nicodemus, like the Samaritan woman, is invited to consider the eschatological significance of Jesus' claims – and in this instance, eschatological reality is associated with God's love in sending his Son into the world (3.16). Core convictions about who Jesus is seemingly need to be established; it is on this theological foundation that discipleship is built. If John's project is to outline the attractiveness of following Jesus the miraculous healer, he is careful to associate Jesus' earthly ministry with the love of the Father who sent him. The Father loves the Son; the Son loves the Father; Jesus loves his followers, who in turn should love one another. Barrett notes that this sequence shows how John 'develops the conception of love as the nature of God himself and as the means by which the divine life, the relation of the Father and the Son, is perpetuated and demonstrated in the community'.[12] So an appreciation of the love that God demonstrates to the world is based upon recognition of Jesus as Messiah; to love, for John, is to follow Jesus and to continue to reflect this love through the quality of relationships at the heart of the church. When Christians disagree, the continued reflection of that mutual love into the world is too easily threatened.

The claim that the Gospel and Epistles of John contain a foundational world view about the centrality of love within Christian discipleship is, then, rooted in a theological conviction about eschatology, expressed through narrative and story rather than explicit moral injunctions. But such views need to be expressed carefully if they are not to slip into vague generality. Richard Hays is alert to this danger: 'John's emphasis on intracommunal love is sometimes construed as a license for sentimental complacency within the church.'[13] Hays insists that such a conclusion is not inevitable, not least if the counter-cultural reality of the Johannine community is recognized alongside its call to costly service. But this avoidance of 'sentimental complacency' is achieved, in particular, by reading the Epistles alongside the Gospel, with a focus on the ways in which the command to love is intensified and clarified in 1 John. Although the focus on love within the community is maintained and indeed restated, in 1 John 3.17–18 we find an emphasis on offers of practical action – help for a brother or sister in need – as being part of what it means to reflect God's love. It is true that the debates around whether John 13.35 implies a sharing of love beyond the community are echoed here; Hays suggests that 'even though their primary mandate is to manifest love and service within the community, the disciples who share in Jesus' mission in the world can hardly remain indifferent to those outside the community of faith.'[14]

The claim that God is love: 1 John 4

A further dimension to our understanding of love offered by 1 John comes in the affirmations of 1 John 4.8 and 4.16 – that God *is* love. Just before this statement, in 4.7, mutual love has been affirmed 'because love is from God'; the later two verses intensify this association between loving action and engagement with the divine. To love is to associate profoundly with the very essence of God, and to carry out his most basic will in the world. Raymond Brown's consideration of the vocabulary used by John to indicate love is worth noting: 'a careful study of the Johannine uses of *agapan* and *philein* shows that the verbs are often used interchangeably, so that scholars like Bernard, Bultmann, and Barrett are not at all convinced that the verbs are not synonymous.'[15] Several recent scholars have concluded, with Brown, that 'there does not seem to be any significant difference in meaning'.[16] But this love is not without a hard edge, in that 1 John 4.20 binds together love for God with the love of brothers and sisters. With characteristic dualism, loving God and hating fellow Christians is denounced: 'those who love God must love their brothers and sisters also' (1 John 4.21b), offering an inescapable challenge to Christians content to disagree unlovingly.

Across Gospel and Epistles, John repeatedly asserts that the love of God shown in Jesus should flow into the life, and particularly the mutual love, of the Christian community. A world view is proposed; a foundational ethic for Christian relating is put forward in a body of writing otherwise often lacking more specific ethical teaching. Ruth Edwards sums it up thus: 'Though obedience to God's (or Christ's) commands is frequently enjoined, it is never spelt out what these commands are: the only one mentioned is the command to love. This is both a strength and a weakness of Johannine ethics.'[17] Her conclusion is found repeatedly in discussions of the (lack of) ethical material in the Gospel and Epistles of John, but it is one that rests too heavily on the notion that ethics is only about specificities of moral action. As we noted both Wright and Boersma observing at the start of this section, the positing of a world view is both challenging and attractive – as well as being a statement of ethical intent. This book argues that prioritizing mutual love as an ethical imperative is neither naive nor impossible to take seriously, even if Christians have often struggled to meet such an ideal. As Richard Hays notes: 'Given the actual level of conflict and struggle within the church historically … John's vision of a community living in loving fellowship is hardly to be disparaged as trivial.'[18] As we consider the ethical basis of a theology of disagreement, this Johannine emphasis on the importance of loving community is foundational. And as we move on to a discussion of the Johannine understanding of the concept of 'unity', we will begin to anticipate the Gospel's Farewell Discourses, where – in imagery of vine, and through the enactment of footwashing – love and unity are combined, to form the heart of a Johannine conception of the church.

The pursuit of unity

Three factors may be borne in mind as we consider the concept of unity within the Gospel and Epistles of John: first, that the Word of the Gospel's Prologue points to a *theological* unity at the heart of John's project which is reflective of the unity of a trinitarian God, where the eternal word takes on human form; second, this theological unity leads to a new kind of unity being made visible among those who choose to follow this path; third, it is a unity of relevance not merely for a Johannine church or community but for the church throughout the ages as it continues to fashion its life as the Body of Christ.

Our discussion of the Johannine conception of unity thus begins with the Prologue's foundational theological claims. We then consider the work of the Spirit, as the force that inspires the unity to which disciples are called. Focusing on our understanding of the context in which John wrote, we examine the more negative, sectarian notions of unity present within the Gospel, before finally considering the development of these themes within the Epistles.

The unity of the Prologue: John 1

The Prologue to John's Gospel is important for our purposes because it grounds the whole of the Gospel in theological territory – but on a cosmic scale. It locates Jesus as the incarnate Word at the heart of God's salvific activity in creation; so Jesus is demonstrably the Son of God, united with God and 'full of grace and truth' (v. 14). The ultimate theological significance of Jesus is affirmed in words which, through their poetic quality and immediacy, have resonated for Christians down the centuries – with the force of the very first verse inviting the follower of Jesus to recognize, in the Word, the God of eternity: 'In the beginning was the Word, and the Word was with God, and the Word was God. He was in the beginning with God' (vv. 1–2). This claim of a deep interconnectedness between the life and ministry of Jesus and the eternal work of God is a central claim for John, and a foundational one for Christianity. The pursuit of 'unity' in the Gospel is integral to these core theological convictions. John's narrative, with its careful characterization and often extended detail about Jesus' healing ministry, guides its reader with the aim of communicating the importance of faith in Jesus the Messiah.

The call of the Christian disciple towards unity, received in faith, is central to this theological project. As James D. G. Dunn observes, 'Jesus does pray for the unity of believers ... the unity John has in mind is comparable to the unity of the Father and the Son and is both rooted in and dependent on the believer's union with Jesus.'[19] This theological dimension, for John, of any understanding of unity is inescapable. As we later consider how these themes inform the ethical dilemmas confronting the contemporary church, not least in relation to the persistence of damaging disagreement, it will be important to be reminded that within the Johannine Gospel and Epistles, both 'love' and 'unity' are concepts that have to be appraised in a firmly theological context – that of the claims those texts make about the person of Jesus. Disagreement is a problematic concept when it undermines the security, or even the very existence, of the unity to which disciples of Jesus are called. To stray deliberately from that path of unity is to risk losing sight of the very relationships that bind the persons of the Trinity; we might observe that apparently cheap disagreement comes at a hefty theological price.

Unity in the Spirit: John 6; 14; 16

The descriptions within the Gospel of the work of the Spirit are also of crucial relevance if we are to appreciate the importance John attaches to unity. Jesus makes quite clear to his disciples – even in the midst of their misunderstanding and confusion about him – that 'the spirit gives life'. It is noteworthy that in the same exchange, 'many of his disciples turned back and no longer went about with him' (6.66). Glib appeals to the importance of church unity in the present can too easily ignore this example of disunity among disciples at this stage in Jesus' ministry. That some disciples should have turned away from Jesus is linked by John to the difficulty of accepting Jesus' teaching; later, this negative is presented positively when Jesus tells the disciples who remain that 'when the Spirit of truth comes, he will guide you into all the truth' (16.13). Here, the unity of believers is grounded in their shared faith convictions; the Spirit will guide those who choose to believe. For Jan van der Watt, this brings theology and ethics together in a fundamental way: 'believing in Jesus thus becomes the basic ethical requirement.'[20] Crucially, it is the Spirit that both enables and deepens faith; as a result of the disciples' love, the Father sends the Advocate, 'the Spirit of truth, whom the world cannot receive, because it neither sees him nor knows him. You know him, because he abides with you, and he will be in you' (John 14.17). Unity among believers is, in part, defined by the presence of the Spirit – a gift from the Father offered in response to the free decision of faith.

This unity of believers is often portrayed in positive terms; but as we have already noted in relation to John 13.35, an intensification of Christian identity, including mutual love among members of the Johannine community, can result in a sharply defined dualistic division between church and world. And this unity should not simply be seen in terms of a coherent body of Christians united against a sinful world; potential diversity and division *among* the earliest Christians has, at the very least, to be borne in mind when we encounter the sharp dualism of the Johannine Gospel and Epistles. Raymond Brown has argued that the enigmatic and unnamed figure of the Beloved Disciple represents Johannine Christianity within the Gospel, with other figures in the narrative representing other Christian groups – so the Samaritan woman represents Samaritan converts, and Peter the emergence of mainstream Catholic Christianity.[21] It is one theory among many but, as Barnabas Lindars notes, 'the possibility that the Johannine church stood apart from the main body should not be denied'.[22] This means that the apparent call to unity within the text is a problematic one, for it may, of itself, reflect the emerging disunity among the earliest Christians.

It is certainly the case that in all three Epistles, the presence of 'antichrists' and others seeking to disrupt the unity of believers is a substantial concern, met with strident affirmations of orthodoxy.[23] Wayne Meeks suggests that in these writings we encounter a community that has moved on from the primarily Jewish context of the Gospel, to a setting where a Christianity distinct from Judaism has emerged. The task is no longer about defining Christianity in relation to Judaism; the key concern is to assert true Christianity in the face of heresy.

> The battle against the threatening world is now waged not so much in the public confrontations in synagogues and court, as the Gospel portrays it, but in the little houses where the Christians meet, by the lines drawn between followers of one charismatic and those of another.[24]

D. Moody Smith cites 1 and 3 John as examples of the fragmented reality of these earliest Christian communities, with various factions claiming to be the true church. He concludes that such fragmentation has to be acknowledged if the presence of division in the church is to be considered from a theological perspective:

the Johannine literature does not solve the problem of church unity so much as it poses it in an acute and fundamental way. The indispensability of unity is not negated by its absence, and John insists upon its indispensability. The perfection of that unity, with Jesus and among themselves, makes sense of Jesus' seemingly extravagant promises about the fulfilment of his disciples' prayers.[25]

We thus recognize in the church described in the Epistles strikingly similar challenges to those faced in the contemporary church, and are forcefully reminded that division and disunity is seemingly as old as the church itself. But we should not lose sight of the fact that true unity is clearly defined within both Gospel and Epistles as being rooted in theological conviction: the unity of God as expressed in the Prologue to the Gospel is the same unity that reflects the unity of Father and Son. Neither the Gospel nor the Epistles suggest that unity is easily achieved or sustained, but the importance of striving towards it is repeatedly asserted. Ruth Edwards regards 'an ideal of a community of friends bound together in mutual love'[26] as a core articulation of the life of discipleship John proposes to his readers. It is an undoubtedly ambitious hope for any human community – and, to look at the history of the church, it seems an unrealizable one. But this book's contention is that because the core values of love and unity as hallmarks of discipleship have too often been overlooked, their importance within the life of the Christian disciple has been downplayed. As we move to consider the significance of the imagery of the vine and the act of footwashing, we consider their potential role in the formulation of a theology of disagreement.

Love and unity combined in the Farewell Discourse

Imaged: The vine: John 15

The image of the vine reveals much about John's conception of both Jesus and discipleship. Its imaginative force has continued to resonate in the life of the church; its core significance for our study lies in the way that it brings together the concepts of love and unity, combining them to underline their importance as hallmarks of discipleship. The vine becomes a paradigmatic image of the mutual interdependence of Christian believers as they abide in Jesus – apart from him, they lose their connection with the life that sustains the entire plant. John's depiction of the vine is the imaged moment when the inseparability of love and unity is emphasized. D. Moody Smith writes:

Unity with Jesus, and with the Father, is living one's life in, and on the basis of, love ... Jesus as the vine obviously provides the essential support and sustenance for the disciples, who are the branches. As branches, they are not simply passive, but must bear fruit of love or suffer the pain of excommunication.[27]

Here we face once more the stark presentation of Christian fellowship found consistently within Gospel and Epistles: an engaging affirmation of life lived within the community of faith, sustained by mutual love, but lived conscious of the significance of separation from this community. Love is celebrated at the same time that the pain of separation from God is articulated.

It is worth highlighting the key theological moves found within John's discussion of the vine, before we consider their implications. Jesus once more asserts his close relationship with the Father (v. 1) and sets this self-understanding in the context of the Father's removal or pruning of the vine's branches, depending on whether they are bearing fruit (v. 2). The relationship between Son and Father is one also open to disciples: fruitfulness is absolutely connected to the believer's abiding in Jesus, as branches relate to the vine (vv. 4–5). The consequences for branches that do not 'abide in me' are clear and stark (v. 6) and are contrasted with the prospects for those that remain: 'If you abide in me, and my words abide in you, ask for whatever you wish, and it will be done for you' (v. 7). Abiding in love means keeping Jesus' commandments, and the centrality of 13.35 is restated here, with mutual love once again underlined as a response to the love of Jesus (v. 12). Significantly, 'No one has greater love than this, to lay down one's life for one's friends' (v. 13) – so the call to love is associated with Jesus' calling to sacrifice his own life. Those who follow his commands are to be called not servants but friends (vv. 14–15). These people, chosen by him, are appointed 'to go and bear fruit, fruit that will last' (v. 16), and all of these commands have been offered so that his followers 'may love one another' (v. 17).

The focus on the Son as the true vine, constituted in part by its branches, raises important questions about notions of mutuality and interdependence in John's vision of Christian life. Rudolf Schnackenburg emphasizes the significance of the admonition to abide in Christ – for without him the disciples can do nothing:

This is a fundamental statement for the Christian's understanding of himself and his function and activity ... it occurs within the wide context of 'bearing fruit' and makes it clear that only the Christian who lives from his communion with Christ can produce the fruits of his Christian condition.[28]

The emphasis is on each individual Christian relating their own journey of discipleship to their relationship with Jesus. In the vine imagery, we do not find a clear articulation of the value of being part of a Christian community per se, but, rather, the emphasis is always on the mutual love of members of that community who, *as individuals*, abide in Christ. Disagreement is dangerous for the well-being of the church when it undermines the integrity of that communion with Christ; John's concern is to articulate the importance of a fruitfulness that is evident when the individual disciple is united both with Christ and with fellow believers.

The vine holds faith and love *in* unity, but is an image that also expresses the unity at the heart of God, into which believers enter when they choose to abide in Jesus. The vine thus states emphatically that the mutual relationships within the body of Christ are a crucial, foundational part of what it is to constitute that body, not an optional extra. As Victor Paul Furnish notes, 'Unity is given by a love which courses through the whole plant as its life force and enables the plant to bear fruit.'[29] The image of the vine is, therefore, central to our emerging understanding of the importance of loving relationships among Christians as part of the Johannine conception of what it is to be a Christian community. Potentially divisive, sectarian implications do, of course, remain – we should not forget that the image of vine is followed by Jesus' teaching on the world's hatred of him and his disciples (15.18–25) – but recognition of this intense self-identification of the Johannine community in relation to the wider world should not, of itself, mask interest in its internal relationships. The image of the vine establishes, with theological force, that whatever the nature of the Christian community's engagement with the wider world, its internal relationships should be characterized by the love that comes from abiding in Christ.

Enacted: Footwashing: John 13

The loving unity towards which God calls his people is not explained by Jesus only through the use of analogy or image. In John's account of the Last Supper, we find in chapter 13 what Richard Hays refers to as an 'enacted parable';[30] through his deeds as well as his words, the disciples discover foundational information about what it is to be a follower of Jesus. So our discussion considers the role of footwashing in the formation of the identity of the disciples as a distinct group, and how this, in turn, has a role in forming their ethical 'world view' as they contemplate the beginnings of mission in Christ's name. Assessing the implications of footwashing as an example of how authentic discipleship can be both embodied and then lived, we can note the role that footwashing plays in the life of L'Arche communities.[31] Reflecting on the extent to which we find in it an example of an embodied commandment of Jesus with an inescapable ethical dimension, we note that a consideration of the relationship between ethics and contemporary liturgy is unavoidable.

Our focus is quite specifically on Jesus' action in washing his disciples' feet; other questions that arise around this action, important as they are, will not be discussed here. By concentrating our attention on the action that Jesus performed, we have cause to reflect on Jesus' desire to communicate not merely through words but by the performance of an act that embodies servanthood. We recognize that this action was designed to be repeated: 'I have set you an example, that you also should so as I have done to you' (13.15). Marianne Meye Thompson cautions that a primarily ethical reading of the action of footwashing is not the only legitimate one; she points to two prevailing interpretations, one soteriological (with a focus on 13.6–11) and the second ethical (13.12–18). She notes that several commentators have argued for the apparently irreconcilable nature of these two interpretations, but she suggests that to regard them 'as existing in conflict with each other or as having nothing to do with each other severs the intrinsic connection between God's action in Christ, which constitutes the community of his followers, and the life of that community'.[32]

Meye Thompson's concern articulates an issue of core importance for this book: the danger that biblical texts can be analysed outside of their theological context, so that ethics and soteriology or eschatology become unhelpfully separated from one another. In the case of footwashing, we encounter another example of John's desire to express ethical and theological concerns together. So Jesus' sacrificial love becomes a model for his disciples: if they can learn to abide in him and show that love to one another, they will begin to offer a true witness to the wider world. Footwashing is offered as a vivid example of what such loving service can look like in reality. Even though in the midst of the action it is misunderstood (13.7), and even if the recipients of this act of service try to reject it (13.8), Jesus tells the disciples that 'servants are not greater than their master, nor are messengers greater than the one who sent them. If you know these things, you are blessed if you do them' (vv. 16–17). Old orders are overturned; the master washes his servant's feet.

Importantly, we do not find here the commendation of good works alone; note that the scenario begins with a reminder that all that follows is grounded in love: 'Having loved his own who were in the world, he loved them to the end' (13.1b). Instead, we encounter another Johannine example of action flowing from intention. Jesus' task has been to convince his disciples of his purpose on earth; as chapter 14 demonstrates, it is once he is acknowledged as Messiah that his disciples receive the Spirit that will animate their future work. Footwashing thus is an expression of faith. This is what leads Jan van der Watt to suggest, 'If you ask why one disciple should wash the feet of another, the answer takes you right back to the worldview of that particular person.'[33] We can certainly say that John is suggesting that to be a faithful Christian is to become the sort of person who, if a master, washes their servants' feet. But the emphasis is on the *type* of action, rather than on specific repetition of this exact action. So we can agree with van der Watt when he writes of Jesus' engagement with the disciples in John: 'Jesus does not address particular physical external actions, but the way they think (i.e. their mental world). If things change there, at the beginning, the whole continuum will be influenced accordingly ... the basic ethical action in John is expressed in faith in Jesus.'[34]

Right action follows as a result of right faith: this point is repeatedly asserted in John, and assumes a greater degree of significance given the Gospel's relative lack of ethical specificities. Footwashing seems to offer a rare worked example of how, in practice, the disciples might act in response to all that that they have received from Jesus. It is an example within its own right, but with even greater force as a paradigm for their emerging understanding of servanthood. In this sense, their 'world view' is being formed – though van der Watt's adoption of the term to describe the ethic Jesus inaugurates is not without its problems. Van der Watt insists that 'actions are the result of worldviews, or belief systems',[35] and it is this claim that demands qualification. Given than John 13 concludes with Jesus foretelling Peter's denial of him, despite Peter's clearly articulated 'world view' as a faithful disciple, we are reminded that it is only too easy for someone with a clearly articulated 'world view' to betray those convictions in a particular set of circumstances. Van der Watt's simplistic appeal to the value of 'world views' falls short; but his point is worth taking seriously, in the sense that it reminds us that ethical content can be found in John's Gospel as a result of the way that Jesus shapes the foundations of the disciples' moral landscape, attempting to change the way they think rather than bombarding them with specific injunctions about how to act.

This is why footwashing has a special potential significance in relation to a theology of disagreement: it provides a unique articulation within John of a specific ethical norm – that of loving servanthood – that Jesus is attempting to instil in his disciples. This self-denying, graceful act is undertaken by those who abide in Jesus and thus abide together on the vine; the presence of disagreement inevitably highlights the fragility of that vine and the ease with which it can be broken when Christians fail to work to sustain the quality of mutual relationship to which Jesus calls them. Through the act of washing his disciples' feet, Jesus anticipates his own sacrifice, while making clear what it is to act in service within a community of mutual love. All who confess Christ as Lord are welcome to take part – however great their doubts, or impending their betrayal. And in the context of human communities that unavoidably become places of tension and disagreement, Jesus offers a sacramental ritual that overturns convention and emphasizes mutuality and solidarity. Thus the ethical imperatives repeatedly restated throughout the Gospel and Epistles of John are expressed in an intimate, physical way that takes followers of Jesus beyond existing ways of relating. Footwashing outlines for the disciples an example of how to live in love and unity: prioritizing this physical fellowship, treating servants as masters, and doing to others as Jesus has done to them.

Conclusion

Our exploration of the Gospel and Epistles of John has revealed the fundamental interconnectedness and significance of love and unity as themes that show Jesus' disciples how to relate both to God and to each other. This appeal to love is an appeal to adopt a world view that sees relationships with others as flowing from the relationship that the Christian believer has with God; just as the vine and its branches are inseparable, so too the Body of Christ is knit together in such a way that it becomes recognizable as a result of the love that sustains its common life. This intensified sense of self-understanding for the Christian community can, of course, lead to a sectarian inward turn. But to focus our attention on whether the affirmation of love *within* the community has a negative effect on those *beyond* it risks missing the importance of that love itself. It is the love that Jesus calls his disciples to abide in; a key characteristic of the God who *is* love in 1 John. The question that remains is how this clear affirmation of the importance of love can translate into the ongoing life of the church amid its complexity, frailty and disagreements.

It is in Part 2, examining all the relevant New Testament texts together, that we will explore that question in its broadest terms, applying some of Richard Hays' methodology to the instances of disagreement before us. At this point in these Johannine texts, a tone has been set, rather than a rule clearly established. To read the Gospel and Epistles of John is to encounter a community with love at its heart, and where the maintenance and deepening of that love is central to the church's very conception of itself. It is this prioritizing of the pursuit of loving unity which a theology of disagreement must take extremely seriously. If this love is as essential to the well-being of the Body as John maintains, then disagreement can represent the beginnings of conflicts that easily lead to schism and the fragmentation of the church. To honour the theological vision outlined by John must surely involve taking very seriously the safeguarding of this love, especially when threatened by disagreement. As we shall see in some of the later New Testament texts before us, such an approach does not mean an abandonment of debate, nor a complete aversion to separation, but it does mean that disagreement is not undertaken lightly and without sober consideration of its potential outcomes. John repeatedly cherishes a vision of the church as a dynamic community sustained by its mutual love. In contemporary churches sometimes overwhelmed by conflict, this vision is one that demands to be taken seriously; a theology of disagreement can make a contribution towards the establishment of ethical conduct that faces disagreements without being overwhelmed by them, always seeking to safeguard the loving unity that is a hallmark of authentic Christian community.

Notes

1 Given that this chapter considers the New Testament's Johannine writings, it is worth pointing out that it is the judgement of this author that the Revelation to John, in all its apocalyptic splendour, does not contain any material that is directly relevant to, or straightforwardly assists, an exploration of a theology of disagreement.

2 John Ashton, 1991, *Understanding the Fourth* Gospel, Oxford: Clarendon Press, p. 458.

3 John Ashton, ed., 1986, *The Interpretation of John*, London: SPCK.

4 Stephen Smalley, 1998, *John – Evangelist and Interpreter*, Carlisle: Paternoster Press, pp. 34, 271.

5 C. H. Dodd, 1953, *The Interpretation of the Fourth Gospel*, Cambridge: Cambridge University Press, p. 406; Dodd's later *Historical Tradition in the Fourth Gospel*, 1963, Cambridge: Cambridge University Press, makes no mention of the verse at all.

6 Raymond E. Brown, 1979, *The Community of the Beloved Disciple: The Life, Loves and Hates of an Individual Church in New Testament Times*, London: Geoffrey Chapman, p. 61.

7 Brown, *Community*, p. 62.

8 Ruth Edwards, 2003, *Discovering John*, London: SPCK, p. 36. The italics are mine.

9 Tom Wright, 1991, 'How Can the Bible be Authoritative?', *Vox Angelica* 21, p. 22.

10 Hans Boersma, 2003, 'A New Age Love Story: Worldview and Ethics in the Gospel of John', *Calvin Theological Journal* 38,1, p. 105.

11 Richard B. Hays, 1996, *The Moral Vision of the New Testament*, New York: HarperCollins, p. 138.

12 C. K. Barrett, 1978, *The Gospel According to St John*, London: SPCK, pp. 215–16.

13 Hays, *Moral Vision*, p. 145.

14 Hays, *Moral Vision*, p. 145.

15 Raymond E. Brown, 1966, *The Gospel According to John*, New York: Doubleday & Co., p. 498. Brown writes in relation to the Gospel; in the Epistles, the question doesn't arise, for as Ruth Edwards notes, 'in 1–3 John the idea of "love" is expressed exclusively by *agapē* (21 times) and its cognate verb *agapaō* (31 times) and adjective *agapētos*, "beloved" (10 times)'. Ruth Edwards in Barnabas Lindars, Ruth R. Edwards and John M. Court, 2000, *The Johannine Literature*, Sheffield: Sheffield Academic Press, p. 176.

16 Brown, *Gospel*, p. 498.

17 Ruth Edwards in Lindars, Edwards and Court, *Johannine*, p. 200.

18 Hays, *Moral Vision*, p. 145.

19 James D. G. Dunn, 2006, *Unity and Diversity in the New Testament: An Inquiry into the Character of Earliest Christianity*, London: SCM Press, p. 128.

20 Jan van der Watt, 2010, *Thou shalt... do the will of God: Do New Testament Ethics have anything to say today?*, Nijmegen: Radboud University Nijmegen Press, p. 28.

21 See Brown, *Community*.

22 Barnabas Lindars in Lindars, Edwards and Court, *Johannine*, p. 74.

23 As considered variously at 1 John 2.9, 18–28; 2 John 7—8; 3 John 9—12.

24 Wayne A. Meeks, 1993, *The Origins of Christian Morality: The First Two Centuries*, New Haven and London: Yale University Press, p. 61.

25 Moody Smith, 1995, *The Theology of the Gospel of John*, Cambridge: Cambridge University Press, p. 152.

26 Edwards, *Discovering*, p. 146.

27 Moody Smith, *Gospel*, pp. 146–7.

28 Rudolf Schnackenburg, 1982, *The Gospel According to St John*, Tunbridge Wells: Burns & Oates, vol. 3, p. 100.

29 Victor Paul Furnish, 1972, *The Love Command in the New Testament*, Nashville: Abingdon Press, p. 145.

30 Hays, *Moral Vision*, p. 144.

31 'At L'Arche we celebrate people with learning disabilities and build circles of support around them. We go beyond supporting people's basic needs to attend to their emotional and spiritual lives, too.' See www.larche.org.uk/what-wedo (accessed 7 May 2020). Jean Vanier, the founder of L'Arche, has faced posthumous disgrace following the disclosure of his sexual abuse of women who visited him for spiritual direction. But the pioneering work of L'Arche as a movement continues.

32 Marianne Meye Thompson, 2003, '"His Own Received Him Not": Jesus Washes the Feet of His Disciples' in Ellen David and Richard Hays, eds, *The Art of Reading Scripture*, Grand Rapids: Eerdmans, p. 259.

33 Van der Watt, *Thou shalt ... do the will of God*, p. 34.

34 Van der Watt, *Thou shalt ... do the will of God*, p. 29.

35 Van der Watt, *Thou shalt ... do the will of God*, p. 35.

3

Disagreements Faced on Mission within the Acts of the Apostles

We now turn to the 'descriptive' task of assessing the narrative of the Acts of the Apostles as it relates to a theology of disagreement. Our focus is on those instances within the text that can resource our consideration of the place of disagreement within the life of the church. It is within the book of Acts that key paradigmatic examples for a Christian approach to disagreement can be discerned. We begin with examples of disagreement concerning those beyond the existing scope of the church's life, before considering disagreements about the relative status of Jewish and Gentile believers; finally, we explore three facets of disagreement occurring among believers as recorded by Luke.

Disagreement with those beyond the church: Peter and John defend their faith

While the ultimate focus of this book is questions of disagreement among Christians, some examples from the New Testament of engagement in disagreement with those beyond the church help to establish key theological parameters for our study. Peter and John's defence of their faith before the religious authorities in Acts 4 is a key example. Having healed the lame man at the Beautiful Gate in the preceding chapter, certain aspects of the interaction between Peter and John and the high priestly family are noteworthy. Verse 8 is crucial: we are told not merely Peter's response to the question, 'By what power or by what name did you do this?', but that his response was made 'filled with the Holy Spirit'. Relatively early on in the disciples' ministry post-Pentecost, this observation is significant because it points to the way in which a disagreement was faced with reference to God, not undertaken using human intellectual power alone. This verse also offers another striking example of the scholarly phenomenon that we have already explored in relation to John's Gospel, the apparent unwillingness of some commentaries even to mention verses of clear theological significance where a text is linguistically unremarkable; here, Jaroslav Pelikan's commentary on Acts makes no mention of verse 8.[1] As explored further in Part 3, a seemingly widespread reluctance among theologians to focus on the actual and potential work of the Holy Spirit, in the context of disagreement and in relation to the pursuit of unity, has impoverished theological reflection on this aspect of Christian relating.

The biblical text itself does, however, speak with clarity about the role of the Spirit in this instance: Peter addresses his opponents with 'boldness', and it became clear that these 'uneducated and ordinary men' were companions of Jesus (Acts 4.13). Luke thus begins to outline what it might look like for those who are filled with the Sprit to face occasions of disagreement. That Peter and John are uneducated, ordinary men is insignificant if they are among those chosen by God to grow his kingdom; the presence of the Spirit enables them to speak boldly in circumstances where such a confident response would seem humanly unlikely. Moreover, the combination of their words and the presence with them of the man who had been healed meant that their interlocutors 'had nothing to say in opposition' (v. 14). Nonetheless, as Richard Longenecker observes, 'even the miraculous is not self-authenticating apart from openness of heart and mind; and the Sadducees' preoccupation with protecting their vested interests shut them off from really seeing the miracle that had occurred'.[2] That said, from the perspective of Peter and John, the assurance of God's presence with them is linked explicitly with their ability to speak boldly when necessary. When ordered not to speak or teach in the name of Jesus, their response is forthright: 'Whether it is right in God's sight to listen to you rather than to God, you must judge; for we cannot keep from speaking about what we have seen and heard' (4.19b).

Despite having been threatened, Peter and John are then released and able to return to their friends. Having told of their recent experience, the theme of God enabling confident speech is underlined by all those present who then praise God saying:

> it is you who said by the Holy Spirit through our ancestor David, your servant: 'Why did the Gentiles rage, and the peoples imagine vain things? The kings of the earth took their stand, and the rulers have gathered together against the Lord and against his Messiah.' (4.25–26)

For these early Christians, confidence can be found in the identification of their struggle with that of their ancestors; at this early point in the book of Acts, the fact that God has spoken through his chosen people throughout history, and continues to do so, reassures and inspires the disciples as they face opposition in their ministry. In verse 29 they petition in prayer specifically that they might be enabled to 'speak your word with all boldness', and this section concludes with a brief account of the place where they prayed being 'shaken; and they were all filled with the Holy Spirit and spoke the word of God with boldness' (4.31b).

There was among the apostles a clear twofold expectation: that they could be filled with the Holy Spirit, and that it was this impartation which enabled their confident speech. This clear connection, made twice in the course of Acts 4, is important for us to note as we consider the ethics that might underpin Christian public speech. This example has the potential to offer an important grounding for a theological ethic concerning disagreement; one that places significant emphasis on those parties in a disagreement seeking the presence and inspiration of the Spirit, confident about its ability to inspire speech that nourishes rather than undermines the work of the kingdom. Indeed, read in isolation, the account of Peter and John before the high priestly family could prompt a confident Christian ethic based upon the notion that Christians have the capacity to speak with boldness and evade their opponents; we may well regard this as an instructive observation that can be made from the text and applied to the life of the contemporary church as it undertakes its mission. But such an example does not assist with the problem that represents our primary focus – those instances where *internal* Christian disagreements are themselves distracting the church from its mission and impeding its ability to model Christian unity to the wider world.

In this troubled context, where Christians disagree among themselves, the broader biblical narrative swiftly reminds us that any confidence that might be gained from the specific example of Peter and John can swiftly dissipate when consideration moves to intra-Christian disagreement. Following Richard Hays, this is an example where – for now – a tension within the biblical narrative needs to be allowed to stand, while more evidence is gathered. Later, my hope is to be able to assess how the example of Peter and John's approach to disagreement might inform an emerging theological ethic. Meanwhile, other instances within the Acts of the Apostles broaden our perspective on the conduct of debate within the church. The repeated examples of disagreement concerning the status of Gentile believers offer important insights into the complexity faced by early Christians unable to avoid the challenge of adjudicating on questions concerning authentic religion and faithful religious practice; it is to such examples that I now turn.

Disagreement concerning the relative status of Jewish and Gentile believers

The conversion of Cornelius in Acts 10 offers a helpful narrative prelude to our discussion of the debates about emerging Gentile Christianity, given that followers of Jesus were increasingly being drawn from beyond Jewish communities. For C. K. Barrett, the incident 'was important as marking the climax of the extension of the Gospel – to Jews, to Samaritans, to the Ethiopian who was all but a proselyte, and now to a Gentile'.[3] Scholars understandably focus on the significance of the Holy Spirit being poured out beyond the confines of Judaism. But for our purposes, it is one particular aspect of Peter's words in verse 28 that demands attention: 'You yourselves know that it is unlawful for a Jew to associate with or visit a Gentile; but God has shown me that I should not call anyone profane or unclean.' One could focus here on the seismic theological shift that occurs as Christian mission expands to include Gentiles. But such an approach risks overlooking the fact that Peter has not merely been shown by God to regard Jew and Gentile impartially: he has been shown by God that he should not *call* anyone profane or unclean.

In the wider context of the book of Acts, to highlight this specific reference to speech in relation to Peter's attitude towards Gentile believers may seem unnecessary; but as an example that can resource a theology of disagreement, its significance is considerable. As the map of missionary potential is redrawn, Peter emphasizes that no one should be verbally demeaned in the course of the work of the church. We might well observe the consonance of this observation with the ethical concerns outlined by Jesus, not least as he called his followers to a life of loving unity; as we consider how disagreements concerning the status of Gentile believers are approached in the early church, it is worth us bearing in mind that Peter has outlined a potential principle for the approaching of difference. However unclean or profane someone is thought to be, God showed Peter that he was not to speak of them in this particular way. An understandable conclusion is that this is a noble aim, but one not easily held to – not least when Peter is challenged by fellow Christians about the legitimacy of Gentile faith.

The scandalous notion that Gentiles might have 'also accepted the word of God' – the bold claim with which Acts 11 begins – creates a sense of urgency, as Peter is depicted returning to Jerusalem to face strident opposition from those who had heard of events in Caesarea. In response to their direct question, 'Why did you go to uncircumcised men and eat with them?' (11.3), Peter offers a lengthy testimony of the events narrated in the previous chapter; Darrell Bock is one of several commentators who regard this restatement as a clear indication, by Luke, of the event's significance.[4] We should note that Peter sought to explain 'step by step' (11.4) – a certain degree of patient exposition is suggested, and his words prove convincing. As with the earlier response to the bold words spoken by him and John, in this instance, too, trustworthy testimony was met first with silence and then the offering of praise. The conclusion of Peter's hearers is absolute in its certainty: 'Then God has given even to the Gentiles the repentance that leads to life' (11.18).

The tensions that accompanied this process of Gentile inclusion are well documented, and by chapter 13 'almost the whole city gathered to hear the word of the Lord' (13.44). But the size of these crowds prompted Jewish jealousy, 'and blaspheming, they contradicted what was spoken by Paul' (13.45b). In response, we again encounter bold speech, this time including within it the undeniably courageous decision that Paul and Barnabas would focus their missionary efforts in Gentile contexts. But it is not just this announcement of a revised mission strategy that should interest us; we should also consider the nature of the response made by Paul and Barnabas to those who have heard the word of God but chosen to reject it. The apostles do not feel the need to prolong their disagreement with such people, nor do they agree to differ; rather, they clarify that their words, clearly expressed, have been rejected, and they choose to move on. That this approach should be made by Paul and Barnabas is worthy of note given the significance of the sharp disagreement and parting of ways that occurs between the two of them in chapter 15.[5]

As we shall see, the Acts of the Apostles does not prize unity as the greatest good in Christian mission, whether within or beyond the church. Disagreement is an inevitable part of the life of disciples, and Acts offers clear examples of occasions when disagreement has to be faced and a new start made. The closing verses of chapter 13 vividly illustrate Paul and Barnabas' enforced departure from Antioch in Pisidia and the surrounding region (13.50). Echoing Jesus' words in Matthew 10.14, 'they shook the dust off their feet in protest' (13.51) and went to Iconium. But there is a final aspect to this departure that should not be overlooked: verse 52's observation that 'the disciples were filled with joy and with the Holy Spirit'. Luke's narrative is shaped to underline that Jewish opposition to the proclamation of the gospel troubled, but did not ultimately dismay, the disciples. They left this dramatic encounter filled with joy and conscious of the presence of God. So at the very least we can observe that they did not regard their mission as one that necessitated agreement with everyone they met; rather, their task was to express clearly their convictions, however unsettling to their hearers, always ready to journey on to a more receptive audience.

Disagreement among believers

Having reflected on examples of disagreement beyond the church, and disagreement concerning where ecclesial boundaries might be set, we now turn to arguably the most fraught context for a theology of disagreement: instances within the church, among believers, where external forces are often secondary and the challenge is the very fact of disagreement in an institution that seeks to live in loving unity. The extent to which this uncontroversial theological aim of unified Christian living leads to the twin presence of idealism and ambiguity is explored in the first section that follows. This discussion offers a significant narrative context for our understanding of a theology of disagreement among the earliest Christians, identifying aspects or fragments within the Acts narrative that illustrate some theological priorities for Christian relationship. We then turn to Acts 15 – pivotal for our purposes – and consider in detail both the council at Jerusalem and the disagreement between Paul and Barnabas.

Idealism and ambiguity: Ananias and Sapphira; Apollos, Priscilla and Aquila; Paul's engagement with Ephesian church elders and with Agabus

We have already considered the earlier part of chapter 4 in relation to the boldness of speech of Peter and John; but now it is to the vision of Christian common life, articulated towards the end of the chapter, that I turn. Verse 32 has to rank among the most optimistic assessments of Christian life within the New Testament: 'the whole group of those who believed were of one heart and soul, and no one claimed private ownership of any possessions, but everything they owned was held in common.' As Joseph Fitzmyer notes, 'this generic statement idyllically describes the unity and harmony of the Jerusalem Christians ... Luke may well be idealizing the situation.'[6] That idealized vision is shattered by the perplexing account of Ananias and Sapphira that immediately follows it. But the narrative significance of the claims of verse 32 should not be overlooked. Attention tends to fall, understandably, on the common ownership described – perhaps not least because, ever since, it has represented a strident challenge to the church on matters of material wealth.[7] But in relation to a theology of disagreement, it is the earlier part of the verse that is more striking, with its affirmation that those who believed were 'of one heart and soul'.

Luke offers a vision of Christian unity that is emphatic in its comprehensiveness: a unity of heart and soul leads to a uniting of material goods. Thus the similar observation about belongings at 2.44–45 is intensified here and given an intimately personalized theological grounding. As Jaroslav Pelikan notes, this approach to possessions 'appears to be identifying not a general trend or statement of average but a total and comprehensive phenomenon'.[8] The account of the dramatic, sudden deaths of Ananias and Sapphira stands as caution against those who undermine this idealized vision, disagreeing with the communitarian ethos at the heart of early Christian community. Peter's questions underline the spiritual dimension that is identified in the couple's deceit: 'How is it that you have agreed together to put the Spirit of the Lord to the test?', he asks (5.9). But this incident also qualifies the sense in which Luke offers an idealized account of the early church, for the inclusion of this episode graphically illustrates the presence of sin and disunity. From our perspective, the challenge offered by these passages is the way in which they stand alongside each other; the optimism of 4.32 has not been moderated in response to the deaths of Ananias and Sapphira. This tension offers a crucial example of the challenge facing Christians seeking to engage with the biblical text when it simultaneously upholds both an ideal and an example of human failure in the context of the life of the church.

A more nuanced, less idealized approach to an incident of potential disagreement or conflict can usefully be identified in the brief discussion of the arrival in Ephesus of the Alexandrian Jew named Apollos (Acts 18.24–28). Commentary tends to focus on questions of Apollos' understanding of doctrine and the extent to which he can be understood to be a Christian prior to the intervention of Priscilla and Aquila, but the consideration of such questions risks overlooking an important ethical move in verse 26: 'He began to speak boldly in the synagogue; but when Priscilla and Aquila heard him, they took him aside and explained the Way of God to him more accurately' (18.26). It is surely significant that this couple (clearly regarded by Luke as having authority to teach) *take him to one side* to explain the Way to him. Here we do not see commended the fiery approach to doctrinal debates evident in Jesus' interaction with religious leaders; rather, as the church develops and refines its theological understanding, Apollos is taken aside and reasoned with for the good of the church as a whole. It is a model worth bearing in mind as we consider appropriate responses to disagreement within the church.

As we consider how the early church acknowledged the existence of moral and doctrinal ambiguity within itself, while still upholding firm ideals, we should also note some of Paul's words to the elders of the Ephesian church:

'Keep watch over yourselves and over all the flock, of which the Holy Spirit has made you overseers, to shepherd the church of God that he obtained with the blood of his own Son. I know that after I have gone, savage wolves will come in among you, not sparing the flock.' (20.28–29)

These verses are important for our purposes in that they are candid about the potential fragility of the church – and, crucially, indicate that opposition and destruction will be *in among* believers in future. C. K. Barrett outlines the complexity inherent in this realization:

> It is clear that a time is contemplated when orthodoxy and heresy would be clearly differentiated, and when the church would be an institution with clearly defined frontiers. It did not always appear so simple. Gnostic teachers, for example, emerging within the church would often regard themselves as its most faithful, or at least its most intelligent and advanced members.[9]

It hardly needs stating that the discernment and articulation of the boundaries of orthodoxy has been an ongoing challenge throughout Christian history; but the contention of this book is that too often the deliberation and debate that accompany such processes of theological discernment fail to seek and guard the unity so consistently prized within the New Testament. The presence of disagreement is inevitable, as is the potential for such disagreement to be rooted in an attempt to undermine the work of the kingdom; the challenge is to consider how such disagreements may be faced in ways that do not undermine the mission of the church.

It is for precisely this reason that Paul's engagement with the Judean prophet named Agabus is so telling (21.10–14). It may come as little surprise to us that the New Testament is short on explicit instruction about the facing of disagreement within Christian community, but verse 14 might be regarded as offering a helpful pointer, as we read of Paul's reluctance to heed Agabus' warning of impending danger in Jerusalem: 'Since he would not be persuaded, we remained silent except to say, "The Lord's will be done."' The context is that there has clearly been a disagreement with Paul regarding how he might respond to Agabus' prophetic warning of future suffering in Jerusalem. Agabus' credentials do not seem to be in doubt – he is introduced as a prophet with no further elaboration – and he is confident that his words emanate from the Holy Spirit. Paul's response is uncompromising: 'What are you doing, weeping and breaking my heart? For I am ready not only to be bound but even to die in Jerusalem for the name of the Lord Jesus' (v. 13). Paul's words are met with silence, which has followed from a realization that any attempt at persuasion would be ineffective. It is a mere vignette, but one that highlights the potential place for discretion and reserve in Christian disagreement. Whether or not Paul was misguided, at this particular point the only constructive contribution that can be made is to pray for God's will to be done.

Joseph Fitzmyer suggests an echo here of Jesus' prayer in Gethsemane: 'Father, if you are willing, remove this cup from me; yet, not my will but yours be done.'[10] There comes a moment when submission to the will of God becomes the only course left to take – but such an observation can move beyond its apparent status as a Sunday school truism when applied to ecclesial disagreement. To pray for God's will is, in these two examples, to admit that human potential has been exhausted; in faith, an appeal to divine providence constitutes an acceptance that the will of God may take one into unknown territory but with the ultimate assurance of divine presence, whatever earthly challenges are faced. One of the contentions of this book is that too often debates and disagreements within the church are undertaken only at a human level of grounded political possibility, where the will or potential of God to transform a given situation is either disregarded entirely or reduced to the realm of practical impossibility. And yet, in the lives of both Jesus and Paul, a repeated motif is the deep significance of reliance on the will of the Father, even when this act of submission necessitates an unwanted or unforeseen journey.

When Christians disagree, they are caught in the midst of a tense spectrum, finding themselves somewhere between, at one extreme, the lofty ideals of ecclesial life, and its often disappointing reality at the other – a spectrum outlined so strikingly within the book of Acts. As we notice this tension between aspiration-in-faith and frustration-in-life, we might do well to reconsider the sort of context in which Luke repeatedly directs his readers to view instances of disagreement. As we have seen, they are always to be viewed through the lens of faith: Ananias and Sapphira lied and paid the price; Apollos was encouraged towards orthodoxy; Agabus' prophecy was challenging precisely because of his fidelity. Thus the book of Acts lives in this tension between idealism and ambiguity, sharing with its readers some of the complexity of corporate Christian life; and within it, in relation to a theology of disagreement, chapter 15 is of unparalleled significance.

The council at Jerusalem

We have already noted that examples of disagreement within the life of the early church are not documented with great frequency in the New Testament, so a close reading of Acts 15.1–35 is useful in documenting a key instance of a disagreement being faced and resolved in the emerging Christian community. It is a narrative that explains with candour the challenge presented by certain individuals from Judea who are proclaiming, 'Unless you are circumcised according to the custom of Moses, you cannot be saved' (v. 1b). Notwithstanding all that has already been addressed within Acts concerning the validity of Gentile faith, Paul and Barnabas seemingly exhibit no apparent resistance to the task of addressing those responsible for this teaching; and after 'no small dissension and debate with them' (v. 2), the decision is made that Paul and Barnabas should go to Jerusalem to discuss the matter with the apostles and elders. It is worth noting that already two observations can usefully be made: first, a disagreement is acknowledged and faced; second, it is resolved to discuss the matter with those in an acknowledged position of oversight and authority within the church.

The meeting of apostles and elders is notable as an occasion of 'much debate' (v. 7) – there was seemingly no concern about the contentious matter being explored and discussed. In his address, Peter reminds them of the recent history whereby he took the good news to the Gentiles: 'And God, who knows the human heart, testified to them by giving them the Holy Spirit, just as he did to us; and in cleansing their hearts by faith he has made no distinction between them and us' (vv. 8–9). Peter emphasizes that both Jew and Gentile 'will be saved through the grace of the Lord Jesus' (v. 11), and through that alone; his and Barnabas' testimony of the signs and wonders seen among the Gentiles offers a compelling argument in favour of the reality of their faith despite a lack of circumcision. James' response seeks to set his words in the context of 'the words of the prophets' (v. 15), underlining the notion that even Gentiles fall within the remit of the rebuilding of the dwelling of David: 'Therefore I have reached the conclusion that we should not trouble those Gentiles that are returning to God' (v. 19); rather, they are to adopt a moderated dietary code. Of inescapable interest here is the compromise nature of James' proposal. Although Mosaic customs need not be followed in full, Gentiles should still abstain 'from things polluted by idols and from fornication and from whatever has been strangled and from blood' (v. 20).

The judgement reached, the apostles and elders – *'with the consent of the whole church'* (v. 22) – appoint leaders to accompany Paul and Barnabas to Antioch with the letter that sets out their conclusions. The unanimity of the church's decision to send such representatives is affirmed within the letter itself, which then goes on to set its moral conclusion in pneumatological perspective: 'For it has seemed good to the Holy Spirit and to us to impose on you no further burden than these essentials ... If you keep yourselves from these, you will do well' (vv. 28–29). We note that the letter was received with rejoicing (v. 31) alongside the words of encouragement and strengthening from Judas and Silas. The concluding words of this section offer a picture of calm restored and ministry once more able to flourish: 'Paul and Barnabas remained in Antioch, and there, with many others, they taught and proclaimed the word of the Lord' (v. 35). A disagreement has been resolved, following reference to authority figures within the church; human interaction has been a significant factor in the resolution of disagreement, including the presence with Paul and Barnabas of others from Jerusalem as they returned to Antioch; and the ministry of the church has not been fatally undermined by a debate that could have ended more problematically.

We can hardly ignore the significance of the Jerusalem council as a paradigm for the resolution of ecclesial disagreement in general, and for the work of official church structures in particular. Jaroslav Pelikan regards it as 'a charter both for authority *at* church councils and for the authority *of* church councils'.[11] He notes that the phrase, 'it has seemed good to the Holy Spirit and to us', has developed particular significance in the self-validation of such decision-making entities; in chapter 9 we will consider whether churches tend towards the downplaying of the expectation that the Holy Spirit informs and can even guide their disagreements. That the church has the ability to resolve disagreement is clearly expressed here; and, crucially, this is disagreement resolved in a way that demonstrates the willingness to discriminate between issues of foundational importance where uniformity of approach is required and those where a degree of variation is permissible. This is, of course, a principle that then creates its own tensions, and the subsequent Christian disagreements – about whether certain issues can be matters of compromise or agreed difference in approach – are well known. But as Darrell Bock observes, 'Christian fellowship means that grace should be shown for differences that are not central to the truth of salvation, as an expression of love. This deference preserves the church and prevents it from fragmentation.'[12]

Central to the effective pursuit of this strategy of holding the church together is the approach taken by key characters in the narrative. Paul's willingness to confront disagreement has already become clear within the book of Acts; but here, James is of particular interest – as the broker of the settlement, invoking Hebrew Scriptures and thus giving his conclusion an authoritative edge. Joseph Fitzmyer regards James as a 'broadminded leader who, while basically agreeing with Peter about no circumcision and no obligation to observe the Mosaic law for Gentile Christians, seeks to preserve the unity and peace of the church ... a church official who seeks a reasonable compromise in the interest of the church at large'.[13] Richard Longenecker points out that such compromise can be seen to be at work at two levels, with two necessary questions being addressed:

> The first had to do with the theological necessity of circumcision and the Jewish law for salvation, and that was rejected. The second had to do with the practical necessity of Gentile Christians abstaining from certain practices ... the major work of the council had to do with the vindication of Gentile freedom, while a secondary matter was concerned with the expression of that freedom in regard to the scruples of others.[14]

The work of the council is important in relation to a theology of disagreement because it introduces questions of discrimination and nuance into our theological reflection. If Jesus' approach was often to set an ethical bar so high that the life of discipleship can be regarded as a constant striving towards the practically unattainable, here in the life of the early church we see leaders grappling with the complexity of human diversity and seeking to arrive at conclusions that honour certain aspects of that diversity without undermining the mission of the church as a whole. John Perry has highlighted the potential for this episode to resource contemporary reflection on sexuality within the church in the West, acting as an analogy that promotes the recognition of difference while maintaining at least a degree of ecclesial unity.[15] Perry critiques various scholars' approaches to the use of the Gentile analogy in relation to contemporary sexuality, but maintains that analogy can offer a useful grounding for debate and disagreement in a Christian context – if those with opposing viewpoints are willing to consider seriously the position they reject. Such willingness is 'what ensures that a conversation is possible, for the analogy itself supplies a rich common language. It is this rich language that has been recently exchanged for the cheap barbs of a culture war.'[16]

Whatever the contemporary challenges concerning the application of the Gentile analogy, a final comment is needed on the extent to which the text of Acts itself betrays a desire to exaggerate the unity found within the early church on this matter. C. K. Barrett observed in 1974 that 'the historical study of the last 100 years has not shown that the conflicts, tensions and resolutions described by F. C. Baur are imaginary'.[17] It is clear that for New Testament scholars, the legacy of Baur's reading of Acts is considerable; reflecting on it, James Dunn concludes:

Baur's understanding of Acts was not so far from the truth after all, despite its dogmatic overstatement. Luke's picture of earliest Christianity and of Paul's role in it is after all something of a compromise between Jewish and Gentile Christianity, a smoothing of the wrinkles and a disguising of the tears that disfigured the cloth of first generation Christianity and made up into a suit which both might find reasonably acceptable.[18]

Dunn's comments serve as a useful reminder to us as we undertake scripturally grounded ethical reasoning. The textual debates highlighted are worthy of study, but to focus on them can risk losing sight of our specific task, which is the consideration of the canonical biblical text as we have received it in relation to the ongoing challenge facing the church concerning how it approaches its inevitable disagreements. Whatever Luke's motives, we cannot deny the theological emphasis placed on the importance of resolving disagreement and promoting unity in the church – and that is precisely why the disagreement between Paul and Barnabas that concludes chapter 15 is so significant.

The disagreement between Paul and Barnabas

This episode, recorded with brevity by Luke, is of inescapable significance for a theology of disagreement – not least because Acts 15.39 offers a rare example of that specific word being used: 'the disagreement between them became so sharp that they parted company'.[19] In the New Revised Standard Version, 'disagreement' appears on only two other occasions,[20] but Darrell Bock offers a revealing insight in relation to the original Greek: 'The term *paroxysmos*, when used negatively, describes anger, irritation, or exasperation in a disagreement. In Hebrews 10.24 it is used positively of stimulating or stirring someone to love.'[21] It is worth quoting in full this verse from Hebrews and the one that follows it: 'And let us consider how to *provoke* one another to love and good deeds, not neglecting to meet together, as is the habit of some, but encouraging one another, and all the more as you see the Day approaching' (Heb. 10.24–25). The provocation to love found here in Hebrews is etymologically similar to the 'disagreement' of Acts 15.39, and while one would not wish to overload the significance of such an observation, we can at least note that the context in Hebrews – the encouragement of Christian virtue – gives this notion of provocation a positive element. We might thus also consider that this notion of disagreement found in Acts need not be regarded as inherently negative. To disagree does not necessarily undermine the realization of God's call to loving unity.

The partnership in the gospel of which we have read in Acts 13 and 14 breaks down dramatically in this short incident. The reader is offered a salutary reminder that however effective the council's deliberations witnessed earlier in the same chapter, human relationships are always prone to fracture. As Joseph Fitzmyer notes, 'even though the decisions made at Jerusalem contributed to the harmony and peace of the church, dissension may still be part of Christian life. That life has its ups and downs, and this episode gives an instance of that. Now the difference of opinion that develops has nothing to do with doctrine, but with personalities.'[22] This final point is particularly important. The separation between Paul and Barnabas is precipitated by a difference of opinion concerning who should accompany them on their future mission. John called Mark is thought to have been a cousin of Barnabas, though it was his desertion in Pamphylia rather than questions of family ties that led Paul to oppose Barnabas in this regard. The disagreement leads to Barnabas and Mark sailing to Cyprus, while Paul takes Silas 'through Syria and Cilicia, strengthening the churches' (15.41).

There are some intriguing variations in the interpretation of these events. Richard Longenecker's glass is at least half full when he writes: 'far from letting the disagreement harm the outreach of the gospel, God providentially used it to double the missionary force.'[23] Notwithstanding the potential danger of inferring that all disagreement might represent God's providential hand at work, Longenecker does helpfully point out that this difference of opinion led to two separate missionary journeys rather than one, with Paul having identified Silas as 'a congenial colleague ... Silas was a leader in the Jerusalem congregation and was explicitly identified in the Jerusalem letter as one who could speak with authority on the attitude of the Jerusalem church.'[24] But such a positive gloss is not the only legitimate reading of these events; Paul Achtemeier urges serious consideration of the presence of ongoing tension in the early church, 'a tension at which Luke again hints when he reports no reconciliation between Paul and Barnabas'.[25] That tensions existed, threatening church unity, is undeniable, but the suggestion that Luke's lack of a recorded reconciliation between Paul and Barnabas is a clear example of such tension argues too much from biblical silence.

A more nuanced reading might recognize the severity and significance of this disagreement – while noting that its focus was personality rather than doctrine – but also see the episode as offering a glimpse of how disunity might be faced with maturity by the church. It is true enough to say that we do not read of any reconciliation; but we do read of the church's mission proceeding as Paul and Barnabas go their separate ways. Darrell Bock regards these events as an example where 'a disagreement was so great that the ability to work side by side was affected. What resulted was a solution that allowed the advance of the gospel to continue, but in a way that recognized a need for distinct ministries. Sometimes this is the best solution.'[26] Jaroslav Pelikan, dismissively brief in his treatment of this disagreement, also risks reading rather too much into the text. He concludes that what we find is 'a pragmatic solution of mutual toleration and an agreement to disagree'.[27] He may be right; we can never know. But what we can say with confidence is that a disagreement between two Christians reveals even at this early point in the church's mission the existence of debate and disunity. Even though this disagreement did not centre on theological questions, it reminds us that the church has never wholly succeeded in living out Jesus' repeated call to be a community united in love. Whether or not Paul and Barnabas regarded each other with mutual toleration, or agreed to disagree, their disagreement of itself reminds us that the gospel message has always been borne by flawed human beings.

Paul Achtemeier is candid about the need for the contemporary church to reflect seriously on instances of tension like that between Paul and Barnabas. He regards such work as a prerequisite for mature theological reflection on the testimonies of emerging Christian community found within the New Testament:

> Unless we are aware of the problems the early church faced concerning its unity, we will inevitably romanticize that period and either give up in despair at the course taken by subsequent developments in the history of the church, or else assume in a naive way that all it takes to recover that lost, original unity is a little good will and some pleasant negotiations.[28]

Of course, as Achtemeier goes on to suggest, neither alternative is appropriate; rather, the task is to learn from the church's history of threatened unity: 'Only a clear, hard-eyed view of the kind of problems that have beset the Christian community from its beginning will enable that community to move forward, under the guidance of God's spirit, to that unity to which it is called.'[29]

Conclusion

The book of Acts has presented us with some key observations for our emerging theology of disagreement. While to disagree, of itself, is not to undermine the work of the church, the extent to which disagreement can be justified seems closely related to the extent to which those disagreeing are acting in recognizably Christian ways in and through their debates. In Acts, the very question of what constitutes recognizable Christianity is – as throughout the New Testament – both emerging and being tested. But we have repeatedly witnessed Luke's desire to portray those events that affirm loving unity between Christians as being foundational for life within the community of the church. Open to and inspired by the Spirit, the early Christians depicted in the book of Acts are thus called to discern the will of God in and through their disagreement. At the Jerusalem council, debate is regulated rather than avoided; the importance of those entrusted with oversight of the church reaching mutually acceptable conclusions, even when presented with seemingly irreconcilable perspectives, is established.

Perhaps most significantly, in Acts we cannot but confront both the idealism and ambiguity to be found in the earliest Christian communities. While the vibrancy of Pentecost promoted deep unity and a sense of shared purpose, such qualities were quickly tested and the human frailty of the church swiftly exposed. And yet, in the response of leaders such as Peter, John, James and Paul to the challenges they faced, we discover the emergence of mature reflection on theological complexity, held in tension with a continuing desire to follow Jesus' repeated invitation to the highest moral standards. Instances of disagreement might thus be regarded as unavoidable sparks of energy in a human institution; the question surrounding each spark is whether it prompts kingdom fire, or opens the way for the undermining of mission. As we have seen, disagreements *of themselves* do not indicate whether they bode ill or well for the church, but Christians engaged in disagreement face the challenge of discerning how to speak and act in ways that honour their calling in the midst of human and political pressure. Following Richard Hays, for now some of the tensions that we have uncovered in Acts can be allowed to stand; this descriptive task, assessing approaches to disagreement within the New Testament, now continues within the Pauline literature.

Notes

1 Jaroslav Pelikan, 2006, *Acts*, London: SCM Press, p. 73.

2 Richard Longenecker, 1995, *The Expositor's Bible Commentary: Acts*, Grand Rapids: Zondervan, p. 102.

3 C. K. Barrett, 2002, *Commentary on Acts*, London: T&T Clark, p. 152.

4 Darrell L. Bock, 2007, *Acts: Baker Exegetical Commentary on the New Testament*, Grand Rapids: Baker Academic, p. 406.

5 Acts 15.36–41; see pp. 56–8.

6 Joseph A. Fitzmyer, 1998, *The Acts of the Apostles: A New Translation with Introduction and Commentary*, New Haven: Yale University Press, p. 313.

7 We should also note that this communitarian vision is challenged even within Acts itself; the complaint that Hellenist widows were being neglected in the daily food distribution (6.1) offers one example of the failure to live as described in 4.32.

8 Pelikan, *Acts*, p. 79.

9 Barrett, *Acts*, p. 317.

10 Luke 22.42; see also Fitzmyer, *Acts*, p. 690.

11 Pelikan, *Acts*, p. 175.

12 Bock, *Acts*, p. 508. Note also our discussion of Galatians 2 that follows in Chapter 4.

13 Fitzmyer, *Acts*, pp. 553–4.

14 Longenecker, *Acts*, p. 244.

15 John Perry, 2010, 'Gentiles and Homosexuals: A Brief History of an Analogy', *Journal of Religious Ethics* 38,2, pp. 321–47.

16 Perry, 'Gentiles', p. 347.

17 C. K. Barrett, 1974, 'Pauline Controversies in the Post-Pauline Period', *New Testament Studies* 20,3, p. 243.

18 James D. G. Dunn, 2006, *Unity and Diversity in the New Testament: An Inquiry into the Character of Earliest Christianity*, London: SCM Press, p. 389.

19 A few English translations of Acts 15.39 – notably the King James Version and the Revised Standard Version – use 'contention' instead of 'disagreement'. In addition to the New Revised Standard Version, 'disagreement' is used in versions including the English Standard Version, the New International Version, and the New Living Translation.

20 Acts 25.19, in words spoken by Festus to King Agrippa, and at 2 Maccabees 3.4.

21 Bock, *Acts*, p. 519.

22 Fitzmyer, *Acts*, p. 571.

23 Longenecker, *Acts*, p. 250.

24 Longenecker, *Acts*, p. 250.

25 Paul J. Achtemeier, 1987, *The Quest for Unity in the New Testament Church*, Philadelphia: Fortress Press, p. 58.

26 Bock, *Acts*, p. 520.

27 Pelikan, *Acts*, p. 178.

28 Achtemeier, *Unity*, p. 2.

29 Achtemeier, *Unity*, p. 2.

4

Pauline Ethics of Relationship
within the Body of Christ

There is no escape from the breadth and volume of potential material as we move to consider how the writings of Paul might inform a theology of disagreement. Indeed, there is no small challenge in first determining which writings found within the canonical New Testament are to be regarded as Pauline for our purposes.[1] But a potential double fear – of the sheer amount of material under consideration, and the authenticity of its authorship – represents exactly the sort of legitimate scholarly investigation that could easily distract us from our chief concern. One might even argue that it is part of the duty of biblical ethicists to join dots between different texts given the (understandable) tendency for biblical scholars to develop relatively narrow expertise in a small proportion of their field. The pursuit of a theology of disagreement necessitates careful consideration of the New Testament text *as a whole*, notwithstanding the challenging nature of such a study. We might usefully be reminded of how Richard Hays himself defends the purpose of his own scripturally based, moral-theological enquiry: 'The goal of this entire project is to encourage the church in its efforts to become a Scripture-shaped community, to allow its life to be more fitly conformed to the stories narrated in the New Testament.'[2]

This book, while seeking to modify Hays' particular methodological approach, nonetheless retains confidence in the reading of Scripture as the primary source of wisdom in Christian ethics. So as we consider the Pauline literature of the New Testament, it is worth us noting, in particular, Richard Hays' engagement with the work of Victor Paul Furnish (one of his first teachers in New Testament studies) on Pauline ethics. Hays writes that Furnish

> proposes that the thing we need to understand, if we are to understand Paul's ethics, is *an underlying set of theological convictions*, which can then be observed in action as they *give particular shape* to the concrete advice he sends to his congregations. It is the *structure* of this

dynamically integrative movement from theology to ethical discernment that is at the heart of Paul's distinctive ethic.[3]

This observation represents an important point for us to note, for it reminds us that any conclusion we might reach about an emerging theology of disagreement in Paul's writings will be authentic if it flows from the theological convictions that underpin his writing as a whole.

Victor Paul Furnish helpfully encapsulates this move while writing the foreword to a recent critique of his own work. He notes that any claimed moral principle or scriptural precept must be subject to a twofold test:

> First, does it *conform to the gospel norm* – to the call for God's people to be agents of the love by which their lives have been graced and claimed for God's service in the world? Second, is it also *credible*, in that it takes account of what is presently understood about the realities of God's creation and our human existence within it? Where these two criteria are met (a matter, to be sure, of discernment, not certainty), I believe that the church may and must speak of a 'binding' scriptural principle or precept.[4]

Such a comment acknowledges the possibility of finding wisdom within Scripture that retains clear ethical force in a contemporary context, if that context has been taken sufficiently seriously; as this book aims to show, part of the problem with current Christian approaches to disagreement is that they often lack an ethical framework for the exploration and discussion of inevitable difference within the church.

Before we consider specific instances of disagreement within the Pauline corpus, and the possibility of good disagreement, we must first develop a clear picture of the kind of ethical grounding to Christian community that Paul champions – as a context within which disagreements can be faced. Following Richard Hays, this constitutes a task of description, investigating instances of ethical reflection within Paul's writings that offer insights into how disagreements within Christian community might best be faced. We will notice, perhaps with some surprise, that this appears to be an area of ethical conduct within the life of the church where Paul's various letters speak with unanimity. The priority of loving unity is repeatedly asserted, as a good of community in itself and as a key means whereby that community can reach beyond its current parameters. We thus now turn to considering four key attributes of such communities, before noting the encapsulation of this vision in Paul's letter to the Colossians.

Towards a Pauline ethic of relating within the Body of Christ as a place to disagree Christianly

Godly speech

If the sort of Christian disagreement that fractures churches, and under-mines mission, has always been an unavoidable dimension of ecclesial life, we might appropriately ask whether this situation is indeed inevitable, or whether it is reflective of a widely adopted politics of speech that fails to live out key principles of a Christian ethic of relating. The first letter to the Thessalonians speaks eloquently to any church that routinely fails to consider whether its public speech, including its disagreement, is under-taken in a way that might (even tentatively) be described as recognizably Christian. Paul offers a foundational challenge to his readers concerning the fundamental orientation of Christian speech: 'For our appeal does not spring from deceit or impure motives or trickery, but just as we have been approved by God to be entrusted with the message of the gospel, even so we speak, not to please mortals, but to please God who tests our hearts' (1 Thess. 2.3–4). The place of speech in the life of the church – and for our purposes, we might broaden the notion of 'speech' to con-sider all forms of Christian public communication – is one of fragility, where a human desire to please others too often trumps the purpose of speech articulated by Paul, as a means of communicating the gospel. The orientation of Christians, therefore, when they speak, should be towards God, considering how their speech is reflective of the gospel hope they are called to convey; when speech falls short of this high purpose, that inadequacy should be acknowledged.

A question of priorities is also articulated. When in his first letter to the church in Corinth Paul chastises some of his readers for becoming arrogant having thought that he was not going to visit them again, he insists: 'But I will come to you soon, if the Lord wills, and I will find out not the talk of these arrogant people but their power. For the kingdom of God depends not on talk but on power' (1 Cor. 4.19–20). All human speech, including verbal disagreement, is emphatically put in its place by Paul, as he draws a sharp contrast between the relative importance within the kingdom of talk versus spiritual power. Indeed, recalling his previous visit to the Corinthian church, Paul writes:

> When I came to you, brothers and sisters, I did not come proclaiming the mystery of God to you in lofty words or wisdom ... My speech and my proclamation were not with plausible words of wisdom, but with a

demonstration of the Spirit and of power, so that your faith might rest not on human wisdom but on the power of God. (1 Cor. 2.1, 4–5)

Paul articulates a vision of the church where engagement with spiritual reality is a significantly greater priority than the articulation of speech of itself; proclamation is regarded as at its most effective when it constitutes interaction with the Spirit. At the very least, such words might prompt important questions for Christians who prioritize the pursuit of debate within the church over the pursuit of God himself: an ethic of Christian relating begins and ends in and through a relationship with God.

Mutual love

If Christian speech risks becoming politicized and too easily detached from God as the source of true life for the church, then mutual love also stands as a fragile component of authentic Christian community, too often pursued as a simplistic end in itself rather than as a by-product of an appropriate orientation towards God. Paul might, admittedly, stand accused of overoptimism when he writes to the Thessalonians, 'Now concerning love of brothers and sisters, you do not need to have anyone write to you, for you yourselves have been taught by God to love one another' (1 Thess. 4.9). These words come shortly after an appeal to the importance of mutual love: 'may the Lord make you increase and abound in love for one another and for all, just as we abound in love for you. And may he so strengthen your hearts in holiness that you may be blameless before our God and Father at the coming of our Lord Jesus Christ with all his saints' (1 Thess. 3.12–13). This eschatological context for mutual love should be noted. The church is encouraged to appeal to God for an increase in love, rooted in the pursuit of holiness, such that 'the coming of our Lord Jesus Christ' should be faced blameless. For us, the important point to note here is that mutual love is regarded as a core dimension of the holiness that followers of Christ should always seek to pursue – it should not be regarded as an optional extra.

This mutuality is given grounded expression in Paul's letter to the Romans, when the strong are encouraged 'to put up with the failings of the weak, and not to please ourselves' (Rom. 15.1). Disciples should seek to build up their neighbour, following Jesus' example of not seeking to please himself: 'May the God of steadfastness and encouragement grant you to live in harmony with one another, in accordance with Christ Jesus, so that together you may with one voice glorify the God and Father of our Lord Jesus Christ' (Rom. 15.5–6). This harmony is nowhere more striking for Paul than in the new relationship between Jew and Gentile, reconciled 'to God in one body through the cross' (Eph. 2.16) as fellow disciples of Christ, who are 'built together spiritually into a dwelling place for God' (Eph. 2.22). The Body of Christ is seen as a place where once sworn enemies become fellow citizens, committed to a life characterized by loving unity. I consider later how such a community might face its inevitable disagreements. But for now we must simply acknowledge the way in which this notion of unified, loving Christian community is found consistently within Paul's writings – and we can hardly fail to note how far the church easily departs from this clearly stated ambition.

Reconciled diversity

We have already begun to see how Paul views the Body of Christ as a place of reconciled diversity. Galatians 3.28 is probably the best-known summation of the varied origins of the unified people of God: 'There is no longer Jew or Greek, there is no longer slave or free, there is no longer male or female; for all of you are one in Christ Jesus.' Similar sentiments are given a more pneumatological grounding in 1 Corinthians: 'For in the one Spirit we were all baptized into one body – Jews or Greeks, slaves or free – and we were all made to drink of one Spirit' (1 Cor. 12.13). The people of God are affirmed as those who have chosen to follow the Way, regardless of their origins; their new unity – though not uniformity – is found in and through the God they worship. The unavoidable conundrum is why this theological unity, clearly stated, so often fails to permeate into the lived experience of the church throughout its history.

A short passage in the letter of Paul to the Philippians offers a helpful insight, while resisting an idealized vision of the church. Notwithstanding the evident affection with which he writes to the Christian community at Philippi, Paul is keen to point out the mixed motives of some disciples: 'Some proclaim Christ from envy and rivalry, but others from goodwill … What does it matter? Just this, that Christ is proclaimed in every way, whether out of false motives or true; and in that I rejoice' (Phil. 1.15, 18). As we consider the ethical foundations upon which a robust theology of disagreement might be built, this observation is of real importance, for it plainly recognizes the presence of human failure in and among Christian proclamation. Envy and rivalry coexist alongside genuine goodwill within the church; the question is whether those who are envious will be distracted from the task before them. This wide variety of motives – like disagreement itself – only becomes problematic when it distracts the church from the pursuit of God. We should not fail to note that

Paul is consistently confident about the ability of diverse followers of Jesus to cooperate effectively in mission, so long as their focus remains on their creator. Having offered a candid admission about an aspect of the ethical diversity of the Philippian church, Paul then calls all members of the church to 'live your life in a manner worthy of the gospel of Christ, so that, whether I come and see you or am absent and hear about you, I will know that you are standing firm in one spirit, striving side by side with one mind for the faith of the gospel' (Phil. 1.27).

Emergent maturity

It is also within the letter to the Philippians that this theme of reconciled diversity becomes closely related to the pursuit of Christian maturity, which of itself then leads to unity. The opening words of the second chapter highlight once more the intensity of this call to a faithful discipleship whose fruit is a united church: 'If then there is any encouragement in Christ, any consolation from love, any sharing in the Spirit, any compassion and sympathy, make my joy complete: be of the same mind, having the same love, being in full accord and of one mind' (Phil. 2.1–2). Clearly appreciating the imperfect reality of Christian community, Paul later exhorts the Philippians to 'do all things without murmuring and arguing, so that you may be blameless and innocent, children of God without blemish in the midst of a crooked and perverse generation, in which you shine like stars in the world' (Phil. 2.14–15). Even if we fear that Paul has risked hyperbolic flourish in this description of the Philippians and their context, we must note his absolute opposition to 'murmuring and arguing': members of the church should resist such emotions, modelling peaceable loving unity to those around them.[5]

A wholly legitimate concern is that Paul presents an idealized ethic of human relating, practically unachievable and too far removed from the reality of ecclesial life. Such a charge can certainly be made against him – but risks overlooking an important sense in which he articulates a degree of moral complexity within the letter to the Philippians, when he writes of his own pressing on towards a goal that he has not yet obtained. The prize is 'the heavenly call of God in Christ Jesus. Let those of us then who are mature be of the same mind; and if you think differently about anything, this too God will reveal to you. Only let us hold fast to what we have attained' (Phil. 3.14b–16). Of key interest here is the assertion of the place of maturity. It is those who are mature in their discipleship who can envisage being of the same mind; and when differences are articulated, the response should focus on the anticipation of revelation from

God. The implications of such anticipation are considerable. A Christian ethic of disagreement rooted in an attitude of expectancy towards the reconciling work of the Holy Spirit offers a potentially transformational approach to the early stages of conflict within the church.

A vision encapsulated: Colossians 3

The four aspects we have identified as being foundational for 'a Pauline ethic of relating within the Body of Christ' – godly speech, mutual love, reconciled diversity and emergent maturity – can be identified alongside one another in this passage from the letter to the church at Colossae. Here, in chapter 3, the characteristically Pauline fusion of theology and ethics highlighted by Victor Paul Furnish is clearly articulated.[6] The ethical actions of Christians in community are inextricably linked to the theological underpinning of their common life – or, at least, that is the vision to which Paul calls them. Hence a theological beginning, recalling that those who have been raised with Christ should 'seek the things that are above' (Col. 3.1). Earthly matters, meanwhile, risk distracting the disciple from the reality that they have died, and that their life is 'hidden with Christ in God' (v. 3). It is from this theological premise that ethical implications flow: 'Put to death, therefore, whatever in you is earthly: fornication, impurity, passion, evil desire, and greed (which is idolatry)' (v. 5).

The Christian faith brings with it a heavenly perspective; new life demands a new ethical outlook and the abandonment of former earthly failings: 'you must get rid of all such things – anger, wrath, malice, slander, and abusive language from your mouth' (v. 8). In a community where mouths are cleansed, the diversity of its people is also seen in a fresh perspective: 'In that renewal there is no longer Greek and Jew, circumcised and uncircumcised, barbarian, Scythian, slave and free; but Christ is all and in all!' (v. 11). The letter's hearers, like us, might query the extent to which a life of Christian discipleship brings with it the abandonment of former vices with the absolute finality that Paul depicts; but whatever our reservations, the clarity of ethical demand is clear. As Tom Wright observes, 'differences of background, nationality, colour, language, social standing and so forth must be regarded as irrelevant to the question of love, honour and respect that are to be shown to individuals and groups'.[7]

This love compels 'God's chosen ones' to bear with one another and to forgive: 'Above all, clothe yourselves with love, which binds everything together in perfect harmony' (Col. 3.14). The church, as a place of reconciled diversity, is a location of mutual love where a true focus on Christ enables onetime enemies to cooperate in the work of the kingdom. But Paul does not resist highlighting the process of maturation that will involve challenging speech within the context of this harmonious community:

> let the peace of Christ rule in your hearts, to which indeed you were called in the one body. And be thankful. Let the word of Christ dwell in you richly; teach and admonish one another in all wisdom; and with gratitude in your hearts sing psalms, hymns and spiritual songs to God. (vv. 15–16)

The Body of Christ is called to a process of maturing that involves the pursuit of wisdom and, at times, the necessity of admonition; but all this is to be undertaken in the context of worship, expressing gratitude to God. F. F. Bruce is candid about the pastoral implications of Paul's teaching for the Colossian Christians:

> when differences threaten to spring up among them, the peace of Christ must be accepted as *arbitrator*. If members are subject to Christ, the peace which he imparts must regulate their relations with one another. It was not to strife but to peace that God called them in the unity of the body of Christ.[8]

Finally, it is worth noting that the following chapter contains a significant observation on the subject of the spoken word, now focused on how the Colossians might interact with those beyond their existing community: 'Let your speech always be gracious, seasoned with salt, so that you may know how you ought to answer everyone' (Col. 4.6). Jerry Sumney notes that 'a clear tension exists between the church's existence as a group that stands apart from the surrounding culture and the church's evangelistic efforts. Believers must remain distinct and separate, yet at the same time they must remain open enough to invite others into the community of faith.'[9] The Christian is called to balance graciousness and saltiness – but these two qualities are held within a greater confidence, that serious devotion to God will bring with it the knowledge of how to answer anyone. Such confidence may well strike us as overly idealistic; as such, it echoes the teachings of Jesus, constantly setting the ethical bar higher than seems practically attainable in order to inspire the highest possible level of commitment. The third chapter of Colossians encapsulates Paul's vision of effective human interaction within the life of the church, creating firm foundations for missionary activity. As we shall now see, such activity does not and should not involve shying away from the facing of disagreement.

On facing disagreement

Recognizing the relative undesirability of disagreement

Before we can consider the place of disagreement within Pauline writing – even the potential for good disagreement – we must first give appropriate acknowledgement to the repeated instances where it is *agreement*, not disagreement, that is strongly affirmed as a hallmark of effective Christian relationship. This first 'facing' of disagreement is one which acknowledges frankly that its appearance in the common life of Christian believers can point to the ever-present reality of human frailty; as such, Paul repeatedly asserts unified vision and visible unity as evidence of fidelity to the gospel message. Indeed, in his correspondence with the Corinthian church, this exhortation is made emphatically, and at the very start of the first letter:

> Now I appeal to you, brothers and sisters, by the name of our Lord Jesus Christ, that all of you should be in agreement and that there should be no divisions among you, but that you should be united in the same mind and the same purpose. (1 Cor. 1.10)[10]

The internal rivalries within the Corinthian church drew stern criticism from Paul; as Joseph Fitzmyer notes, Paul's concern is that surface disunity points to a deeper theological problem:

> the lack of unity in the community implies a misunderstanding of Christ among them. He fears that such a situation might even empty the very cross of Christ of its meaning (v. 17). Implied in his argumentation is the conviction that Christ died for all human beings, and not only for those who pledge allegiance to one of his preachers.[11]

Fitzmyer argues that Paul's concern is to establish his apostolic credibility among the Corinthians and that this relies on his ability to adjudicate between factions while reminding all parties of their fundamental Christian allegiance. One might suggest that bishops have been attempting similar interventions ever since; Fitzmyer argues that Paul's forceful call to unity represents 'a challenge to Christians of all ages, who also have to consider the dangers of liberal or conservative thinking within the communities in which they live'.[12]

The seriousness with which Paul views Christian disagreement is underlined when he later poses this question: 'For as long as there is jealousy and quarrelling among you, are you not of the flesh, and behaving according to human inclinations?' (1 Cor 3.3).[13] Craig S. Keener identifies a Stoic-influenced dualism here, which has unambiguous implications for those who have chosen to follow Christ, a commitment that 'demands that those converted to truth walk in a manner consistent with that truth'.[14] Again we see the way in which an ethical demand flows from a point of theological recognition. For Paul, those who indulge in worldly, un-godly dissension and debate risk being diverted from an engagement with the spiritual reality of God, which should be their priority. He later asserts this line of argument when he reminds his readers that 'the kingdom of God depends not on talk but on power' (1 Cor. 4.20).

Dealing with opposition and opponents within the church

Having noted the way in which Paul outlines the desirability of agreement among Christians, we can now turn to a consideration of those instances where, that hope of agreement notwithstanding, disagreement is faced within the church. An important initial observation, which develops some of the conclusions we have already reached in relation to the book of Acts, underlines that the facing of disagreement does not entail the pursuit of unity at all costs. In his closing remarks within the letter to the Romans, Paul envisages at least a degree of separation between those holding to orthodox faith and those promoting disunity:

> I urge you, brothers and sisters, to keep an eye on those who cause dissensions and offences, in opposition to the teaching that you have learned; avoid them. For such people do not serve our Lord Christ, but their own appetites, and by smooth talk and flattery they deceive the hearts of the simple-minded. (Rom. 16.17–18)

Once more the link is made between sincere faith and speech that builds up Christian community. Such communities must be alert to the subtlety with which those seeking to undermine their foundations may speak – though there is, perhaps, some consolation in Paul's estimation here that they will only convince the 'simple-minded'.

The second letter to the Thessalonians contains a similar warning against full association with those who fail to heed orthodox teaching: 'Take note of those who do not obey what we say in this letter; have nothing to do with them, so that they may be ashamed. Do not regard them as enemies, but warn them as believers' (2 Thess. 3.14–15). We should recognize that in both these examples, a disagreement is faced – certainly not ignored – but there is not an expectation that those deemed to be the source of the disagreement should be excluded from the church. They might be avoided, but they are not to be seen as enemies; rather, they should be warned 'as believers'. Their dignity within the Body of Christ is maintained. What becomes clear is that Paul's overriding concern is that the gospel in its authentic form should continue to be propagated, in the face of the tensions and alternative perspectives hinted at in many of the letters to new churches.[15] Disagreement, for Paul, represents a significant but surmountable problem in the life of the church. As we shall see in the examples that follow, Christians should not be afraid of their disagreements, but neither should they be content to let them fester or, worse, distract them from what Paul sees as gospel priorities.

Lawsuits among believers: 1 Corinthians 6.1–11

There is no hiding Paul's exasperation at the litigious culture that has emerged within the church at Corinth. Joseph Fitzmyer highlights the two stages of argument in this passage: verses 1–6 criticize Christians for taking each other to court, while from verse 7 onwards Paul argues wholly against the pursuit of such practices: 'In fact, to have lawsuits at all with one another is already a defeat for you. Why not rather be wronged? Why not rather be defrauded?' (1 Cor. 6.7). The initial amazement at the actions of the Corinthian Christians rests on their apparent inability to resolve grievances among themselves. Verse 2 highlights Paul's concern that this inability to resolve internal disagreement impedes the effectiveness of the church's witness: 'Do you not know that the saints will judge the world? And if the world is to be judged by you, are you incompetent to try trivial cases?' (1 Cor. 6.2).

Paul thus challenges the Corinthian church to consider their disagreements over apparently trivial matters in the broader context of their engagement with the world. Listing ten examples of wrongdoers who will not inherit the kingdom of God, Paul calls his readers to live up to their calling as Christians rather than continuing to act is if unconverted. For Fitzmyer, this vice list

> enables Paul to formulate his basic conviction about the vocation of a Christian: you have been washed, sanctified, and justified in the name of the Lord Jesus and by God's Spirit. Such a calling summons Corinthian Christians to a mode of life that cannot be marked by trivial lawsuits or other questionable conduct.[16]

The undesirability of public disagreement is emphasized in relation to the missionary effectiveness of the church; internal disagreements of themselves need not be of concern, but the way that they are handled is crucial. Christians in Corinth have risked losing sight of the implications for mission of their public wrangling. Paul longs to call them back to the core of their vocation as the sanctified people of God who reveal to the world a different way to face the disagreements that will inevitably affect any community.

Paul opposes Cephas: Galatians 2.11–21

Paul's encounter with Cephas (Peter) offers another example of a disagreement being faced candidly. Cephas' apparent fear of the 'circumcision faction' has led to his refusal to eat with Gentiles, meaning that others, including Barnabas, were 'led astray' by him. Paul is forthright in his response: 'when I saw that they were not acting consistently with the truth of the gospel, I said to Cephas before them all, "If you, though a Jew, live like a Gentile and not like a Jew, how can you compel the Gentiles to live like Jews?"' (Gal. 2.14). David Horrell has noted how this exchange highlights the way in which Paul distinguishes between areas of potential ethical flexibility, and the need for a rootedness as disciples of Christ: 'Paul's tolerance operates only within the framework of an intolerance that insists on Christ alone as the basis for community solidarity, a basis which also implies the proscription of actions deemed to threaten this union.'[17]

Although it is unclear exactly how these events relate to the depiction of Paul and Barnabas in Jerusalem at Acts 15, they certainly emphasize once more that Christian identity is to be found in baptism rather than the continued observance of Jewish law. Paul writes: 'We ourselves are Jews by birth and not Gentile sinners; yet we know that a person is justified not by the works of the law but by faith in Jesus Christ' (Gal. 2.15–16a). The status of believers is not affected by their birth, and as such Paul argues that Cephas has gravely misunderstood a key aspect of the emergent tradition. Justification comes through faith, not the law; righteousness is found through trust in Christ, not legalistic observance. Paul thus underlines his willingness to disagree publicly in order to guard the faith that he seeks to pass on to the Galatians. However uncomfortable this may be for Jewish converts, he is unwavering in his commitment to the public pursuit of the truth as he sees it. The strident rhetoric of the following chapter further illustrates Paul's refusal to mollify the 'foolish Galatians' at that point he fears they could fall away from Christian orthodoxy (Gal. 3.1–5).

Observing the Lord's Supper: 1 Corinthians 11.17–22

Paul's intemperate response to division in the Corinthian church concerning the celebration of the Lord's Supper reminds us that even in this early Christian gathering, disagreement and conflict could be found at the very heart of the church's ritual life: 'Now in the following instructions I do not commend you, because when you come together it is not for the better but for the worse' (1 Cor. 11.17). Robin Scroggs has pointed out that this highlighting of division is particularly significant in relation to Paul's concern for the 'eschatological body': social relationships damaged through improper eating undermine the common life of the church and distract believers from their fundamental unity in Christ. Having also considered various other failures of the Corinthian church, Scroggs regards one principle, for Paul, as being dominant: 'the determination that ritual acts should lead to the upbuilding of the community ... If one can speak of "eschatological worship", then such worship occurs when individuals through their bodily actions show acceptance of, and bestow insight and encouragement upon, other members.'[18] This is a call to a unity that works hard to transcend superficial tensions – though, of course, the determination of what constitutes a tolerable tension is by no means straightforward.

In confronting the Corinthian Christians' apparent inability to order their commemoration of the Last Supper appropriately, David Horrell notes that 'their meal fails to be an enactment of oneness, of corporate solidarity, and instead demonstrates a despising of the fundamental character of the ecclesia'.[19] Horrell suggests that this episode is crucial in forming an understanding of Paul's sacramental theology: baptism and holy communion become the means by which it is possible to 'convey as the central theme of the Christian ethos the notion of a solidarity in Christ which transcends former distinctions'.[20] Here, then, disagreement has been highlighted and faced in order to invite a community to return to a right ordering of its priorities. It is difficult to imagine how any avoidance of this disagreement could have enabled the Corinthian church to consider its failure in this regard and amend its ways; Paul issues a direct and fulsome corrective such that their common life might be fashioned in a way properly reflective of the Christian call to a life of loving unity.

On the weak eating only vegetables: Romans 14

This final consideration of engagement with opponents and opposition within the church involves Paul cautioning his readers:

> Welcome those who are weak in faith, but not for the purpose of quarrelling over opinions. Some believe in eating anything, while the weak eat only vegetables. Those who eat must not despise those who abstain, and those who abstain must not pass judgement on those who eat; for God has welcomed them. (Rom. 14.1–3)

Paul does not immediately convey his own particular view in this scenario, beyond the encouragement to welcome all; but as Arland Hultgren points out, 'he does, however, make an emphatic point, and that is that passing judgements and despising one another have no place in the household of God, before whom each person is finally accountable'.[21] Those of 'weak faith' are to be engaged with, but not to the detriment of the unity to which the church is called. Here Paul implies that a degree of disagreement is inevitable within the household of faith, but the poisoning of mutual relationships should be avoided through a recognition that all stand equally before the judgement of God.

It is also worth noting Paul's affirmation at the beginning of the following chapter: 'We who are strong ought to put up with the failings of the weak, and not to please ourselves. Each of us must please our neighbour for the good purpose of building up the neighbour' (Rom. 15.1–2). Paul's hope is that 'together with one voice' (15.6) they might glorify God. Perhaps most tellingly, he exhorts them to 'welcome one another therefore, just as Christ has welcomed you, for the glory of God' (15.7). Colin Kruse notes that this concern is articulated by Paul in relation to the context of a communal meal: 'In that setting, if the believers were not accepting one another, they could hardly bring praise to God. It is implied that for Paul glorifying God and bringing praise to him is not just an individual but also a communal thing.'[22] Inevitable disagreement *among* Christians should, then, be considered alongside the call for all Christians to worship *alongside* one another. Paul encourages an upward turn to God in worship, rather than an inward turn to a fellow believer in judgement or disagreement. He is not suggesting that disagreements or divisions can easily disappear, but he is urging his readers to concentrate on their shared acts of praise, confident of the transformation that can result: 'May the God of peace fill you with all joy and peace in believing, so that you may abound in hope by the power of the Holy Spirit' (Rom. 15.13).[23]

Tom Wright considers this passage, as well as 1 Corinthians 8—10, in relation to the question of *adiaphora* – how it is determined whether a point of difference is of central importance, in this instance to a community's self-identity in Christ. Wright notes, in relation to Romans 15.7–13, that Paul's appeal to the value of united worship signifies the importance he attaches to mutual respect: 'He does not here ask the different groups to give up their practices; merely not to judge one another where differences exist ... Paul is here applying pastoral wisdom to contentious situations.'[24] It is such pastoral wisdom that is sought in a theology of disagreement, and it is worth noting that Wright himself concedes that even when the question of whether something is *adiaphora* or not has been ruled upon, 'this again neither reflects or produces a stable situation', because the contemporary church persists 'in dialogues of the deaf or, worse, the lobbing of angry verbal hand grenades over walls of incomprehension'.[25]

It is important, therefore, to note that an attempt to discern whether a given issue is or is not *adiaphora* does not resolve the disagreement being faced. At best, it moves the argument back one stage – but varied ongoing debates about sexuality demonstrate that disagreement over whether a particular issue is of fundamental doctrinal significance can itself swiftly lead to entrenched conflict, threatening schism. Paul's priority is to encourage appropriate discernment of the seriousness of a particular issue prompting disagreement, but also to do so in a way that does not lose sight of the pursuit of loving unity, held alongside a generosity towards those whom he deems to be 'weak in faith'. A theology of disagreement seeks to resource disagreeing Christians, whose arguments often risk turning toxic, whether or not the issue under consideration is deemed to be *adiaphora*.

On the possibility of good disagreement

We now move to a consideration of instances where Paul outlines the possibility of good disagreement, and engage by means of introduction with some of his words in the letter to the Colossians. Its celebrated claim about Jesus Christ, 'He himself is before all things, and in him all things hold together' (Col. 1.17), once more reminds us that disagreement within the church is contained within a framework known, loved and ultimately enfolded by God. All things can and do hold together in God. As Tom Wright notes, 'Through him the world is sustained, prevented from falling into chaos.'[26] But, Paul cautions, Christians are not to regard themselves as powerless in the face of their inevitable disagreements: they are urged to 'continue securely established and steadfast in the faith, without shifting from the hope promised by the gospel that you heard, which has been proclaimed to every creature under heaven' (Col. 1.23). Each believer must take responsibility for their response to the pressures they will face to accept alternative teaching or a divisive path.

Ultimately, Paul's call is to a loving unity rooted in the knowledge of God:

> I want their hearts to be encouraged and united in love, so that they may have all the riches of assured understanding and have the knowledge of God's mystery, that is, Christ himself, in whom are hidden all the treasures of wisdom and knowledge. I am saying this so that no one may deceive you with plausible arguments. (Col 2.2–4)

Paul regularly articulates his concern that the churches to whom he writes should not be attracted by unorthodox teaching. But this negatively expressed anxiety is always to be seen in the light of the positive sense of encouragement and unity to be found in the love of God, which is the very basis of Christian community. As Jerry Sumney notes, 'Love here designates the sphere within which believers live and has its source in God. Since the phrase "in love" depends on the participle "united", this love involves relations within the church and so concerns the attitude one takes toward fellow believers.'[27] This, then, is the context in which Paul envisages disagreements being faced – a community rooted in the love of Christ that is called and re-called to know that love and in that love confront all forms of human frailty.

2 Corinthians 7.8ff.

A brief comment is worthwhile on Paul's regret for sending an earlier letter, now presumed lost, to the Corinthian church: 'For even if I made you sorry with my letter, I do not regret it (though I did regret it, for I see that I grieved you with that letter, though only briefly)' (2 Cor. 7.8). Several commentators have noted the tension within this verse, as Paul seems to equivocate about the impact of his actions. As Frank Matera observes, 'Paul may have had second thoughts about the harsh letter ... more importantly, however, the tension and ambivalence are further indications of his love and concern for the community – for he realises the sorrow the letter produced among them.'[28] Disagreement is implicit here, but this passage is helpful for our purposes in that it offers an example of discord among Christians being resolved fruitfully in Paul's opinion:

'Now I rejoice, not because you were grieved, but because your grief led to repentance; for you felt a godly grief, so that you were not harmed in any way by us' (2 Cor. 7.9).

The letter to Philemon

Another intriguing instance worthy of note is found in the letter of Paul to Philemon. The enigmatic discussion concerning the future of Onesimus, Philemon's slave, is revealing of Paul's approach to a disagreement – even when he is arguing from a personal position of authority: 'though I am bold enough in Christ to command you to do your duty, yet I would rather appeal to you on the basis of love' (Philemon 8–9). Later, Paul asserts that he 'preferred to do nothing without your consent, in order that your good deed might be voluntary and not something forced' (v. 14). Tom Wright underlines that this exchange highlights Paul's understanding of how Christians might best relate to one another in community:

> Merely obeying an order might not necessarily elicit from Philemon that increase in understanding and love for which Paul has prayed ... Behind this choice of the right sort of appeal lies an all-important point: living Christianly makes people more human, not less. No Christian should grumble at extra demands of love.[29]

Notwithstanding the complex context of this exchange, Paul does point here to the value of disagreement being resolved through fruitful negotiation, always undertaken 'in Christ' (Philemon 8, 20, 23).

Ephesians 4

It is in this chapter of the letter to the Ephesians that we find crucial material within the Pauline literature that can resource a theology of disagreement. Paul urges the Ephesians 'to lead a life worthy of the calling to which you have been called, with all humility and gentleness, with patience, bearing with one another in love, making every effort to maintain the unity of the Spirit in the bond of peace' (Eph. 4.1b–3). The ethical implications of Christian life are inescapable; the call of Christ is inseparable from a call to loving unity. It is worth quoting the section that follows in full:

The gifts he gave were that some would be apostles, some prophets, some evangelists, some pastors and teachers, to equip the saints for the work of ministry, for building up the body of Christ, until all of us come to the unity of the faith and of the knowledge of the Son of God, to maturity, to the measure of the full stature of Christ. We must no longer be children, tossed to and fro and blown about by every wind of doctrine, by people's trickery, by their craftiness in deceitful scheming. But speaking the truth in love, we must grow up in every way into him who is the head, into Christ, from whom the whole body, joined and knitted together by every ligament with which it is equipped, as each part is working properly, promotes the body's growth in building itself up in love. (Eph. 4.11–16)

First, the diversity of the church is affirmed (v. 11). The role of the saints, in this diversity, is to build up the body of Christ, and this process is undertaken with confidence, for it leads to unity, knowledge and maturity. Christians must be alert to the danger of a childlike willingness to be persuaded inappropriately – people will oppose the work of the church with deceit and trickery. But, crucially, *speaking the truth in love* acknowledges the place of disagreement and debate in the life of the church, but encourages the communication of truth within a context of love.

The practical outworking of these verses is hardly straightforward, whether the context is Paul's first readers or contemporary Christians. To 'speak the truth in love' can be issued as a glib claim, built on slippery definitions of both 'truth' and 'love' and with unhelpful pastoral consequences following. But we should resist being distracted by these concerns, and instead recognize the significant extent to which Paul is placing the quality of internal relationship within the church at the heart of his Christian ethic. Disagreement can and will be part of the life of the church, but it should be part of the life of a church that is confident about its corporate journeying towards the heart and truth of Christ. The Body grows when it is built up in love. David Horrell has argued that 'other-regard' constitutes a key moral norm in Pauline ethics: 'a pattern of behaviour which constitutes a conformity to the pattern of Christ's self-giving'.[30]

In considering a theology of disagreement, this concern for the other, modelled on Christ, points to the potential transformation of disagreements. Paul then offers to his Ephesian readers an unusual degree of practical instruction: 'So then, putting away falsehood, let all of us speak the truth to our neighbours, for we are members of one another. Be angry but do not sin; do not let the sun go down on your anger' (Eph. 4.25–26). There is a frank recognition that the pursuit of truth may bring with it anger and falsehood, but even in fraught circumstances, the community should seek reconciliation at the end of each day. Furthermore, Paul urges his readers to be channels of grace: 'Let no evil talk come out of your mouths, but only what is useful for building up, as there is need, so that your words may give grace to those who hear' (v. 29). Fundamentally, Paul is challenging his readers to recognize that if they are fully to appreciate Jesus' sacrifice for them, they in turn need through their own mutual relationships to make sacrifices for the good of the Body as a whole: 'Put away from you all bitterness and wrath and anger and wrangling and slander, together with all malice, and be kind to one another, tender-hearted, forgiving one another, as God in Christ has forgiven you' (vv. 31–32). We may well wonder how any church at any time is to live up to such a calling – but we cannot ignore the significance Paul attaches to the quality of relationships within Christian community.

Galatians 5

The summation of the law at Galatians 5.14[31] has intrigued scholars to a degree that need not detain us here, but it is important for us to note the way in which a concern for the neighbour's well-being is given priority among Paul's ethical teachings. For James Dunn, 'to fulfil the law of Christ is to bear one another's burdens, which is a particular example of loving the neighbour, which fulfils the law'.[32] What should detain us is a consideration of the implications of this claim for an emerging theology of disagreement. For the neighbour with whom one disagrees is the neighbour whose well-being is paramount for the Christian committed to an imitation of Christ. To dismiss or anger or break relationship with such a neighbour is to conform to the world's pattern of broken relationships. Paul is calling his readers to a more complex and costly path for the good of the church as a whole: 'For in Christ Jesus neither circumcision nor uncircumcision counts for anything; the only thing that counts is faith working through love' (v. 6).

Paul then introduces an explicitly spiritual dimension to the discussion, when he challenges the Galatians to consider the source of any encouragement to deviate from the gospel: 'You were running well; who prevented you from obeying the truth? Such persuasion does not come from the one who calls you' (vv. 7–8). A church riven with disagreement and division might well be urged to consider whether the voice of God alone is being heard; a church can all too easily become consumed by such temptations (v. 15). Thus follows Paul's well-known contrast between the works of the flesh and the fruit of the Spirit. Verse 20 happens to include the vices most relevant to Christian disagreement – 'idolatry, sorcery, enmities, strife, jealousy, anger, quarrels, dissensions, factions'[33] – whereas 'the fruit of the Spirit is love, joy, peace, patience, kindness, generosity, faithfulness, gentleness, and self-control. There is no law against such things' (vv. 22–23).[34] As Richard Hays notes, 'When the community suffers division, the temple of God is dishonoured. But the presence of the Spirit in the community should produce unity rather than conflict.'[35]

The key question that follows for us concerns how disagreements are faced when there is a clear acknowledgement of the desirability of unity and the danger of falling into division – and whether disagreement undertaken with due regard to Paul's encouragement to Christians to live in loving unity can have a positive impact on the way disputes are approached. Too often, an initial disagreement merely represents the beginning of a seemingly inevitable slide into entrenched conflict, which in turn all too easily leads to disunity and separation. We will later explore whether an awareness of Paul's ethical imperatives in this respect really can have a bearing on ethical conduct; for now, we can usefully note James Dunn's observation in this regard: 'diversity that abandons the unity of the faith in Jesus the man now exalted is unacceptable; diversity that abandons the unity of love for fellow believers is unacceptable.'[36] Dunn's own wrestle with this tension between unity and diversity is candid about the internal contradictions and varied views to be found within New Testament Christianity – but, crucially, he returns repeatedly to an acknowledgement that the pursuit of loving unity is a consistent theme within the New Testament canon. It might be suggested that in Galatians we find an exhortation to disagree fruitfully, always journeying together and towards Christ: 'So then, whenever we have an opportunity, let us work for the good of all, and especially for those of the family of faith' (Gal. 6.10).

Romans 12

Romans 12 offers some final glimpses of how Paul envisages the place of disagreement within the body of Christ. Once again, a concern for Christian mutuality is asserted, as is the call to approach division in a way consonant with discipleship, rather than merely adopting an approach to it that might as easily be found in the rest of the world. Paul thus urges an openness to renewal that enables an appreciation of divine purpose: 'Do not be conformed to this world, but be transformed by the renewing of your minds, so that you may discern what is the will of God – what is good and acceptable and perfect' (v. 2). Paul's confidence in the Christian's ability to discern God's will may well appear overly optimistic to a contemporary reader. But this book aims to show that Paul's repeated call to his readers to return to a potentially costly path of loving unity is not mere idealism; rather it speaks of an ethical grounding to Christian life which he regards as non-negotiable. It is a call to humility that necessitates a recognition of the gifts of others: 'we, who are many, are one body in Christ, and individually we are members one of another' (v. 5).

Paul asserts the individual responsibility of each Christian when it comes to building a community of genuine love. Followers of Jesus are to 'love one another with mutual affection; outdo one another in showing honour' (v. 10). Those who may persecute – including in the course of disagreement and conflict – should be blessed in return; harmony should be pursued; humility is affirmed (vv. 14, 16). Crucially, the call of Christ demands self-examination, concerning to what extent any individual believer is responsible for promoting damaging disagreement and the resulting disunity: 'If it is possible, so far as it depends on you, live peaceably with all. Beloved, never avenge yourselves, but leave room for the wrath of God; for it is written, "Vengeance is mine, I will repay, says the Lord"' (vv. 18–19). Disciples of Christ are not barred from engaging in debate or even disagreement – Paul's 'if it is possible' leaves a self-autonomous door open – but they are to consider very carefully those instances when they will choose potentially damaging debate over the pursuit of mutual affection. Ultimately, Paul reminds them that vengeance should not be sought on their own behalf, since God as judge 'will repay'; as we shall consider later, a key question concerning a theology of disagreement concerns the extent to which any individual Christian is willing to choose self-denying gracious restraint over active participation in acrimonious debate.

Conclusion

David Horrell has suggested that 'building ecclesial solidarity and fostering other-regard' are the most basic goals of Paul's ethical outlook.[37] This chapter has shown that Paul repeatedly asserts that the pursuit of God and the up-building of his church rest upon a commitment to ethical goods that promote the flourishing of the Christian community's common life. I have suggested that there are four characteristics that are foundational for a Pauline ethic of relating within the Body of Christ: godly speech, mutual love, reconciled diversity and emergent maturity. This community on a journey towards holiness will never be free of disagreement this side of heaven, but when disagreements occur it has a responsibility to consider whether it is approaching such debates in a way remotely consonant with these four characteristics of internal ecclesial relationship. As I shall consider later in this book, the church's historic and contemporary willingness to set aside this ethical call to loving unity, in the midst of disagreement, represents a damaging move away from a core aspect of its true vocation. Paul does not offer a blueprint for the handling of disagreement, but he does acknowledge its existence – and offers a theological-ethical framework within which it can be faced fruitfully.

Notes

1 See, for example, Christopher Tuckett, 1987, *Reading the New Testament: Methods of Interpretation*, SPCK: London, pp. 53–62. For the purposes of this study, following Luke Timothy Johnson and others, I have treated the Pastoral Epistles as non-Pauline texts; as such they are considered in Chapter 5.

2 Richard B. Hays, 1996, *The Moral Vision of the New Testament*, New York: HarperCollins, p. 463.

3 Richard B. Hays, 2009, 'Introduction to Victor Paul Furnish, *Theology and Ethics in Paul*' in Victor Paul Furnish, *Theology and Ethics in Paul*, Louisville: Westminster John Knox Press, p. 13.

4 Victor Paul Furnish, 2005, 'Foreword' in Michael Cullinan, *Victor Paul Furnish's Theology of Ethics in Saint Paul: An Ethic of Transforming Grace*, Rome: Editiones Academiae Alfonsianae, p. 17.

5 See also Philippians 4.5: 'Let your gentleness be known to everyone. The Lord is near.'

6 It should be noted that Furnish focused his attention on Romans, 1 and 2 Corinthians, Galatians, Philippians, 1 Thessalonians and Philemon, arguing that 'the soundest procedure methodologically is to limit oneself to the letters of indisputable authenticity' (Furnish, *Theology and Ethics in Paul*, p. 11). Our preference is to approach the canonical New Testament text as received by the contemporary church. In overlooking Colossians, Furnish misses the opportunity to reflect on the extent to which the letter's third chapter offers a grounding for Pauline ethics in general, and for an emerging ethic of Christian relating within the Body of Christ, in particular.

7 N. T. Wright, 1986, *Colossians and Philemon*, Nottingham: InterVarsity Press, p. 144.

8 F. F. Bruce, 1984, *The Epistles to the Colossians, to Philemon, and to the Ephesians*, Grand Rapids: Eerdmans, pp. 156–7.

9 Jerry L. Sumney, 2008, *Colossians*, Louisville: Presbyterian Publishing Corporation, p. 264.

10 A similar view is expressed at Romans 15.5–6.

11 Joseph Fitzmyer, 2008, *First Corinthians: A New Translation with Introduction and Commentary*, New Haven: Yale University Press, p. 138.

12 Fitzmyer, *First Corinthians*, p. 140.

13 Paul voices similar concerns at 2 Corinthians 12.20.

14 Craig S. Keener, 2005, *1–2 Corinthians*, Cambridge: Cambridge University Press, p. 40.

15 See also Galatians 1.6–9, where 'deserting the one who called you in the grace of Christ and ... turning to a different gospel' is condemned in the strongest possible terms.

16 Fitzmyer, *First Corinthians*, p. 249.

17 David G. Horrell, 2005, *Solidarity and Difference: A Contemporary Reading of Paul's Ethics*, London: T&T Clark, p. 195.

18 Robin Scroggs, 1996, 'Paul and the Eschatological Body' in Eugene H. Lovering and Jerry L. Sumney, eds, *Theology and Ethics in Paul and his Interpreters*, Nashville: Abingdon Press, pp. 24–5.

19 Horrell, *Solidarity*, pp. 109–10.

20 Horrell, *Solidarity*, p. 110.

21 Arland Hultgren, 2011, *Paul's Letter to the Romans: A Commentary*, Grand Rapids: Eerdmans, p. 509. See also Corneliu Constantineanu, 2010, *The Social Significance of Reconciliation in Paul's Theology: Narrative Readings in Romans*, Edinburgh: T&T Clark. He notes that 'to live according to the logic of the gospel and in the light of the life of Christ is to be community oriented. Everyone is to nurture and embody reconciling practices – harmony and solidarity, peace, love, and regard for others – which enhance and enrich life together' (p. 174).

22 Colin Kruse, 2012, *Paul's Letter to the Romans*, Nottingham: Apollos, p. 532.

23 For an extended analysis of this passage, see Philip Esler, 2003, *Conflict and Identity in Romans: The Social Setting of Paul's Letter*, Minneapolis: Fortress Press, pp. 339–56. He notes that 'Paul plainly views the strong as those who must give way most. The weak are not to judge them, but the initiative for resolving the disputes rests with the strong' (p. 355). For Wolfgang Schrage, writing in relation to Romans 14, Paul 'has no choice but to leave most specific decisions about everyday matters to the resourcefulness and responsibility of love' (Wolfgang Schrage, 1988, *The Ethics of the New Testament*, Edinburgh: T&T Clark, p. 193). It is an enigmatic observation, but striking in relation to my subsequent suggestion in Part 2 that the double love command should form a basis for the discernment of a theology of disagreement.

24 Tom Wright, 'Pastoral Theology for Perplexing Topics' in Atherstone and Goddard, eds, *Disagreement?*, pp. 76–7. See also Ben Witherington III with Darlene Hyatt, 2004, *Paul's Letter to the Romans: A Socio-Rhetorical Commentary*, Grand Rapids: Eerdmans, pp. 325–45.

25 Wright in Atherstone and Goddard, eds, *Disagreement?*, pp. 81–2.

26 Wright, *Colossians*, pp. 77–8.

27 Sumney, *Colossians*, p. 115.

28 Frank J. Matera, 2003, *II Corinthians: A Commentary*, Louisville: Westminster John Knox Press, p. 175.

29 Wright, *Philemon*, p. 186.

30 Horrell, *Solidarity*, p. 241.

31 'For the whole law is summed up in a single commandment, "You shall love your neighbour as yourself".'

32 James Dunn, 1996, '"The Law of Faith," "the Law of the Spirit" and "the Law of Christ"' in Lovering and Sumney, eds, *Theology and Ethics in Paul*, p. 76.

33 James Dunn's commentary suggests that Paul is here referring to a concern 'that the factionalism which disfigured late second-Temple Judaism might be

imported into the new movement by the activities of the other missionaries. Since that factionalism was characteristically exclusive and judgemental of other Jews, discounting them as "sinners" and as those whose actions had effectively put themselves outside the covenant people ... Paul had every reason to resist such censorious factionalism in his own churches.' (James Dunn, 1993, *The Epistle to the Galatians*, Grand Rapids: Baker Academic, p. 305). Dunn's observation only underscores the relevance of this passage in relation to a theology of disagreement.

34 In our context, Ben Witherington's affirmation of Paul's concern for the upbuilding of the corporate church community, rather than merely individual morality, is worth noting: 'a corporate and communal effort is required to win these sorts of battles against the flesh. That is why we have all the discussion here about burden bearing and loving neighbour. These are the bases of forming a resilient and enduring community.' See Ben Witherington III, 1998, *Grace in Galatia: A Commentary on St Paul's Letter to the Galatians*, Edinburgh: T&T Clark, p. 415.

35 Hays, *Moral Vision*, p. 34.

36 James D. G. Dunn, 2006, *Unity and Diversity in the New Testament: An Inquiry into the Character of Earliest Christianity*, London: SCM Press, p. 416.

37 Horrell, *Solidarity*, p. 280.

5

The Priority of Holy Speech and Conduct in Other New Testament Texts

In the Preface to their commentary on the Pastoral Epistles, Robert Wall and Richard Steele acknowledge candidly that the texts under their consideration are often exiled by biblical scholars, who regularly conclude that the general unlikelihood of the letters to Timothy and Titus having been written by Paul renders them of little interest to most students of the New Testament. Moreover, these same letters contain some of the Bible's most apparently obnoxious and offensive 'texts of terror', which have 'been used or abused to push sisters and brothers to the harsh margins of a community called to instantiate God's love in the world'.[1] Wall and Steele refuse, however, to allow such concerns to sideline these texts. Indeed, given their place within the biblical canon, the letters taken as a whole may, for the contemporary reader,

> confidently target holy ends – deeper communion with God and holy fellowship with others – not on the conditions that a text's attributed author is confirmed by historians or that its original meaning can be reconstructed by the tools of modern criticism, but on the belief that God's spirit sanctifies and uses these same texts to lead Jesus' followers into truth about God's providential way of ordering the world.[2]

For a theology of disagreement, these sometimes marginalized texts offer some of the richest insights into how early Christians faced the challenge of disagreement. While we may wish to ask exactly how Wall and Steele's notion of 'God's providential way of ordering the world' is understood, not to mention translated across gaps of time and cultural context, we can, with them, affirm the value of engaging with potentially disruptive or inconvenient narratives. In this chapter we thus consider certain thematic aspects of disagreement that recur in these later New Testament texts. As we shall see, the character ethics evident in both the way Christians speak and the words they use was a key concern in the life of these young churches – though we will also note the lack of unanimity of approach, and begin to consider how the tensions that exist between some of these texts can be faced appropriately as we explore the construction of a theological ethic of disagreement.

The cost of disagreement: key observations in the letters to Timothy

A call to godly speech: 1 Timothy 4 and 6

The sixth chapter of 1 Timothy offers an apposite example of a text set in such an uncomfortable narrative context – the need for slaves to respect their masters – that there is a risk of the text as a whole being overlooked by readers reluctant to engage with the author's seeming contentment with the institution of slavery. There is no easy way for the contemporary reader to soften the reading of the instruction to respect believing masters and 'serve them all the more' (1 Tim. 6.2); but however appalled we might be at these sentiments, it is a shame if our response leads to a lack of engagement with the verses that follow:

> Whoever teaches otherwise and does not agree with the sound words of our Lord Jesus Christ and the teaching that is in accordance with god-liness, is conceited, understanding nothing, and has a morbid craving for controversy and for disputes about words. From these come envy, dissension, slander, base suspicions, and wrangling among those who are depraved in mind and bereft of the truth, imagining that godliness is a means of gain. (vv. 3–5)

There is an interpretative challenge here, concerning whether we see an ethical value in the words of these three verses that transcends their specific (and uncomfortable) context. Some readings seem intent to pro-ceed from verse 3 as if the content of the immediately preceding verses were immaterial, or simply not present. Raymond Collins comments: 'sound teaching does not stand alone. It leads to a way of life, identifi-able patterns of appropriate behaviour. That behaviour can be summed up as a 'godliness' (*eusebia*), the kind of religious devotion that leads to a corresponding way of life.'[3] There is no doubt that such conclusions can be drawn from the text – but Collins seems unclear as to whether these conclusions from verse 3 onwards have any impact on the preced-ing discussion of slavery. For our purposes, it is verse 4's warning of the danger of 'a morbid craving for controversy and for disputes about words' that surely highlights the ease with which Christians can be distracted from the heart of their faith, lured by the superficial attractiveness of the pursuit of the latest ecclesiastical controversy. Such disputes breed the behaviour lacking in virtue outlined in verse 4: contentment is elusive while scores are settled, and a failure to 'agree with the sound words of our Lord Jesus Christ' is evident (6.3).

It is worth underlining that these verses consider the implications of heterodoxy; it does not seem conceivable, from the author's perspective, that Christians *themselves* might develop a morbid craving for controversy and for disputes about words. Alas, it hardly needs saying that the history of the church, from the pages of the New Testament onwards, reminds even a figure as early in Christian history as the author of the letters to Timothy that it is precisely because Christians engage with one another in destructive disputes that an assumption such discourse only happens outside the church is naive at best. The grave danger is that the church loses all sight of the importance of the kind of conduct urged earlier in the letter: 'set the believers an example in speech and conduct, in love, in faith, in purity' (1 Tim. 4.12b). The words that come from Christian lips need, of themselves, to be recognizably Christian, and Timothy and those around him are urged to take seriously the notion that the gospel hope to which they hold will be made visible in part through the kind of words they choose to use with each other and in the wider community: the believers need to be set a godly example, and the use of appropriate speech is key to the pursuit of that end.

On the care of widows, and other household instructions: 1 Timothy 5

The need for appropriately Christian speech is also in evidence in verses that immediately precede a lengthy consideration of the treatment of widows: 'Do not speak harshly to an older man, but speak to him as to a father, to younger men as brothers, to older women as mothers, to younger women as sisters – with absolute purity' (1 Tim. 5.1–2). Robert Wall notes that such concerns have a missiological dimension, in that they point to a church that needs to be seen to order its life with care: 'central to the political ideology of antiquity, the well-run family household is a necessary condition of civil society; likewise, an orderly congregation of believers is a necessary condition for maintaining a covenant-keeping relationship with God.'[4] The complexity of the pastoral concern for widows evident here is not directly relevant for our purposes, but it is worth noting the level of detail with which the place of widows in the life of the church is considered. There is a clear expectation of order and regulation in the Christian life, even in the midst of inevitable disagreements – and the church needs to organize itself in this regard: 'Never accept any accusation against an elder except on the evidence of two or three witnesses. As for those who persist in sin, rebuke them in the presence of all, so that the rest also may stand in fear' (1 Tim. 5.19–20). Although the key concern here is how to deal with potentially false accusations against church leaders, and the presence of persistent sinners within the community, the value of time being given to consider how difficulties in church life might be faced is important to note as we consider theological approaches to disagreement.

Attributes of a worker approved by God: 2 Timothy 2

The repeated concern for godly speech outlined in the first letter to Timothy is restated in the second, with unambiguous force: 'Remind them of this, and warn them before God that they are to avoid wrangling over words, which does no good but only ruins those who are listening' (2 Tim. 2.14). It may be that we read this verse with a wry smile, such can be the dependence of scholarly endeavour on wordy wrangles. But this exhortation is part of a broader plea that Timothy and those with him should pursue all that makes for a close relationship with God. As Raymond Collins observes in relation to verse 14, 'verbal warfare results in no advantage at all; rather, it results in great disadvantage, that is, utter destruction'.[5] It is important to note the gravity of concern associated with speech that leads people away from gospel truth. Timothy is urged to 'avoid profane chatter, for it will lead people into more and more impiety' (2 Tim. 2.16). The challenge seems to be to steer church members away from disagreements that risk distracting them from the core purposes and concerns of Christian life. They must 'have nothing to do with stupid and senseless controversies; you know that they breed quarrels' (v. 23). There is a frank recognition of the corrosive impact that controversy can have on the life of the church and the way in which one argument feeds off another. This is not to suggest that truth should not be argued for vigorously and defended candidly; but Timothy must recognize that 'the Lord's servant must not be quarrelsome but kindly to everyone, an apt teacher, patient, correcting opponents with gentleness' (vv. 24–25). Such a list of attributes may be offputtingly exacting in its demands, but Timothy is left in no doubt about the character ethics that should be fundamental in effective Christian life and ministry.

Alexander the coppersmith: 2 Timothy 4

Notwithstanding the encouragement to Timothy to engage in godly speech and conduct, moments of tension remain from the perspective of the letter's author, with one brief observation worthy of our consideration: 'Alexander the coppersmith did me great harm; the Lord will pay him back for his deeds' (2 Tim. 4.14). We do not know the specifics of the incident with Alexander, but we should note two implications that flow from this verse. First, harm is acknowledged – shortcomings in the life of the church are not to be airbrushed out of its discourse. Second, the resolution of this problem is not a matter for human judgement but for God. An inevitable question that follows concerns how to determine if a situation demands the sort of church regulation witnessed in 1 Timothy 5, or whether human withdrawal in the hope of divine judgement is appropriate. We know only too well that the history of the church is littered with examples where that tension remains unresolved. A recurring challenge for Christians facing complex instances of disagreement involves determining when an instinct to speak out or intervene should give way to a deliberate commitment to gracious restraint, trusting in the possibility of divine rather than human resolution to the issue in question.

Godly speech and Christian disagreement: instances from 1 Peter and James

Speaking so that God may be glorified: 1 Peter 3 and 4

Having considered the repeated ways in which the letters to Timothy highlight the gravity of disagreement as a potentially negative force within the life of the church, we now examine texts that underline the call to godly speech, and the very particular capability of the spoken word as a means for undermining the work of the gospel in the midst of disagreement and debate. The first letter of Peter calls its readers 'who desire life and desire to see good days' to 'keep their tongues from evil and their lips from speaking deceit' (1 Peter 3.10). It is worth noting that this caution almost immediately precedes words (in)famously used as an encouragement to personal evangelism:

> Always be ready to make your defence to anyone who demands from you an account of the hope that is in you; yet do it with gentleness and reverence. Keep your conscience clear, so that, when you are maligned,

those who abuse you for your good conduct in Christ may be put to shame. (3.15b–16)

Although this is advice concerned with Christian interaction with non-believers, it is offered by Peter in a context of an assumed 'unity of spirit', 'sympathy' and 'love for one another' as described in verse 8. The Christian brother or sister with whom one disagrees must surely also be worthy of the 'gentleness and reverence' to be accorded to those beyond the church. As Peter notes in the following chapter:

Whoever speaks must do so as one speaking the very words of God; whoever serves must do so with the strength that God supplies, so that God may be glorified in all things through Jesus Christ. To him belong the glory and the power for ever and ever. Amen. (1 Peter 4.11)

Christian speech ethics: James 1 and 3

The letter of James contains some of the most sustained consideration of the ethics of speech within the New Testament, and in its exploration of the relationship between anger and speech it offers useful material for a theology of disagreement: 'You must understand this, my beloved: let everyone be quick to listen, slow to speak, slow to anger; for your anger does not produce God's righteousness' (James 1.19–20). This pithy call affirms time taken for thoughtful consideration rather than angry retort, and is followed by a curt reminder of the value of not speaking at all: 'If any think they are religious, and do not bridle their tongues but deceive their hearts, their religion is worthless' (1.26). This generalized observation challenges those who speak without self-restraint to examine the authenticity of their claims to religious status. As Douglas Moo notes, 'a person whose religion is the "genuine article" will manifest that fact by being careful in what he or she says. Failure to control one's speech, James asserts, means that one is "deceiving" oneself about having true religion.'[6]

The bridling of the tongue is one image that is further developed in chapter 3, whose opening verses are worth quoting in full:

For all of us make many mistakes. Anyone who makes no mistakes in speaking is perfect, able to keep the whole body in check with a bridle. If we put bits into the mouths of horses to make them obey us, we guide their whole bodies. Or look at ships: though they are so large that it takes strong winds to drive them, yet they are guided by a very small rudder wherever the will of the pilot directs. So also the tongue is a small member, yet it boasts of great exploits.

How great a forest is set ablaze by a small fire! And the tongue is a fire. The tongue is placed among our members as a world of iniquity; it stains the whole body, sets on fire the cycle of nature, and is itself set on fire by hell. For every species of beast and bird, of reptile and sea creature, can be tamed and has been tamed by the human species, but no one can tame the tongue – a restless evil, full of deadly poison. With it we bless the Lord and Father, and with it we curse those who are made in the likeness of God. From the same mouth come blessing and cursing. My brothers and sisters, this ought not to be so. (James 3.2–10)

These are uncompromising words. In the dual images of a horse's bit and a ship's rudder, we find examples that may well have had proverbial resonance to their first hearers, and that still powerfully convey the sense that the tongue, though small in relation to the body, has huge influence for good or ill. Moreover, James emphasizes that this same part of the body can effortlessly switch from spreading joy to spreading poison; so the scale of the challenge facing the Christian who dares to teach or speak in public is a considerable one. James Adamson suggests that 'to bless God is the sublimest function of the human tongue',[7] and the letter of James deplores the ease with which those within the church fail to embrace this opportunity, still less the opportunity to bless one another. They can choose to curse, but they can also choose to bless; the pressing need, for James, is that his readers will acknowledge the potentially destructive power of their words and consider how changed behaviour might result in an improved situation. The possible implications for a theology of disagreement are clear: the way that Christians choose to speak, as well as the specific words they use, are crucial factors in enabling disagreement that sustains rather than undermines the Body of Christ.

The impact of disagreement on relationships in the church

A call to peaceful co-existence: Hebrews 12 and 13

The letters of James and Peter both articulate specific concerns about inappropriate speech that undermines the life of the church; a more general desire for visible loving unity among Christians is articulated widely in the texts of the early church under consideration in this chapter. The Hebrews are instructed to 'pursue peace with everyone, and the holiness without which no one will see the Lord' (Heb. 12.14). Marie Isaacs cautions that 'it is unlikely that this is an injunction to find accord with all ... rather it is an encouragement to make common cause with others (presumably members of the Christian community) in their quest for God's peace'.[8] This pursuit of peace is emphasized in a context where threats to orthodox holiness are in evidence – 'Do not be carried away by all kinds of strange teachings' (13.9) – and where ultimately the call is to faithful conformity: 'Obey your leaders and submit to them, for they are keeping watch over your souls and will give an account' (13.17a). The challenge of this verse, in relation to Christian disagreement, is inescapable: it urges a submissiveness that might be seen to presuppose that no faithful member of a church would disagree with their leader.

Embody virtue: Titus 3

This notion is also found in the letter to Titus, where ethical directives concerning both speech and relationships are stated boldly: 'Remind them to be subject to rulers and authorities, to be obedient, to be ready for every good work, to speak evil of no one, to avoid quarrelling, to be gentle, and to show every courtesy to everyone' (Titus 3.1–2). Philip Towner points out the way in which these two verses first address the Christian's relationship to the state, and, second, their relationship with other people:

> in the civic arena Christians are to be as responsible as the best citizens. Where believers, more generally, come into contact with other people, they are to embody the highest ideals of human virtue as they imitate the pattern of behaviour embodied by Christ himself.[9]

As discussed previously in relation to the Synoptic Gospels, it is in fact important to distinguish between a simplistic biographical imitation of Jesus and a response to his commands; the former could easily include behaviour flatly contradicting the gentle avoidance of quarrelling outlined in Titus 3.2.

The reader is left in no doubt about the concern Titus should have for the unity of the church in the face of fragmentation, and the danger of damage to its public image as a result of its disputes.[10] Indeed, such concerns are restated and then followed by a practical proposal for the facing of disagreement:

> avoid stupid controversies, genealogies, dissensions, and quarrels about the law, for they are unprofitable and worthless. After a first and second

admonition, have nothing more to do with anyone who causes divisions, since you know that such a person is perverted and sinful, being self-condemned. (3.9–11)

Jerome Quinn notes that this approach combines a desire to see the problem addressed with a commitment to ensuring it does not, of itself, become a distraction: 'The apostolic minister envisioned here is dealing with fellow Christians as individuals with their frailties and limitations. The procedure submitted ensures a hearing and "due process" as well as forestalling wasting time in pointless argument.'[11] Of crucial significance is the expectation that an unrepentant dissenter will be excluded – in some way – from continuing fellowship. It is, of course, unclear what degree of separation or exclusion from the church is intended, and their self-exclusion is implied at the end of verse 11; but, nonetheless, this instance of disagreement (and worse) not being tolerated needs to be noted carefully as we continue to build our picture of approaches to disagreement found across the canvas of the New Testament.

Pursue mutual love: 1 Peter 1 and 4

One cannot escape the tensions that exist between different texts in relation to the impact of ecclesial disagreements on the health of the church. While Titus has been urged to distance himself from controversy and, if necessary, to exclude those responsible for stoking it, in the first letter of Peter a notably different approach is found. Peter regards mutual love as flowing from sincere commitment in faith: 'Now that you have purified your souls by your obedience to the truth so that you have genuine mutual love, love one another deeply from the heart' (1 Peter 1.22). The theological significance of this statement should not be overlooked: Peter believes that obedience has led to genuine mutual love, and the challenge for the church that then follows is to ensure that such love is deeply and sincerely expressed. This represents an association between theological orthodoxy and loving unity that has offered an important challenge to fractured churches ever since; if mutual love really does come about as a result of obedience to truth, then the importance of disagreement being rooted in a desire to uncover the truth is inescapable. This transforms a call to loving unity into a call to faithful discipleship, where unity is a fruit of faithfulness and where the pursuit of mutual love is paramount: 'Above all, maintain constant love for one another, for love covers a multitude of sins' (4.8).

Submit to God: James 4

Having already studied the exacting commands in the letter of James concerning the self-regulation of the tongue, we may not be surprised to find in the same epistle an extended consideration of the impact of conflicts and disputes within the body of Christ. The letter's fourth chapter begins by asking where such disagreements originate, and rapidly answers its own question with a forceful dualism cautioning against 'friendship with the world' (4.4). It is only as a result of submission to God that sin and the devil can be resisted: 'Humble yourselves before the Lord, and he will exalt you' (v. 10). A constituent part of this call to humility is the warning to resist judging others that follows: 'Do not speak evil against one another, brothers and sisters. Whoever speaks evil against another or judges another, speaks evil against the law and judges the law; but if you judge the law, you are not a doer of the law but a judge' (v. 11). This statement has radical implications for a theology of disagreement. Marie Isaacs underlines that judgement of another is understood here in a condemnatory sense, which stands alongside speaking evil of them. To speak ill of others 'is singled out as an especially grave offence'.[12]

It is worth noting that some scholars who have paid particular attention to the letter of James point out that its distinctive speech ethics are just as prominent as its consideration of questions concerning wealth and poverty, but the former topic routinely receives less attention. Richard Bauckham, sympathetic to this argument, nonetheless devotes only two pages to 'Speech Ethics' in James, calling it 'a topic rarely discussed today'.[13] He does, however, highlight William Baker's claim that 'James has made control of speech the premier ethical and spiritual task of man'.[14] While we may be sympathetic to Bauckham's criticism that solidarity with the poor surely remains the priority, or at least of equal importance, for James, we can hardly ignore the way in which this letter places the quality of speech and the impact that such speech has on ecclesial relationships as a key ethical concern within the life of the church. James repeatedly cautions his reader to think carefully about the potentially grave impact of wounding words on the health of the Body of Christ. It is the contention of this book that such arguments still tend not to be taken sufficiently seriously by churches routinely wounded by damaging disagreements.

Disagreement and the safeguarding of doctrinal truth

Sound doctrine and its preservation: Hebrews 2, 3, 4, 6 and 10

One of the inescapable questions concerning disagreement in the church is how the presence of such disagreement relates to an understanding of the development of doctrine. Disagreement can be seen as a useful process whereby mutual understanding is established and difference faced; but we should not overlook the extent to which it can also be regarded as a fraught and inherently negative process, where the doctrinal integrity of the church is perceived to be – or actually is being – threatened. The letter to the Hebrews offers an insight into how such tensions were experienced in the early church, when a concern is raised that some have departed from the truth: 'Therefore we must pay greater attention to what we have heard, so that we do not drift away from it' (Heb. 2.1). The clear expectation is that a careful rehearsal of teachings received will result in fidelity to the truth – though we might well question whether such a stance is overly optimistic. It is also noteworthy that, in the following chapter, departing from the truth is perceived markedly more negatively: 'Take care, brothers and sisters, that none of you may have an evil, unbelieving heart that turns away from the living God' (3.12). The earlier notion of 'drifting away' has been replaced by the harsher reference to an 'evil, unbelieving heart'; those who might dare to disagree are forced to recognize that the very act of disagreement might be perceived as damaging to the health of the Body.

If Hebrews hints at a general discouragement of disagreement, it also repeatedly encourages its readers to model themselves on Jesus, which is, as we have previously discussed in relation to the Synoptic Gospels, an unstraightforward task. The Hebrews are reminded that they 'do not have a high priest who is unable to sympathize with our weaknesses, but we have one who in every respect has been tested as we are, yet without sin' (4.15). The theological implications here are complex, and in relation to a theology of disagreement we are forced to consider the moral weight of instances such as Jesus' angry attitude towards Pharisees and other religious leaders. Gareth Lee Cockerill notes: 'Because Jesus has experienced and overcome every kind of temptation to which humans are subject, he is able to empower his people in their human weakness.'[15] An intriguing question about Jesus' own anger in the midst of disagreement nonetheless remains: even if his anger towards the Pharisees wasn't sinful, it is hard to see how it can represent a model for Christian behaviour consonant with his overall teaching. The Hebrews may take some consolation from the reassurance that Jesus was tested as they are, but that identification alone does not sanction an imitation of Jesus' intemperate attitude to those with whom he disagreed.

It is in its later discussion of journeying towards perfection that the letter effectively cautions against any church becoming too comfortable with the presence of disagreement within it. Chapter 6 offers a vision of dynamic movement within the life of the church, always striving towards a fulfilment of Christian teaching:

> Therefore let us go on towards perfection, leaving behind the basic teaching about Christ, and not laying again the foundation: repentance from dead works and faith towards God, instruction about baptisms, laying on of hands, resurrection of the dead, and eternal judgement. (6.1–2)

The Hebrews are called to build on the foundations of faith, rather than undermine them; so if they are to disagree well, they will do so in a way that enables the clarification and appreciation of such foundations. The importance of an agreed doctrinal basis to the life of the church is affirmed, and in terms that anticipate a clear sense of development in discipleship beyond the foundational beliefs and practices cited; the grave alternative, outlined in verses 4–8, is a falling away that leaves little scope for restoration. Thus the Hebrews are called to 'hold fast to the confession of our hope without wavering, for he who has promised is faithful. And let us consider how to provoke one another to love and good deeds' (10.23–24).[16]

Sound doctrine and love: 1 Timothy 1 and 6

This close association between doctrinal certitude and the pursuit of mutual love is expressed in uncompromising terms in a passage from 1 Timothy:

> I urge you, as I did when I was on my way to Macedonia, to remain in Ephesus so that you may instruct certain people not to teach any different doctrine, and not to occupy themselves with myths and endless genealogies that promote speculations rather than the divine training that is known by faith. But the aim of such instruction is love that comes from a pure heart, a good conscience, and sincere faith. Some people have deviated from these and turned to meaningless talk, desiring to be teachers of the law, without understanding either what they are saying or the things about which they make assertions. (1 Tim. 1.3–7)

At the very start of the letter, Timothy is urged to safeguard the doctrinal unity of the church and dissuade people from speculation that distracts from 'divine training' rooted in faith. As we have just seen in the letter to the Hebrews, the purpose of this adherence to truth is the furtherance of love. Perhaps most tantalizingly for our purposes, a concern is outlined that some have 'turned to meaningless talk' – making unfounded assertions that undermine the health of the church. The goal for Timothy's leadership is that he should become one who can 'set the believers an example in speech and conduct, in love, in faith, in purity' (1 Tim. 4.12b). As we have already noted, part of our challenge is to consider how disagreement within the church, inevitable as it is, can avoid being the 'meaningless talk' that risks distracting believers from the truth, and instead initiates a process whereby the frank facing of difference nonetheless initiates a constructive process towards mutual understanding and unity.

The personal instructions offered to Timothy in the final chapter of the letter reassert the challenge that Christian leaders face as custodians of a living tradition: 'guard what has been entrusted to you. Avoid the profane chatter and contradictions of what is falsely called knowledge; by professing it some have missed the mark as regards the faith. Grace be with you' (1 Tim. 6.20–21). While we may not be clear about the specific theological perspective of those who opposed Timothy, we are left in little doubt about the danger that is perceived in the indulgence of profane chatter and its associated false knowledge. Tellingly, that danger has grave potential consequences for the sustenance of faith and the well-being of the community. As Gordon Fee observes, 'the church needed to hear that the deviations were a disease among them and that what Timothy would have to teach would be the words of health'.[17] Timothy's task is to safeguard the gospel message that has been entrusted to him, defending orthodoxy from Gnostic or other attacks; as we shall see, determining how opponents within the church should be engaged with, however unorthodox their theological position appears, remains a key challenge for any Christian seeking to reflect on how disagreement can be faced more effectively and fruitfully within the church.

The pursuit of church order in the midst of disagreement

Appointing reliable teachers: Titus 1 and 2

The letter to Titus relates concerns about doctrinal integrity to the structure and ordering of church life. We read that elders should be appointed in every Cretan town who possess both an understanding of Christian faith and an ability to defend it: 'He must have a firm grasp of the word that is trustworthy in accordance with the teaching, so that he may be able both to preach with sound doctrine and to refute those who contradict it' (Titus 1.9). The presence of 'many rebellious people, idle talkers and deceivers' (1.10), presents a particular problem for Titus – but the solution is clearly expressed: 'they must be silenced, since they are upsetting whole families by teaching for sordid gain what it is not right to teach' (1.11). In stark contrast to some approaches to disagreement or dissent that we have identified elsewhere in the New Testament, Titus is encouraged forcefully to confront such people:

> rebuke them sharply, so that they may become sound in the faith, not paying attention to Jewish myths or to commandments of those who reject the truth. To the pure all things are pure, but to the corrupt and unbelieving nothing is pure. Their very minds and consciences are corrupted. They profess to know God, but they deny him by their actions. They are detestable, disobedient, unfit for any good work. (1.13–16)

In Richard Hays' terminology, this instance of an uncompromising approach to opponents within the church represents a tension with other attitudes we have considered elsewhere, which, for now, we must allow to stand. What we can clearly recognize here is the emergence within the early church of authority structures and an associated expectation that those who hold office within them will act as guardians of orthodoxy. Here, particular concerns about the faith of Jewish Christians are expressed to Titus in the strongest possible terms. But while he is to rebuke them sharply, he is also asked to 'tell the older men to be temperate, serious, prudent, and sound in faith, in love, and in endurance' (2.2). We might ask whether there is an appropriate degree of consistency envisaged in this apparent speech ethic. The sharp rebukes sanctioned in relation to 'those of the circumcision' stand in contrast with the approach commended in relation to the younger men:

> Likewise, urge the younger men to be self-controlled. Show yourself in all respects a model of good works, and in your teaching show integrity, gravity, and sound speech that cannot be censured; then any opponent will be put to shame, having nothing evil to say of us. (2.6–8)

It is this final phrase that is perhaps most telling: Titus is encouraged to speak in ways that defy censure, such that opponents will fall silent. Integrity and gravity are proposed as hallmarks of speech that has the capacity to forestall disagreement.

Work towards an ordered church: 1 Peter 3 and 5; 2 Peter 1 and 2

For the Christian believer, a willingness to submit to those in authority is portrayed as a crucial component of faithful discipleship in the first letter of Peter: 'you who are younger must accept the authority of the elders. And all of you must clothe yourselves with humility in your dealings with one another, for "God opposes the proud, but gives grace to the humble"' (1 Peter 5.5). Such humility forms part of the discipline of faith that might, ultimately, face severe testing: 'Discipline yourselves; keep alert. Like a roaring lion your adversary the devil prowls around, looking for someone to devour' (5.8). David Horrell points out that opposition to the truth of the gospel is usually conceived as coming from other people, but this verse represents the one occasion when it is regarded as the work of the devil himself. Peter's response, Horrell argues, thus depends on the source of attack: 'While human accusers and opponents should encounter blessing and not resistance from the Christian community, and while those in authority, even those who are unjust, should receive due submission, Satan should by all means be opposed and resisted.'[18]

It is certainly worth recalling the appeal made by Peter to all his readers, having (notoriously) offered specific teachings to both women and slaves:

> Finally, all of you, have unity of spirit, sympathy, love for one another, a tender heart, and a humble mind. Do not repay evil for evil or abuse for abuse; but, on the contrary, repay with a blessing. It is for this that you were called – that you might inherit a blessing. (1 Peter 3.8–9)

While Peter has emphasized the need for the respect of offices within the church in order for the Christian community to operate effectively, he places yet greater emphasis on what could be termed the emotional intelligence with which he encourages Christians to face their daily interactions. A distinction is drawn here between blanket resistance to the enemy and a loving forgiveness directed at fellow Christians – though it is unclear when a member of the church might be deemed to be doing the devil's work or to have abandoned orthodoxy.

Peter's second letter affirms the encouraging tone of the first, in respect of its encouragement to live in loving unity: 'For this very reason, you must make every effort to support your faith with goodness, and goodness with knowledge, and knowledge with self-control, and self-control with endurance, and endurance with godliness, and godliness with mutual affection, and mutual affection with love' (2 Peter 1.5–7). This intentional pursuit of virtue, for the good of the whole community, offers the beginnings of a template for Christian living. Peter is well aware of the threats to this harmonious vision, but it is as if he recognizes that as much can be achieved through the gracious self-discipline of Christians as can by their effective engagement with opponents. Those opponents will, after all, 'exploit you with deceptive words. Their condemnation, pronounced against them long ago, has not been idle, and their destruction is not asleep' (2.3). Those receiving Peter's letter are to be encouraged that their plight is not ignored, but that the potential for their exploitation remains real; they are called to reflect on how it is that they can interact with others in their community in ways that model the love of Christ and promote mutual affection – blessing one another, rather than repaying evil for evil or abuse for abuse.

Resist external threats: Jude

It is in the brief letter of Jude that we find many of the themes already discussed restated with pithy clarity. The presence of 'certain intruders' is the presenting challenge – those who 'pervert the grace of our God into licentiousness and deny our only Master and Lord, Jesus Christ' (v. 4). We cannot ignore the extent to which it is the sinful speech of these intruders that is of particular concern: 'These are grumblers and malcontents; they indulge their own lusts; they are bombastic in speech, flattering people to their own advantage' (v. 16). That words are being used to distract people from the heart of the gospel message is a fairly familiar theme in these early church letters, but Jude adds a sharply observed spiritual dimension to these observations:

> It is these worldly people, devoid of the Spirit, who are causing divisions. But you, beloved, build yourselves up on your most holy faith; pray in the Holy Spirit; keep yourselves in the love of God; look forward to the mercy of our Lord Jesus Christ that leads to eternal life. And have mercy on some who are wavering. (vv. 19–22)

A controversial claim about the absence of the Spirit in the lives of 'these worldly people' is held alongside an encouragement to have mercy on those who risk falling away; as a footnote in the Revised English Bible puts it, 'There are some whom you should snatch from the flames.'[19]

Conclusion

The New Testament texts under consideration in this chapter both resource and problematize an emerging theology of disagreement. Given that our task thus far – following Richard Hays – is primarily one of description, we can be content, for now, to allow such tensions to stand. But we should note the extent of those tensions. For example, while James advocates quick listening and slow speech, the letter to Titus encourages confident admonition; while the Hebrews are encouraged to pursue peace with everyone, the letter of Jude implores its readers to 'contend for the faith' (v. 3). It is clear that these later New Testament texts do not begin to speak with one voice about how disagreement might be faced in the complex contexts of emerging Christian community – but that does not mean that there are not useful broader conclusions to draw. Crucially, we should recognize that the presence of disagreement and associated disunity is repeatedly seen as an instance of the church falling short of its calling. Nowhere do we find contented disagreement, or an agreement to disagree; while approaches to disagreement differ in these early Christian communities, a determination to acknowledge its cost and impact is widespread.

We also witness the beginnings of attempts to order the church's response to disagreement and dispute, anticipating conciliar processes to come. The Hebrews were not alone in being encouraged, in the midst of their disagreements, to journey on towards perfection – but the ongoing task of Christian ethical reflection might appropriately be described as an attempt to make theological sense of this familiar gap between recurring human failure and godly ideals. While disagreement is inevitable in any human community, we witness within the church a profound dissatisfaction with the way in which inevitable disagreements risk undermining missionary effectiveness. The New Testament voices we have considered in this chapter, too often sidelined, have offered us an important window on the complexity of the early church not least in relation to these internal doctrinal and ethical tensions. We now proceed to consider these and the other relevant New Testament passages in relation to one another, in the light of Jesus' call to love God and to love one's neighbour as oneself, examining to what extent a coherent theology of disagreement can emerge from these foundational Christian texts.

Notes

1 Wall and Steele nod towards Phyllis Trible, 1984, *The Texts of Terror: Literary-Feminist Readings of Biblical Narratives*, Philadelphia: Fortress Press. While Trible dealt with four Old Testament narratives, here we can assume that reference is being made to those texts affirming the subjugation of slaves and women within the Pastoral Epistles. Robert W. Wall and Richard B. Steele, 2012, *1 & 2 Timothy and Titus*, Grand Rapids: Eerdmans, p. ix.

2 Wall and Steele, *1 & 2 Timothy*, p. x.

3 Raymond F. Collins, 2002, *I and II Timothy and Titus: A Commentary*, Louisville: Westminster John Knox Press, p. 155.

4 Wall and Steele, *1 & 2 Timothy*, p. 127.

5 Collins, *I and II Timothy*, p. 230.

6 Douglas J. Moo, 2000, *The Letter of James*, Leicester: Apollos, p. 96.

7 James B. Adamson, 1976, *The Epistle of James*, Grand Rapids: Eerdmans, p. 146.

8 Marie E. Isaacs, 2002, *Reading Hebrews and James: A Literary and Theological Commentary*, Macon: Smyth & Helwys, p. 146.

9 Philip H. Towner, 2006, *The Letters to Timothy and Titus*, Grand Rapids: Eerdmans, p. 773.

10 See also Titus 2.7–8, where it is hoped that the actions and speech of believers will result in opponents having 'nothing evil to say of us' (v. 8).

11 Jerome D. Quinn, 1990, *The Letter to Titus*, New Haven and London: Yale University Press, p. 249.

12 Isaacs, *Reading Hebrews and James*, p. 229.

13 Richard Bauckham, 1999, *James: Wisdom of James, Disciple of Jesus the Sage*, London: Routledge, p. 204.

14 Bauckham, *James*, p. 205.

15 Gareth Lee Cockerill, 2012, *The Epistle to the Hebrews*, Grand Rapids: Eerdmans, p. 225.

16 Note our earlier discussion of the etymological link between the use of 'provoke' here and 'disagree' at Acts 15.39 (see Chapter 3, p. 56).

17 Gordon D. Fee, 1988, *New International Biblical Commentary: 1 and 2 Timothy, Titus*, Peabody: Hendrickson, p. 10.

18 David Horrell, 1998, *The Epistles of Peter and Jude*, Peterborough: Epworth Press, p. 97.

19 See David Horrell's discussion in Horrell, *Jude*, p. 131.

PART 2

Disagreeing Christianly: Constructing a New Testament Ethic of Disagreement

Introduction to Part 2

My concern to establish a theological ethic of disagreement begins from a recognition that in Jesus' own words, the church is recognizable because its members love each other in a way that is attractive to behold – such is the foundational narrative significance of John 13.35. If such attractive love becomes less visible, the mission of the church is undermined; this book contends that the way in which disagreements are routinely approached contributes to an undermining of missionary effectiveness. Each individual Christian, in the situations of moral discernment within which they find themselves, must consider whether they are approaching instances of disagreement in a way that is consonant with Jesus' own appeal to the centrality of love – of God, neighbour and self.

It is in such a context that our reading of the New Testament proceeds. We now have before us the body of texts from within it that I have determined to be of relevance to a theology of disagreement. But before I analyse what sort of picture emerges from these texts, and to what extent that picture is consistent, both within individual books and from one part of the canon to another, there is a prior evaluative challenge in relation to the methodology proposed by Richard Hays in *The Moral Vision of the New Testament*. Part 2 of this study thus proceeds in two chapters: the first engages in a detailed critique of Hays' approach to the New Testament and proposes modifications to his scheme; the second applies this revised scheme to a theology of disagreement.

The previous five chapters of this book have comprised the first of Richard Hays' four tasks – the 'descriptive' task where the reader is urged to read the text carefully. Notwithstanding our recognition of Christians' ability to disagree about almost anything, we can envisage broad consensus in affirming that a careful reading of Scripture itself is an essential prerequisite for the drawing of ethical conclusions from it; so this book has no methodological quibble with the first task in Hays' model. Nor is any foundational objection raised in relation to the final, 'pragmatic' task of 'living the text', though I will argue that Hays fails to account appropriately for the role of wisdom from beyond the Bible – encompassing the tradition, reason and experience of the church – and its role in the construction of a Christian ethic; illustrative exploration of these applied contexts follows in Part 3.

Our principal concern now, then, is to critique the 'synthetic' and 'hermeneutic' tasks proposed by Hays. Although we will consider both tasks in turn, part of our questioning will be about the extent to which Hays' apparently clear distinction between synthesis and hermeneutics can be sustained. Our modified approach to the model developed by Richard Hays will thus seek to examine what might emerge from the text of the New Testament to resource a theology of disagreement.

Within Part 2 it is proposed that a narrative appeal to the place of the double love command in Christian ethical tradition offers a more constructive foundation than Hays' focal images. While reading the New Testament in relation to the double love command does not miraculously address all its moral inconsistencies, it does offer a mechanism whereby we can consider how a particular text might be read in relation to Jesus' own narrative summary of his ethic. If we acknowledge that it is within the story of Jesus Christ that the people of God find their moral vocation, then it seems logical to examine whether that story itself offers any kind of workable foundation upon which a theological ethic that is both coherent and consistent might be built; so we now turn to a critique of the methodology of Richard Hays, and how that informs our own process of discerning a theology of disagreement within the text of the New Testament.

6

The Recovery of the Double Love Command in New Testament Ethics

Before my own proposal about the utility of the double love command is made, the first task is to analyse Richard Hays' own methodology in the construction of a Christian ethic. He maintains that if such an ethic is to be coherent, and sufficiently rooted in the New Testament, all texts under consideration for inclusion in such an ethic must be subject to a process of synthesis, which ultimately involves the setting on one side of any texts that contradict the overall narrative picture that emerges. He admits that 'the problem, then, is whether we may legitimately speak of a unity that somehow underlies the multiplicity';[1] this book argues that his approach, using filters supplied by key 'focal images', unhelpfully sidelines apparently inconvenient texts – and part of my modification of Hays' scheme will allow the voices of such texts to continue to be heard. But first, we need to explore Hays' own proposal in detail.

The synthetic process relies on the application of three focal images – community, cross and new creation – to any given text under consideration when a particular ethic is being discerned. The three images are designed to encapsulate three foundational themes: the countercultural community at the heart of Christian discipleship; the centrality of Jesus' death on the cross; and the hope and power of life in the resurrection. All texts deemed to be of relevance for ethical reflection are to be viewed through one of these three lenses; by interrogating the extent to which texts resonate with any of these three key 'focal images', the reader can determine whether they should form part of a Christian understanding of the particular moral issue in question, or should be set aside. Hays admits that 'the focal images we choose will become pivotal for our subsequent normative use of the New Testament in ethical argument and formation of the community',[2] yet he is unwilling to admit that his choice of images must necessarily be a response to his own understanding of Christian theology. The pivotal status of the focal images means that they *themselves* influence the sort of picture of Christian ethics that emerges as a result of their application. Although Hays does offer 'three criteria for evaluating themes or images proposed as focal lenses',[3] these criteria are themselves subjective. One asks whether a proposed image stands in *serious* tension with *major emphases* of any New Testament witnesses – hardly a question over which biblical scholars would immediately agree in all instances.

My concern is not about the need for some sort of method that appraises the ethical content of diverse New Testament texts, but whether the 'focal image' approach championed by Hays achieves its stated aim. An exchange between Richard Hays and a fellow New Testament scholar is instructive: Luke Timothy Johnson asks 'whether it is really necessary to articulate a synthesis before the NT texts can be used in ethical reflection',[4] and, in reply, Hays suggests that the church's necessary task of moral discernment 'can most fruitfully be pursued by the community within the framework of some synthetic account of the unity of the canonical witness'.[5] Hays says that both he and Johnson agree that part of the church's calling is to engage in such moral reflection – but unfortunately Hays takes this discussion no further. It is a shame that he does not say more, for this exchange highlights a tension that exists at the core of Hays' project, raising an inevitable question about whether any 'synthetic' attempt to achieve a 'unity of canonical witness' imposes on the text a forced level of coherence that does not actually exist. Hays is reluctant to concede that fruitful ethical reflection might be undertaken even as the complex equivocality of the New Testament is asserted.

Hays offers three 'procedural guidelines' for his synthetic task: the full range of canonical witnesses must be confronted; tensions must be allowed to stand; and the literary genre of texts must be explored. It is not as if textual complexity is being ignored or suppressed, but there is a clear sense in which these three guidelines are designed to enable a coherent, unified New Testament ethic to be articulated. Crucially, Hays employs a metaphor of 'performance', suggesting that each reading of the New Testament in search of its ethical teaching is analogous to the work of a director producing the performance of a Shakespeare play: the end product could appear in a number of ways, but it will be judged on its creative fidelity to the original text. Here, too, we find Hays engaging in frustrating brevity with crucial material that could usefully support the claims he makes. But his own admitted caveats undermine any sense that the moral coherence he aims for is likely to be found:

we cannot escape acknowledging that any synthetic account of the unity of the New Testament's moral vision will be a product of our artifice, an imaginative construct of the interpreter – or perhaps better,

since interpreters do not form their readings in isolation – of the interpretative community.[6]

This seeming ambivalence about his synthetic account of the unity of the
New Testament, accompanied by a clear admission of its 'artifice' and
associated subjectivity, leaves an unresolved question for Hays about how
one is to determine with any coherence the occasions upon which a particular text, that does *not* fit with an apparent synthesis, may be set to one
side. Furthermore, Hays' proposal that the hermeneutical task can only
begin once a synthesis is complete – meaning that inconvenient texts are
excluded from hermeneutical analysis – undermines the rich and diverse
witness of Scripture. Hays does at least concede the difficulty associated
with the claims he makes, and acknowledges Ernst Käsemann's dictum:
'The New Testament Canon does not, as such, constitute the foundation
of the unity of the Church. On the contrary, it provides the basis for the
multiplicity of the confessions.'[7]

Richard Hays is determined to show that the New Testament can provide a basis for coherent ethical teaching of a sort that the church has
historically claimed to be able to affirm. In this sense, Hays is hardly to
be blamed if the church continues to make unsustainable claims about
the moral coherence of the New Testament. But Hays himself risks over-
confidence in his ability to articulate the level of coherence he maintains
can be found. It is as if he has conceived the focal images as a way of
marshalling the text of the New Testament in pursuit of a coherence he
has already decided is identifiable; but to take such an approach risks
imposing a unified facade that fails to do justice to textual richness and
complexity, imposing a lens on the text rather than responding to its
narrative. Hays' desire to synthesize comes rather too close to a desire
to dismiss textual inconsistency, in the pursuit of moral coherence in the
New Testament.[8] It is an approach that should be resisted.

'Specify and distinguish' – Nigel Biggar's critique

A debate between Hays and Nigel Biggar further demonstrates how difficult it is to establish under what conditions the synthetic task, with its
desire to wrest coherence from the equivocality of the New Testament,
can determine how to weigh an irritatingly untidy few verses – ones that
detract from what would otherwise seem to be a body of text that might
exhibit coherence in its moral theology. Biggar challenges the way that
Hays has dealt with Gospel 'soldier narratives':

the awkward presence in the text of soldiers who are neither rebuked for their profession, nor repent of it, makes the stance of the New Testament canon toward the use of violent force less 'unambiguous' – and the ground for arguing that Christian discipleship could include it more robust – than Hays supposes.[9]

Hays concedes that such passages offer 'the one possible legitimate basis for arguing that Christian discipleship does not necessarily preclude the exercise of violence in defence of social order or justice';[10] but for Hays, given the wider context, such texts – as apparent justification for the place of soldiers within the church community – have to be dismissed as anomalous. Biggar, meanwhile, suggests that Hays' method 'generalizes too much and distinguishes too little'.[11]

After two rounds of journal debate, Hays complains that Biggar 'does not engage my overarching methodological assertion that the NT tells a *story* in which we find ourselves situated … We find our identity and our moral vocation as the people of God within the story of Jesus Christ and nowhere else.'[12] We might well agree that Christians should locate themselves in the church's founding narrative, but an appeal to narrative does not, of itself, equate to an appeal to broad brush strokes at the expense of attention to fine detail. Subscribing to the Christian narrative need surely not mean that one loses interest in narrative peculiarities or the plight of particular minorities within the text of Scripture. Hays maintains that the narrative thrust of the New Testament permits the theologian in search of moral coherence to choose to downplay the significance of a text deemed unrepresentative of the overarching narrative in question. But this procedure only undermines any sense of integrity in the biblical text as a whole – something that Hays would doubtless wish to defend. As Nigel Biggar points out, Hays' reliance on metaphor-making, at the expense of other approaches (including casuistry), risks impoverishing ethicists' engagement with the New Testament.

Seeing the New Testament through an inclusive lens – Richard Burridge's critique

A broader but equally prescient critique of Hays' approach can be made through reference to the work of Richard Burridge. His 'inclusive approach' to New Testament ethics, with its 'insistence on the priority of the person of Jesus of Nazareth',[13] echoes Hays' wish to root Christian ethical reflection in a reading of the New Testament, but does so through a narrative focus on the life and teaching of Jesus. Burridge is unconvinced that Hays' detailed methodology can deliver as much as it promises, and instead he proposes a central role for the person of Jesus in New Testament ethical reflection: 'Without him as the catalyst, there would be no New Testament, and no Christian church, let alone Christian ethics.'[14] This desire to focus Christian discipleship on the imitation of Christ, with moral reflection rooted in a response to the life and work of Jesus, calls for a different sort of response to the biblical text. Interpretation of the New Testament is to be undertaken, for Burridge, through a recognition of the inclusive nature of Jesus' humanity, which can lead on to an understanding of how to live a fully Christian life, walking in Jesus' footsteps. We shall consider some limitations of Burridge's approach shortly, but first examine his critique of Hays in relation to questions raised about the genre of New Testament texts.

Burridge argues that Richard Hays views the New Testament primarily from a Pauline perspective, privileging the picture of Christ that emerges from epistles and failing to give the gospel accounts of Jesus' life appropriate prominence in the formation of any ethical response to Scripture. Burridge, by contrast, summarizes his own project in these terms: having undertaken

> an ancient biographical reconstruction of Jesus' words and deeds, we discovered that his rigorous and demanding teaching was actually set within a narrative of his open acceptance of those who responded to his preaching of the sovereign rule of God and, as a consequence, joined the inclusive community of those who were also seeking to follow and imitate his example as his disciples.[15]

In essence, Burridge regards Hays as having misinterpreted the genre of too much of the New Testament, hoping to find rules and paradigms in texts that, for Burridge, are only likely to offer glimpses of a life worthy of imitation.

For Burridge, appropriate hermeneutical responses to the New Testament will thus follow from a biographical appreciation of the person of Jesus as found in Scripture. In this sense, Hays' use of focal images is regarded as an unhelpful methodological step: Hays is 'in danger of imposing prior principles on the text ... If we must have a "focal image", perhaps Christology would be better because it arises directly out of the biographical genre of the gospels and fits into the central concerns of the New Testament writers.'[16] Burridge does not elaborate on this potential alternative to Hays' own 'focal images'; nor is further explanation offered concerning the operation of Christology in this context. While Burridge does provide a brief challenge to Hays' dismissal of 'love' and

'liberation' as potential focal images, his principal concern is to emphasize the importance of underlying trends in Scripture being read in the
light of Jesus' inclusive love of sinners.

This 'inclusive' approach that Richard Burridge favours, while reassert-
ing the central place for Jesus in any attempt to discern a coherent New
Testament Ethic, risks viewing Jesus partially; Burridge is so concerned
to emphasize Jesus' love for all that he risks overlooking Jesus' desire
to see – and prompt – moral transformation. Richard Hays appropriately suggests that Burridge downplays New Testament texts concerning
judgement in order to be able to view it through an 'inclusive' lens, and
fails to account for what Jesus might expect to happen within the life
of one who chooses to become a disciple. In Hays' words, 'the sticky
questions for New Testament ethics have to do not so much with who
is initially welcomed into the community of faith as with the *shape* of
the new life of radical obedience into which all who are welcomed are
summoned to participate.'[17]

In his critique of Hays, Richard Burridge has proposed replacing the
systematic method outlined in *The Moral Vision of the New Testament* –
with its descriptive, synthetic, hermeneutical and pragmatic stages – with
a scheme that is much more dependent on an acceptance that inclusivity lies at the heart of the New Testament, and that appropriate moral
theology can be deduced from responding to the gospels as biographies
of Jesus in the light of that all-embracing welcome. Burridge helpfully
underlines some of the shortcomings in Hays' methodology, but then
suggests replacing it with a scheme that, like Hays, risks imposing its own
criteria on to the New Testament text. Before an alternative approach is
proposed, we should first also consider the third, 'hermeneutical' task
proposed by Hays, not least because this book argues that a division
between the two tasks is difficult to sustain and risks creating false
distinctions within a broad hermeneutical process.

Evaluating Hays' hermeneutical task

As he introduces his third, 'hermeneutical' task, Hays contends that
theologians find in Scripture 'four different modes of appeal to the text in
ethical argument',[18] and he proposes the classification of texts in relation
to these modes. Rules (direct commandments or prohibitions), principles
(general frameworks for moral decision-making), paradigms (narrative
models for good conduct) and a symbolic world ('perceptual categories
through which we interpret reality'[19]) offer four means by which a particular moral text can be evaluated under Hays' scheme. With reference

to the application of this scheme by Willard Swartley, we will consider how helpful this approach to classification actually is; but first we find in Hays' response to extra-biblical authority a further need for clarification in relation to the robustness of his hermeneutical proposals.

The place of extra-biblical authority in Hays' scheme

It is worth noting that it is only as he introduces these four 'modes' that Hays also specifically addresses the role that non-biblical sources of authority might have in the formulation of a Christian ethic, in reflections that have the feel of an extended footnote. The location of this brief discussion is perplexing, for the whole question of how scripturally based ethics relates to non-biblical sources of wisdom – in particular, to themes of tradition, reason and experience – is surely a fundamental one within Hays' project. He concedes that 'the right relation of Scripture to each of these other sources of authority has been a perennial problem for theology',[20] but does not go on to address these questions in any detail. We will now consider the need for Hays to give a stronger account of the place of extra-biblical authority in the formulation of Christian moral theology, but suggest that this can be achieved without abandoning the pre-eminence of Scripture as the foundational source in Christian ethics. Our study proceeds on the basis that a core commitment to biblical authority can be held alongside an openness to wisdom from tradition and reason – recognizing that such extra-biblical wisdom contributes to the construction of a Christian ethic.

In this writer's Anglican context, Richard Hooker's much-cited three-fold appeal to Scripture, tradition and reason is apposite. It is a three-way tension that is in play in all Christian ethical reflection, regardless of denomination, but it receives particular attention in Anglican settings. Indeed, within contemporary Anglican reflection, a nod in Hooker's direction is commonplace, not least in documents seeking to promote agreement in the context of ecclesial fragmentation: 'Anglicans are held together by the characteristic way in which they use Scripture, tradition and reason in discerning afresh the mind of Christ for the Church in each generation.'[21] Importantly, the Anglican notion of a three-legged Scripture-tradition-reason stool supporting the life of the church has sometimes been misread, suggesting that Scripture's authority is to be regarded as equal to that of tradition and reason. A more precise rehearsal of the dictum notes that Anglicanism 'affirms the primary authority of the Holy Scriptures; and – guided by the Holy Spirit – it acknowledges the interplay of Scripture, tradition and reason in the continuing work of interpretation, understanding and discernment'.[22] Martyn Percy suggests that Hooker himself supported this sense of scriptural pre-eminence: 'Reason is applied to Scripture in the humility that sees Scripture as primary. At the same time, reason is freshly formed out of our gracious life within a Church which, again in humility, looks to its tradition as authoritative.'[23]

One of the chief challenges appropriately levelled at Richard Hays is his relative lack of interest in extra-biblical inspiration for Christian moral reflection. But his clear aim, echoing Hooker, is to reassert the primary importance of Scripture – and he regards himself as writing within a context where too much that passes for Christian ethics has lost meaningful touch with the scriptural texts that should be at the very heart of truly Christian moral reflection. He is undoubtedly weak in his analysis of exactly how extra-biblical material might be drawn into the formulation of a Christian ethic, but his priority remains to affirm the construction of an ethic with unashamed pre-eminence afforded to Scripture. In so doing he offers a frank critique of the often fraught interaction between Christian ethicists and the Bible: the problem is not merely a failure of scholars to engage seriously enough with Scripture, but also one where walls have been built between theological sub-disciplines resulting in limited engagement between biblical experts and ethicists. Nonetheless, fundamental questions remain for Hays about how he proposes that Christian ethicists engage with texts beyond the Bible, with church history and with the lived experience of individual Christians.

This book proposes that Hays' scheme should be amended in relation to its understanding of the place of hermeneutical reflection: my argument is that it should also form part of his fourth and final 'pragmatic' task. In particular, engagement with extra-biblical authority – which Hays restricts to his 'hermeneutical task' – should, instead, be regarded as part of the ongoing theological exploration of the pragmatic construction of a Christian ethic. I will demonstrate this approach in Part 3. Hays clearly expresses his view that an ethic should be finalized at the end of his third task, before it can engage pragmatically with the world as it is:

> The final task of New Testament ethics is the pragmatic task ... *After* all the careful exegetical work, *after* reflective consideration of the unity of the New Testament's message, *after* the imaginative work of correlating our world with the New Testament's world, the test that finally proves the value of our theological labors is ... their capacity to produce persons and communities whose character is commensurate with Jesus Christ and thereby pleasing to God.[24] (my italics)

Hays does acknowledge that 'distinguishing the pragmatic task from the hermeneutical is easier in theory than in practice',[25] but in relation to a threefold engagement with Scripture, tradition and reason (with reason including reflection on experience) Hays creates a fixed ethic based on Scripture, with a nod towards tradition but with very little scope for an ongoing conversation in relation to reason and experience. He pays scant attention to the notion that engagement with extra-biblical sources might influence the shape of an ethic itself. He argues that 'the living out of the New Testament cannot occur in a book; it can happen only in the life of the Christian community'.[26] Such an approach suggests that it is once the hermeneutical task has been concluded – and only then – that a finalized ethic interacts with the world; such an approach severely undermines any useful role for theological reflection on Christian practice. But hermeneutics, and theological reflection more broadly, is surely an *ongoing* conversation, and a Christian who values engaging with the insights and challenges of the contemporary world – as well as with the wisdom of tradition – will want continually to test their hermeneutical reflections against the circumstances of their particular context.

The effectiveness of Hays' 'modes' for classifying ethical arguments

It is a mark of the influence of *The Moral Vision of the New Testament* that a monograph such as Willard Swartley's *Covenant of Peace: The Missing Peace in New Testament Theology and Ethics*[27] should owe such a methodological debt to Hays' work, published only a decade earlier. Swartley seeks to expose a recurrent lack of exploration of the theme of peace within New Testament ethics, and does so largely taking as given Hays' assertion that the New Testament text alone can provide a substantive basis for the church's ethical reflection. Swartley makes use of Hays' four modes of hermeneutic appeal to Scripture – but, tellingly, he both conflates and modifies Hays' model: 'I consider three basic paradigms and join principles to the paradigms, since I believe principles are embedded in or develop from paradigms or are derived from the symbolic world.'[28]

Swartley's approach to examining the question of whether peace has been overlooked as a theme in the writing of ethicists focused on the text of the New Testament is undeniably eccentric, placing great emphasis on an analysis of indexes and chapter headings in scholarly works. It is an approach that is over-reliant on the signposting within a theological text, and presumes that peace only exists as a theme when the specific word 'peace' is mentioned – which rather risks undermining the potential for the exploration of metaphor and allegory. Nonetheless, Swartley's engagement with Hays offers a useful example of the fragility of Hays' conceptual framework for a hermeneutical approach to Scripture. Swartley is reluctant to follow Hays' strict demarcation between principles, paradigms and the symbolic world – which leaves only 'rules' as a category intact within Hays' hermeneutical scheme. The implication is that the efficacy of Hays' approach may depend on the question being asked at the time that a particular hermeneutical strategy is employed; it is certainly unclear whether a strict distinction being made between a biblical paradigm and a biblical principle does, of itself, enable Christian moral reflection to proceed with greater efficiency.

These potential shortcomings are further highlighted by an analysis of apparent inconsistencies within Hays' own work. We might consider the conclusions he reaches, first on divorce and remarriage and then in relation to homosexuality. His confident conclusion that biblical prohibitions can be overturned in relation to the former but not the latter suggests a hermeneutical approach that is simply not as rigorous as Hays would have us believe, and is, in fact, all too easily inconsistent in application. Dale Martin concludes:

> Hays does not seem to recognise that his method is not what engenders his results. In each case a different conclusion would result from a slight tweaking here or there of the different factors in interpretation ... The method is too malleable to service as *prescriptive* practice.[29]

It is certainly important to consider the hermeneutical justification that Hays offers for his approach to divorce:

> I would take the New Testament's hermeneutical process of discerning exceptions to the rule of Jesus' teaching to be instructive about the *process* of moral deliberation in the church on this matter. *The canonical witness itself exemplifies a process of reflection and adaptation of the fundamental normative prohibition of divorce.*[30]

This 'process of reflection and adaptation' surely leaves the door so wide open to divergent interpretations that it remains difficult to show how this hermeneutical strategy can deliver consistent, coherent results. We might certainly consider whether, in relation to homosexuality, permanent, monogamous, covenanted same-sex relationships could be tolerated, or even blessed, by the church as a result of 'a process of reflection and adaptation of the fundamental normative prohibition'. When Hays states that 'the New Testament offers no loopholes or exception clauses that might allow for the acceptance of homosexual practices under some circumstances',[31] he flatly contradicts the very hermeneutical approach that allowed him to tolerate divorce and even extend its permissibility to circumstances of domestic violence not even mentioned in Scripture.[32] My point here is not to adjudicate on either issue, but rather to underline the fact that Hays cannot be seen to apply his own hermeneutical strategy with a universally accepted clarity and precision. Rather, he is left in a situation where he has arrived at divergent conclusions on various issues, and in so doing he fails to attract unbridled enthusiasm for a methodology that appears arbitrary in its application.

Affirming the centrality of the double love command: a proposal

It is in relation to Hays' proposed reliance on focal images that neither his own metaphor-based approach nor Burridge's genre-based alternative are ultimately satisfying. I propose that it is, instead, within the foundational ethical principles outlined by Jesus himself that we can locate a groundwork upon which to build ethics from the New Testament, and against which individual texts can be examined and tested. This proposal steers a course between Hays and Burridge, and represents a response to the narrative, rather than the imposition of a particular filter on the text. It certainly affirms the importance of the story of Jesus Christ, and the fact that disciples locate themselves within that story and tradition in order to explore how they might live faithfully in response to the Christian call – and in that sense, Richard Burridge's call towards biography is helpful. But just as Hays' three focal images are open to criticism, so too Burridge's 'inclusivity' lens also risks projecting on to the text a hoped-for foundation that cannot consistently be found.

Our proposal looks to the text itself for some coherent moral theological moorings. Within the double love command issued by Jesus in all three Synoptic Gospels, and further elaborated in the Gospel of John, we can locate an ethical grounding that can withstand the sort of challenges legitimately levelled at Hays and Burridge. Jesus is asked:

'Teacher, which commandment in the law is the greatest?' He said to him, '"You shall love the Lord your God with all your heart, and with all your soul, and with all your mind." This is the greatest and first commandment. And a second is like it: "You shall love your neighbour as yourself." On these two commandments hang all the law and the prophets.' (Matt. 22.36–40)[33]

These words of Jesus constitute his own summation of the law and provide the beginnings of an ethic for Christian relating that can also act as a grounding for the task of moral theology, complemented by his words in the Gospel of John:

> 'I give you a new commandment, that you love one another. Just as I have loved you, you also should love one another. By this everyone will know that you are my disciples, if you have love for one another.' (John 13.34–35)

The point here is that we are not forcing on to the text either a metaphorical lens or a suggested theme by which all other texts should be measured. Rather, in Jesus' own words, and in his own articulation of moral priority, we find a *narrative* foundation to which all other moral reflection rooted in the New Testament can usefully be related. Apparently awkward texts, such as those debated by Hays and Biggar, can now instead be read in relation to how effectively they resonate with this narrative, and to what extent the fundamental basis of the Christian moral call being to show love for God, neighbour and oneself is visible through them.

It is, at this point, worth interrogating Hays' justification neither for choosing love as the lens through which to read the New Testament nor for adding it as a fourth focal image. His argument in this regard suggests that love might only be regarded as having 'central thematic emphasis'[34] – and therefore qualify as a focal image – if it receives sufficient narrative attention across the pages of the New Testament. As such, somewhat extraordinarily, Hays' first argument in this respect is that the double love command is of marginal significance within Mark's Gospel because 'it stands as an isolated element, not supported by other references to love in the story'[35] and so would be an inappropriate basis upon which to construct an ethic. Hays seemingly wishes to ignore the core *narrative* significance of Jesus affirming the summation of the law – hardly a marginal consideration. Jesus' own claim, that he is revealing the greatest commandment, has an inescapable and inherent narrative value. As such, I find it difficult to believe that Hays really does wish to propose that specific instances in the biblical text, however apparently isolated within their narrative context, cannot be of central ethical significance.[36]

It is when Hays articulates his second reason for love being an unsatisfactory focal image that the nature of the problem we are facing is clarified. He proposes that love 'is not really an image; rather, it is an interpretation of an image ... The content of the word "love" is given fully and exclusively in the death of Jesus on the cross; apart from this specific narrative image, the term has no meaning.'[37] But the problem Hays identifies here is one of his own creation, relating to his desire to see his 'focal images' model operate smoothly. While it is certainly the case that 1 John 3.16 shows that love is expressed on the cross, that does not somehow negate the force of John 13.35, affirming mutual Christian love as the means by which the church is recognizable. Love only fails to offer a grounding for New Testament ethics because of the unhelpful imposition on to the text demanded by Hays' focal images. As Brian Brock observes:

> The concept of focal images helps Hays unify the disparate biblical materials and spur analogical reasoning across the temporal gap between our lives and that of the Bible, but it does so by picturing Scripture (or the synthetic 'biblical narrative') as a static template on which our narratives are measured and cut or squeezed to fit.[38]

Hays' ultimate concern is that an appeal to love cannot avoid being overly generalized, lacking in theological rigour and specificity: 'The term has become debased in popular discourse; it has lost its power of discrimination, having become a cover for all manner of vapid self-indulgence.'[39] But contemporary confusion about a particular term is no inherent justification for its lack of status within moral theological reflection, and the textual study of Part 1 of this book has shown the repeated appeals made, across the New Testament, concerning the importance and centrality of mutual love within the church. Jesus' followers are being called to live within the Trinitarian dynamic of the Father's love for the Son, poured out on humankind through the work of the Spirit. This love at the very heart of God may be beyond easy human definition, but it is not inherently confusing: when Justin Welby hopes that the church might learn to 'disagree in love', no one is left wondering if such a statement has erotic undertones.[40] To learn to love the Christian neighbour with whom one disagrees is testing, and the exact details of a loving response are not predetermined; but the New Testament is surprisingly consistent in its affirmation that this love is what lies at the heart of a flourishing church.

Rather than adopting an approach like Hays, where focal images impose an apparatus that risks acting as a distraction, our preference is for a narrative appeal to love as articulated in Jesus' own words. This means that the asking of specific ethical questions, and the reading of particular narratives of moral theological significance, are both tasks that need to be undertaken in the service of the love of God, neighbour and self. Ethical teaching that emerges from the pages of the New Testament needs to be able to show that it is consonant with this call to mutual, self-sacrificial love. We are prompted to ask whether the love of God, neighbour and self is upheld – not merely through the theological con- clusions reached but in the *way* in which those conclusions have been reached. Have neighbours been loved in the way that Jesus commands in and through a particular process of theological reflection?

We might consider the example of Anglican sexuality debates. So often, theological reflection on sexuality focuses on determining a 'right read- ing' of Scripture – with ethicists hoping to convince their readers that they alone have finally solved a particular problem and uncovered the appro- priate Christian response. But if such questions are viewed in relation to the double love command, theological reflection would be undertaken with a determination that the church does not detach itself from a moor- ing in the love that Christ commends to his followers – showing that love in and through the way it arrives at its ethical teaching, as well as in that teaching itself. This does not mean that hard moral choices are ignored for the sake of the promotion of loving unity. It does mean that when Christianity makes seemingly harsh moral demands, it should do so with constant reference back to Jesus' call to his followers to live together in love and reveal that love to the world.

Conclusion

This chapter began by exploring a number of critiques of Hays' method- ology, and it is worth highlighting the key observations I have made, before reviewing my proposed modifications to that methodology. First, in relation to Hays' overall fourfold scheme, I have affirmed its basic integrity while pointing out the potential problems involved in a strict demarcation between the synthetic and hermeneutical processes, particu- larly if that separation prevents hermeneutical reflection on texts deemed by Hays to fall outside of the scope of his synthesis. Second, within the synthetic task, I have considered the limitations of the metaphorical 'focal images' approach, with its ultimate dismissal of marginal perspec- tives. Third, I have examined Richard Burridge's attention to genre, and have remained unconvinced by his proposed 'inclusive' lens with which to read the New Testament. Fourth, I have considered the shortcomings of Hays' limited engagement with extra-biblical authority. And finally, I have noted his arguments about the need for a fourfold classification of ethical 'modes' within the hermeneutical process and have failed to be convinced by the necessity of such an approach.

These observations have led me to relax some of Hays' firmer attempts to marshal the New Testament text. So while I agree with Hays that the New Testament should be read carefully in the pursuit of moral coherence, that pursuit should not lead to a process of synthesis that excludes certain texts that might surprise or seem inconsistent. Similarly, the task of hermeneutics should not be regarded as a process to be concluded within the tightly sealed biblical text, before it engages with other sources of theological wisdom – and Part 3 will offer examples of how moral theology, even when clearly rooted in biblical sources, is enriched through extra-biblical engagement. But perhaps most significantly, I have proposed replacing Hays' 'focal images' with a narrative-based approach to the pursuit of moral coherence, always seeking to refer particular relevant texts to Jesus' own summation of the law.

An approach to New Testament ethics that constantly relates back to Jesus' double love command maintains a confidence that Christian ethical reasoning can be undertaken within a narrative framework of ultimate coherence, but that such coherence is not to be found exclusively in the imposition of metaphorical lenses or other themes on the text as a whole. By constantly relating our ethical norms back to the commands of Jesus, we recognize that *the way we relate* is of significance alongside *the conclusions we reach*: the attractiveness of the Body of Christ is dependent not only on its being led into all truth but on the way it conducts itself on that journey.

It is important to recognize the challenge to moral theological study that such an emphasis presents. Our task is not merely concerned with the transmission of theological knowledge, but one undertaken with a desire to see the church respond more faithfully – and pastorally – to its call, considering *how* it approaches its moral disagreements, and asking itself what impact the way it ordinarily conducts such debates has on the health of its own body. And so while we have modified Hays' methodological basis for the pursuit of moral coherence within the New Testament, we owe him a debt in having strengthened the foundations of an arena where theological reflection on morality, rooted in the study of Scripture, may be undertaken. Markus Bockmuehl notes that Hays

> presents a systematic outworking of the thesis that the New Testament's vision of Christian faith has a clear moral dimension, that this dimension is central to any properly Christian encounter with scripture, and that it has significant practical relevance for Christian life today ... [he] merits unstinting credit for having championed this sorely neglected vision with such infectious courage, grace and conviction.[41]

'Christianly' is an ugly word, but a necessary one. The task before us is to examine whether the call to love God, neighbour and self, mindful of how the presence or absence of such love affects an outsider's view of Christian community, can provide a robust foundation for a theology of disagreement. As we consider how the New Testament resources our discussion of Christian disagreement, we proceed in the hope of finding a coherence rooted in Christian love that might inspire recognizably Christian action.

Notes

1 Richard B. Hays, 1996, *The Moral Vision of the New Testament*, New York: HarperCollins, p. 191.

2 Hays, *Moral Vision*, p. 195.

3 Hays, *Moral Vision*, p. 195.

4 Hays, *Moral Vision*, p. 191, n. 4.

5 Hays, *Moral Vision*, p. 191.

6 Hays, *Moral Vision*, p. 189.

7 Quoted by Hays in *Moral Vision*, p. 192, n. 8.

8 Brian Brock suggests that a reliance on a synthetic approach might impede the process of discernment of Christian ethics: 'the question remains of whether the performance of Scripture is ensured by the systematicity that a synthetic account promises, or whether it might be possible that, in the course of a serious communal wrestling with Scripture and moral issues, some moral judgements can emerge that will only retroactively appear to have been correct for their synthetic accuracy or otherwise. These moral judgements, *ex post facto*, might have been valid, or even prophetic, even though they appeared *ad hoc* when ventured.' Brian Brock, 2007, *Singing the Ethos of God: On the Place of Christian Ethics in Scripture*, Grand Rapids: Eerdmans, p. 42.

9 Nigel Biggar, 2009, 'Specify and Distinguish! Interpreting the New Testament on "Non-Violence"', *Studies in Christian Ethics* 22,2, p. 170.

10 Hays, *Moral Vision*, pp. 335–6.

11 Biggar, 'Specify and Distinguish!', p. 177.

12 Hays, *Moral Vision*, p. 198.

13 Richard Burridge, 2007, *Imitating Jesus: An Inclusive Approach to New Testament Ethics*, Grand Rapids: Eerdmans, p. 4.

14 Burridge, *Imitating*, p. 31.

15 Burridge, *Imitating*, p. 347.

16 Burridge, *Imitating*, p. 359.

17 Richard Hays, 2010, 'Response to Richard Burridge, *Imitating Jesus*', *Scottish Journal of Theology* 63,3, p. 335.

18 Hays, *Moral Vision*, p. 208.

19 Hays, *Moral Vision*, p. 209.

20 Hays, *Moral Vision*, p. 211

21 'The Virginia Report: The Report of the Inter-Anglican Theological and Doctrinal Commission' in Anglican Communion Office, 1999, *The Official Report of the Lambeth Conference 1998*, Harrisburg: Morehouse Publishing, p. 32, is one recent example.

22 The Windsor Continuation Group Report to the Archbishop of Canterbury, 2008, www.anglicancommunion.org/media/39817/wcg_report.pdf, section A.1, p. 1 (accessed 16 December 2020).

23 Martyn Percy, 1999, *Introducing Richard Hooker and the Laws of Ecclesiastical Polity*, London: Darton, Longman and Todd, p. 18. Alison Joyce concurs – 'Hooker is clear that the authority of the Bible is unique and unparalleled within the Christian life' – but she also shows how he steers a 'sophisticated and subtle' course between perceived extremes of approach to Scripture found in Puritan biblicism and Roman Catholic insufficiency. See her *Richard Hooker and Anglican Moral Theology*, 2012, Oxford: Oxford University Press, pp. 103–48. The foundational nature of an Anglican commitment to Scriptural authority is expressed in Article VI of the Articles of Religion of 1562, in a form to which Anglian clergy still assent: 'Holy Scripture containeth all things necessary to salvation: so that whatsoever is not read therein, nor may be proved thereby, is not to be required of any man, that it should be believed as an article of the Faith, or be thought requisite or necessary to salvation' (printed in all editions of the *Book of Common Prayer*, Cambridge: Cambridge University Press). An affirmation of this by the churches of the Anglican Communion was made at the Lambeth Conference of 1888, Resolution 11, which referred to 'The Holy Scriptures of the Old and New Testaments, as "containing all things necessary to salvation," and as being the rule and ultimate standard of faith'. See www.anglicancommunion.org/resources/document-library/lambeth-conference/1888/resolution-11?author=Lambeth+Conference&year=1888 (accessed 14 June 2016).

24 Hays, *Moral Vision*, p. 7.

25 Hays, *Moral Vision*, p. 7.

26 Hays, *Moral Vision*, p. 7.

27 Willard Swartley, 2006, *Covenant of Peace: The Missing Peace in New Testament Theology and Ethics*, Grand Rapids: Eerdmans.

28 Swartley, *Peace*, p. 400.

29 Dale Martin, 1998, 'Review of Hays, *The Moral Vision of the New Testament*', *Journal of Biblical Literature* 117,2, p. 359.

30 Hays, *Moral Vision*, p. 372.

31 Hays, *Moral Vision*, p. 394.

32 Brian Brock, writing in relation to marriage, expresses surprise that Hays' method did not yield 'thicker moral conclusions', given the complexity of the witness of the New Testament. See Brock, *Singing*, p. 47. Allen Verhey raises similar concerns in relation to violence in 'Neither Devils nor Angels: Peace, Justice and Defending the Innocent: A Response to Richard Hays' in J. Ross Wagner, C. Kavin Rowe and A. Katherine Grieb, eds, 2008, *The Word Leaps the Gap: Essays on Scripture and Theology in Honor of Richard B. Hays*, Grand Rapids: Eerdmans, pp. 599–625.

33 See also Mark 12.28–31 and Luke 10.25–28 (and note that Jesus brings together Deut. 6.4–5 and Lev. 19.18). Such an approach stands in a tradition of moral theology rooted in Augustine's observation that 'anyone who thinks that he has understood the divine scriptures or any part of them, but cannot by his understanding build up this double love of God and neighbour, has not yet succeeded in understanding them'. R. P. H. Green, trans., 1996, *St. Augustine: De Doctrina Christiana*, Oxford: Oxford University Press, p. 49. See also William S. Babcock, ed., 1991, *The Ethics of St. Augustine*, Atlanta: Scholars Press; and 'Jesus' Decisive

Action: The Concentration of all Religious Moral Precepts in the Great Commandment of Love of God and Neighbour' in Rudolf Schnackenburg, 1965, *The Moral Teaching of the New Testament*, Freiburg: Herder, pp. 90–109. Lois Malcolm sketches the history of this tradition of Christian ethical thought in 'Divine Commands' in Gilbert Meilaender and William Werpehowski, eds, 2007, *The Oxford Handbook of Theological Ethics*, Oxford: Oxford University Press, pp. 112–27.

34 Hays, *Moral Vision*, p. 200.

35 Hays, *Moral Vision*, p. 200.

36 At no point does Hays explain why Jesus' own summary of the moral law is insufficient as a narrative foundation for the construction of moral theology, rooted in the text of the New Testament. He performs another textual contortion when arguing that love is largely irrelevant to the book of Hebrews, notwithstanding its appeal at 10.24: 'let us consider how to provoke one another to love and to good deeds.' Meanwhile his claim that 'a synthesis of the New Testament's message based on the theme of love drives these texts [Mark, Acts, Hebrews and Revelation] to the periphery of the canon' (p. 202) is equally surprising, implying that – for example – the work of the Holy Spirit in Acts had nothing to do with God's *loving* presence being poured out on the church.

37 Hays, *Moral Vision*, p. 202.

38 Brock, *Singing*, p. 251.

39 Hays, *Moral Vision*, p. 202.

40 The English language's failure to distinguish between 'agape' and 'eros' undoubtedly complicates the picture, and the significant contribution of Anders Nygren, 1953, *Agape and Eros*, London: SPCK, in affirming and exploring this distinction in Scripture and Christian tradition is important to note.

41 Markus Bockmuehl, 1997, 'Review of Hays, *Moral Vision*', *Expository Times* 109,3, p. 86.

7

Living Out the Double Love Command:
A New Theology of Disagreement

Part 1 of this book considered, in detail, New Testament texts of relevance for a theology of disagreement. Having outlined concerns about the methodological approach to the New Testament proposed by Richard Hays in the previous chapter, my task now is to assess the extent to which a coherent theological ethic might emerge from the scriptural texts that we have identified as having relevance for a theology of disagreement. Using my modified version of Hays' methodological approach, I will consider whether a synthesis of the texts can be achieved, reading them in relation to the narrative force of Jesus' own summation of the law. As we have already discussed, it is difficult and sometimes unhelpful to resist hermeneutical reflection at this stage; but following Hays, my initial focus will be the identification of inconsistencies alongside some discernment of common patterns.

Considering the value of a New Testament synthesis in a theology of disagreement

Any attempted pursuit of a synthesis of New Testament texts on disagreement may seem doomed to failure, such is the varied witness of Scripture. But given that I have already outlined my reluctance to follow Hays in deliberately setting awkward texts to one side, I will instead proceed to give an account of the variety of perspectives before us, without anticipating that some must necessarily be excluded from hermeneutical reflection. In fact, we will later observe a striking unanimity in terms of the ethical norms with which disagreement might be approached; but the task, for now, is to consider four particular areas of textual inconsistency that demand attention. These are: the contrast between Jesus as paradigm and teacher; multiple approaches to those who disagree; varied accounts of the emerging authority of the church; and differing affirmations of what constitutes appropriate speech in the context of disagreement.

Jesus: paradigm and teacher

Our first challenge concerns the sheer variance of approach to disagreement visible in Jesus' words and actions, and this phenomenon should be considered carefully. I have already highlighted some of the examples of his intemperate engagement with Pharisees and other religious leaders: 'Is not this the reason you are wrong, that you know neither the scriptures nor the power of God?' (Mark 12.24); or in Luke's Gospel, 'Now you Pharisees clean the outside of the cup and of the dish, but inside you are full of greed and wickedness. You fools! Did not the one who made the outside make the inside also?' (Luke 11.39–40). It is worth noting the purpose of these disagreements. They were all occasions where Jesus' spoken claims or miraculous healings were being challenged; his often angry responses always had as their end a description of the kingdom, following his criticism of the inherited religious law. We might then also recall the contrast between Jesus' attitude to his opponents, and his engagement with his disciples ahead of what becomes the feeding of the five thousand:

> When it was evening, the disciples came to him and said, 'This is a deserted place, and the hour is now late; send the crowds away so that they may go into the villages and buy food for themselves.' Jesus said to them, 'They need not go away; you give them something to eat.' They replied, 'We have nothing here but five loaves and two fish.' And he said, 'Bring them here to me.' (Matt. 14.15–18)

Jesus disagreed with the disciples about the need for the crowds to be sent away, but this exchange was not in any way angry, and instead opened the way for another glimpse of the kingdom through the provision of bread and fish to all present. Disagreement was not avoided here, but nor did it undermine; indeed it might even be regarded as a necessary prelude to the miracle.

Jesus' encounter with the Syrophoenician woman further complicates our picture of Jesus and disagreement:

> Now the woman was a Gentile, of Syrophoenician origin. She begged him to cast the demon out of her daughter. He said to her, 'Let the children be fed first, for it is not fair to take the children's food and throw it to the dogs.' But she answered him, 'Sir, even the dogs under the table eat the children's crumbs.' Then he said to her, 'For saying that, you may go – the demon has left your daughter.' So she went home, found the child lying on the bed, and the demon gone. (Mark 7.26–30)

Her very act of disagreeing with Jesus seems to prompt his compassion and presents an opportunity for the nature of his healing mission to be revealed. Were we slavishly following Hays' desire to synthesize, we would have to consider which of these passages represented an authentic iteration of a theology of disagreement. But considering all these examples in narrative context, relating them back to Jesus' own double love command, enables them to be held in tension without the need to synthesize. We can recognize that in the unique circumstances of his earthly ministry, Jesus was forced to confront the arguments of his opponents – even knowing that ultimately they would send him to his death. While his engagement with the Pharisees represents a very different context from his discussions with his disciples or with the Syrophoenician woman, all are instances where the nature of the kingdom is being revealed.

A theology of disagreement need not shy away from this narrative complexity. Our consideration of Jesus as both paradigm and teacher sets his own diversity of personal approaches to disagreement in the biographical context of his lived existence, proclaiming the kingdom; his teaching, meanwhile, is clear and consistent in its affirmation of the pursuit of loving unity among his disciples. The centrality of John 13.35 to a theology of disagreement is worth restating: it is through the love that is visible among his followers that the church can be identified. There could hardly be a clearer affirmation of the pursuit of loving unity at the heart of the Body of Christ. Those who follow Jesus are commended in the Sermon on the Mount to be peacemakers, loving their enemies and turning the other cheek (Matt. 5.1–12). This sometimes self-denying pursuit of loving unity is made possible because the Spirit dwells in the midst of Jesus' followers; this Spirit inspires the footwashing of servant leadership, guiding faithful disciples into 'all the truth' (John 16.13).

Facing disagreement

The New Testament is also ambiguous in its witness concerning how disagreement should be faced. While there is widespread affirmation of harmonious community that apparently lacks disagreement, those instances where it is faced are dealt with in a variety of ways. The ethic for Christian relating that we have already identified within the Pauline writings – comprising godly speech, mutual love, reconciled diversity and emergent maturity – finds its encapsulation in Colossians 3.12–14:

> As God's chosen ones, holy and beloved, clothe yourselves with compassion, kindness, humility, meekness, and patience. Bear with one

another and, if anyone has a complaint against another, forgive each other; just as the Lord has forgiven you, so you also must forgive. Above all, clothe yourselves with love, which binds everything together in perfect harmony.

There is a recognition here that life in Christian community will not be immune from complaints or disagreements – but the ethical attributes of God's chosen ones are clearly articulated, with confidence expressed in the ability of love to foster harmony.

When disagreement is faced, the New Testament offers a variety of responses. Some texts urge the avoidance of those who promote dissension (Rom. 16.17); Paul urges the Thessalonians to 'have nothing to do' with those 'who do not obey what we say in this letter' (2 Thess. 3.14–15). In both these cases, this distancing from those who promote disagreement does not go so far as excluding them from the church. In Acts, however, we encounter a rather different approach, marked by patient persuasion. Apollos 'began to speak boldly in the synagogue; but when Priscilla and Aquila heard him, they took him aside and explained the Way of God to him more accurately' (Acts 18.26). Meanwhile, notoriously, Paul and Barnabas' disagreement 'became so sharp that they parted company; Barnabas took Mark with him and sailed away to Cyprus' (Acts 15.39). What should be noted in all these examples is that disagreement is faced and although some degree of separation between the parties involved follows, even significant geographical separation, there is no expectation of exclusion from the church itself.

There is also an unresolved question about when it is right to address disagreement and tackle associated challenges prompted by disunity within the church. In Romans, forbearance is asserted: 'We who are strong ought to put up with the failings of the weak, and not to please ourselves. Each of us must please our neighbour for the good purpose of building up the neighbour' (Rom. 15.1–2). In Jude, meanwhile, an altogether more strident approach is commended: 'I find it necessary to write and appeal to you to contend for the faith that was once for all entrusted to the saints. For certain intruders have stolen in among you' (Jude 3–4). This does represent an instance where a referral back to Jesus' narrative summation of his ethic is instructive. We can straightforwardly identify the extract from Romans with the pursuit of neighbour-love; whereas that is not so obvious in relation to Jude. But the value of applying the double love command to the latter text is that it *qualifies* the way that we might interpret the act of contending for the faith. A theology of disagreement does not exclude the facing of difference, but it does urge that such discussion happens in a way that is consonant with the love at the very foundations of Christian faith. So the reader of the letter of Jude is to be encouraged to contend for the faith, disagreeing with opponents where necessary, but always seeking to do so in ways that model love of neighbour.

Authority in the church

We should hardly be surprised that the variety of New Testament texts demonstrates considerable variation in the way the early churches developed and understood their authority structures. Even within Jesus' own teaching, there are apparent ambiguities, to which we turn first. In Matthew 5.23–24, Jesus affirms reconciliation among his followers: 'So when you are offering your gift at the altar, if you remember that your brother or sister has something against you, leave your gift there before the altar and go; first be reconciled to your brother or sister, and then come and offer your gift.' Later in the same Gospel, he addresses how a sinner should be dealt with in a process that passes through a number of stages, culminating in this observation: 'if the offender refuses to listen even to the church, let such a one be to you as a Gentile and a tax-collector' (Matt. 18.17). Although the scenarios are not identical, we can hardly fail to notice the affirmation of reconciliation in the former example and the potential for exclusion in the latter.

The account of the Jerusalem council in Acts has already been considered in some detail, but at this point it is also worth noting that it represents the introduction of reference to a higher ecclesial authority in response to a local dispute. If our two examples from Matthew's Gospel demonstrate the fragility of resolution within the local community, Paul and Barnabas' actions in response to the controversy surrounding circumcision demonstrates a maturing of authority structures and processes: 'after Paul and Barnabas had no small dissension and debate with them, Paul and Barnabas and some of the others were appointed to go up to Jerusalem to discuss this question with the apostles and the elders' (Acts 15.2). It was an occasion of 'much debate' (15.7) but resolved in the context of an affirmation of the work of the Spirit: 'it has seemed good to the Holy Spirit and to us to impose on you no further burden than these essentials' (15.28). As we will consider shortly, the acknowledgement of the role of the Spirit is deemed crucial in an effective theology of disagreement.

Godly speech

My final example of scriptural complexity concerns the witness of the New Testament in relation to what might be termed godly speech – namely, the sort of speech to be commended during instances of disagreement. Acts 21.14 contains a memorable vignette in this regard: 'Since he would not be persuaded, we remained silent except to say, "The Lord's will be done."' We might note that there are relatively few endorsements of silence in the New Testament, and this one represents a unique response to ineffective persuasion – but one that may well deserve wider commendation. Perhaps unsurprisingly, most of the texts we encounter deal not with silence but with the various problems prompted by conflictual speech. In 2 Timothy 2, both 'wrangling over words' and 'profane chatter' are warned against; 1 Peter 3.10 urges that its readers 'keep their tongues from evil and their lips from speaking deceit'; later in the same letter, they are challenged that 'whoever speaks must do so as one speaking the very words of God' (1 Peter 4.11).

My previous discussion of the extensive consideration of speech ethics in the letter of James need not be repeated here, but the contrast between it and the letter to Titus is worth revisiting. James writes, 'You must understand this, my beloved: let everyone be quick to listen, slow to speak, slow to anger; for your anger does not produce God's righteousness' (James 1.19–20). Contrast this with the advice given to Titus, facing the challenge of 'many rebellious people, idle talkers and deceivers' (Titus 1.10). He is urged to

> rebuke them sharply, so that they may become sound in the faith, not paying attention to Jewish myths or to commandments of those who reject the truth. To the pure all things are pure, but to the corrupt and unbelieving nothing is pure. Their very minds and consciences are corrupted. They profess to know God, but they deny him by their actions. They are detestable, disobedient, unfit for any good work. (Titus 1.13–16)

These two passages offer a further example of where an adaptation of Hays' synthetic task can be of value. It is worth restating that Hays stands prepared simply to set an inconvenient text to one side, whereas this book's concern to engage the whole text of the New Testament means such an approach is to be resisted. If we are to read these two texts in relation to the narrative force of Jesus' double love command, it is quite clear that James is far closer than the letter to Titus in affirming a recognizably Christian response. But, Titus does find more than an echo in some of Jesus' forceful engagement with religious opponents. For a theology of disagreement, focused as it is on relationships within the church, we might note the pre-eminence of the call to loving unity while also recognizing the stridency of advice given to Titus as he seeks to defend emerging orthodoxy. Unlike Hays, we should not then simply set Titus to one side; but we can suggest that, in its intemperate approach, it offers an example of the sort of response to disagreement that, elsewhere, the New Testament repeatedly urges faithful disciples to try to resist.

Hermeneutical reflections for a theology of disagreement

Consideration of these examples of textual inconsistency might lead us to wonder whether any vague semblance of coherence can be found among the New Testament's texts that engage with themes of disagreement. But, in part, such a concern is prompted by our attempt to focus initially on following Hays' approach to his synthetic task. We have exposed inconsistency and variation, but to do so without attending to areas of similarity risks distorting the picture. We have already noted the limited value of Hays' strict four-part demarcation of hermeneutical 'modes'; it certainly seems difficult to sustain the distinction Hays seeks to draw between a principle and a paradigm. But the fourth aspect of his scheme, the 'symbolic world', offers fruitful insights for a theology of disagreement.

The symbolic world

The variation between texts concerning disagreement at a surface, narrative level can distract our gaze from the underlying ethic that is consistently articulated in the New Testament, and that offers a *world view* or *orientation* within which disagreement among Christians should be viewed. Whereas in other areas we have identified points of tension within the life and teaching of Jesus, we must also now recognize the rich imagery that resources a theology of disagreement. In particular, my discussion of the Gospel of John emphasized both the vine (John 15) and footwashing (John 13) as images of the interdependence of the Christian community, living in loving unity. Disagreement should be viewed in the context of this community where the master takes on the role of a servant, enacting a ritual that emphasizes mutuality and service. Traditional social barriers are overturned and the inherent value of all humanity is affirmed; Jesus memorably demonstrates the reality of the self-sacrificing love at the heart of his ministry, and in this both accessible and dramatic image we find a resonance with a theology of disagreement's concern for upbuilding speech that nurtures – rather than damages – the Body of Christ.

When Hays describes his own characterization of the 'symbolic world', he uses two examples:

> Romans 1.19–32 offers a diagnosis of the fallen *human condition* without explicitly articulating any moral directives, and Matthew 5.43–48 proffers a *characterisation of God* (who makes his sun rise on the evil and on the good, and sends rain on the just and on the unjust) in order to establish a framework for discipleship.[1]

We might suggest, in turn, that the Johannine images of vine and foot-washing offer symbolic representation of the call to a life of loving unity as a key characteristic of authentic discipleship. Followers of Christ are to be orientated towards a world view where the kingdom is expressed through the love shown among disciples. They depend on each other, and their community is defined by a mutuality that transcends established notions of hierarchy. That they will disagree is inevitable, but this orientation towards a life of loving unity compels them to approach these disagreements in a way that is both distinctive and attractive.

Rules and paradigms

Our remaining question is whether, in their diversity, the texts of the New Testament offer any clear 'rules or paradigms', of the sort commended by Richard Hays, in relation to a theology of disagreement. We should note that Hays defines a 'rule' in this sense as 'direct commandments or prohibitions of specific behaviours'.[2] As my preceding 'synthetic' discussion has shown, it is not as if the New Testament speaks with one clear voice – still less a rule – in relation to the practical outworkings of how disagreement might be approached. But that observation in itself does not leave us without potential rules to follow; rather, our focus shifts to those rules that could shape individual response to the presence of disagreement, prompting Christians to consider the moral framework within which they approach a disagreement. Three rules are proposed.

First, a direct quotation of Colossians 4.6: '*Let your speech always be gracious, seasoned with salt, so that you may know how you ought to answer everyone.*' I have already highlighted the value of Colossians as a text that encapsulates many of the core concerns of this study, and in this one verse we are given a rule that, if applied, could transform ecclesial disagreement. Its opening appeal that speech should always be gracious makes an implied reference to the work of the Spirit, upon which I will build shortly. Second, it is to be speech 'seasoned with salt'. Gracious speech – and loving disagreement – need not be bland or lacking bite. But inherent to such speech is the task of discernment. We may well quibble with the implication that we could know 'how you ought to answer everyone', but if we read this statement in relation to the manner of our response, it helpfully reminds us that effective disagreement will be carefully discerned. It is no small irony that a verse within a brief section directed 'towards outsiders' (4.5) should resource our approach to disagreement *within* the church. The tragedy of Christian disagreement is the damaged nature of relationships within the Body of Christ; the need is for love of neighbour to be asserted even when that neighbour is a fellow Christian.

Our second rule builds on the first: *pursue godly speech, inspired by the Spirit*. While we have highlighted varied approaches to specific instances of disagreement in the New Testament, our hermeneutical reflection must also affirm the consistency with which this theme is articulated. When Jesus warns his disciples about persecution, he also reassures them: 'do not worry about how you are to speak or what you are to say; for what you are to say will be given to you at that time; for it is not you who speak, but the Spirit of your Father speaking through you' (Matt. 10.19–20). Similarly, Luke records Jesus as telling them that 'the Holy Spirit will teach you at that very hour what you ought to say' (Luke 12.12). Within the life of the church after Pentecost, numerous examples are given of the power – and necessity – of speech inspired by the Spirit, such as Acts 4.31: 'they were all filled with the Holy Spirit and spoke the word of God with boldness.' This book argues that Christian public speech undertaken in the midst of disagreement too often ignores any question of whether the wisdom of the Spirit, and its inspiration, is being sought.

A third rule sets these prior two in ethical context, recognizing that an emerging disagreement can quickly descend into a damaging dispute or conflict: *'If it is possible, so far as it depends on you, live peaceably with all'* (Rom. 12.18). This verse anchors an aspiration for gracious, godly speech in a recognition that the individual Christian lives in a context, and that context may change such that their response in conscience to an act of aggression may move beyond the straightforwardly peaceable. In a disagreement, however, the Christian should hold fast to this rule, recognizing that the health of the Body can be influenced substantially by the elements of a disagreement for which they are personally responsible – 'so far as it depends on you'. This requires the adoption of moral self-examination as disagreements emerge. So far as it depends on us as individuals engaged in disagreement, we should proceed to speak peaceably.

These three rules are to be seen in the light of one paradigmatic text: Galatians 5. Paul's sharply drawn contrast between attributes of flesh and spirit may risk being overly dramatic, but any disagreement would be transformed if the parties within it deliberately pursued 'love, joy, peace, patience, kindness, generosity, faithfulness, gentleness, and self-control' (Gal. 5.22–23). To be able to do so requires the individual Christian – so far as it depends on them – to speak with grace, seeking the wisdom of the Spirit. Our concern to demonstrate the importance of theological input from beyond the Bible in shaping Christian moral response will be considered in relation to the fruit of the Spirit in Chapter 9: there we will consider in greater detail the importance of an appeal to pneumatology within Christian ethical thinking. For now, it is sufficient to note the centrality of Galatians 5 in our emerging theology of disagreement.

Conclusion

There can be little doubt about the desire of Richard Hays to assert the primacy of the New Testament in the construction of a Christian ethic. At the end of this second part of our study, we have established the extent to which the New Testament speaks coherently about the facing of disagreement. Our proposal to move an engagement with sources beyond the Bible to the fourth, 'pragmatic' task of Hays' scheme means that at the end of the third, 'hermeneutical' task we can express the content of an emerging Christian ethic, rooted in Scripture, with clarity – but recognizing that this ethic will yet further be shaped by insights from tradition, reason and experience. The extent of this additional shaping will, of course, vary considerably from one ethic to another, not least in relation to the extent to which a particular ethical question is considered directly in the Bible. But given the central place still afforded to Scripture in the life of the church, and the uniquely relevant role of the New Testament as the church's own holy text, it is helpful to clarify the content of a Christian ethic that emerges from the New Testament itself – and *then* bring this into dialogue with other sources of theological wisdom.

A biblically rooted theology of disagreement thus stands ready to engage with sources beyond the New Testament. In the context of this study, that pursuit of loving disagreement will mean engagement with illustrative examples in relation to the church's public witness, its pneumatology and liturgy, as we seek to establish an ethic that sustains the well-being of the Body of Christ even as it engages in debates that threaten its unity. So finally, let us restate the core of our proposed theology of disagreement that we have discerned through our engagement with the New Testament:

'Let your speech always be gracious, seasoned with salt,
so that you may know how you ought to answer everyone.'
(Col. 4.6)

'Pursue godly speech, inspired by the Spirit.'
(Matt. 10.19–20; Luke 12.12; Acts 4.31)

'If it is possible, so far as it depends on you, live peaceably with all.'
(Rom. 12.18)

'Cultivate the fruit of the Spirit.'
(Gal. 5.22–23)

Notes

1 Richard B. Hays, 1996, *The Moral Vision of the New Testament*, New York: HarperCollins, p. 209.
2 Hays, *Moral Vision*, p. 209.

Ecclesiological Implications of a Theology of Disagreement

Introduction to Part 3

It is now time for our emerging theology of disagreement, rooted in the text of the New Testament, to engage in Richard Hays' final, 'pragmatic' task. At this point it is worth being reminded of how Hays introduces this task, which is shaped by what he calls 'the practical question that drives all the others: How shall the Christian community shape its life in obedience to the witness of the New Testament?'[1] Responding to this question is, for Hays, the purpose of his pragmatic task. But to frame a question about the moral shape of Christian life in the way that Hays does carries two risks: a potential overstatement of the clarity and coherence of the New Testament's witness, and a diminution from the outset of the place of tradition, reason and experience in ethical discernment. Furthermore, having asserted that the task of hermeneutical reflection finishes before the engagement with non-biblical authority begins, Hays limits the extent to which the Bible can be brought into a fruitful dialogue with insights from the lived experience – historical and contemporary – of Christian disciples.

This is not to suggest that there is no value in attempting to discern an ethic from the pages of the New Testament; rather, our concern is to highlight the need to set such observations, foundational for Christian moral practice as they are, in the broader landscape of the life of the church and its history of ethical discernment. In this book, our consideration of the New Testament offers a grounding for a Christian ethical response to the challenge of disagreement within the church. With Hays, we can assert that greater clarity about the ethical content of the Scriptures written by early Christians is of particular value, given the authority the Bible – and, in particular, the New Testament – still commands in ecclesial moral debates. But that scriptural material should not be viewed in isolation; rather, it should be read and appraised alongside other sources of Christian ethical inspiration.

We do not have the scope to consider the vast range of contexts and insights, both historical and theological, that would enrich a fuller theological reflection on disagreement. The chapters that follow thus offer illustrative examples of the way in which my proposed theology of disagreement, hitherto rooted exclusively in New Testament soil, can interact fruitfully with voices representing tradition, reason and experience. Hays does commend such a process, but does not foresee any need for the New Testament's engagement with non-biblical authority to prompt further scriptural hermeneutics. This book, in contrast, suggests that Hays' pragmatic task should, in its very pragmatism, allow the Bible to enter into theological dialogue with other voices. Indeed, one might suggest that at moments when the church faces calls from within to revise its position on particular moral issues, the credibility of any process of change depends on effective hermeneutical approaches that successfully bring Scripture into engagement with such voices and perspectives.

As the biblical witnesses found in Part 1 have demonstrated, the quality of speech in the midst of disagreement is a key concern across the text of the New Testament, and so the first chapter of Part 3 is a consideration of the church's public theological witness and how this is undermined by the nature of public ecclesial disagreement. The focus of my proposed theology of disagreement on the fruit of the Spirit, already proposed at the end of Part 2, is examined in greater detail and in relation to some psychological insights in a chapter that follows on pneumatology. I then consider the church's liturgy as a source of wisdom from tradition, which can be brought into instructive dialogue with the text of the New Testament. This set of extra-biblical perspectives on disagreement points to some of the directions in which a theology of disagreement can usefully be developed beyond New Testament foundations; so, first, let us turn to questions concerning the place of disagreement within public theological engagement.

Note

1 Richard B. Hays, 1996, *The Moral Vision of the New Testament*, New York: HarperCollins, p. 313.

8

Public Theological Witness: Theological Ethics for Christians Disagreeing in Public

In Part 1 of this book, our reading of the New Testament led us to conclude that a cogent theology of disagreement needs to be able to offer a robust ethical underpinning to the church's public speech, not least because at the heart of John 13.35 is the notion that Christian community is recognizable to outsiders because of the love visible within it; through distinctly unloving public disagreement, Christians easily undermine such a vision. This chapter seeks to examine the relationship between public disagreement and the church's desire to engage theologically in public, and so proceeds on the basis of a simple claim: *too little attention has been given to the impact of internal disagreement on the ability of the church to speak effectively in public.* As we pursue the 'pragmatic task' described by Richard Hays, seeking to situate our emerging theology of disagreement in the lived experience of the contemporary church, and drawing on theological insights from beyond the New Testament, our discussion here offers an illustrative example of one context where a theology of disagreement can be applied fruitfully – that of the church's public engagement in theology.

My primary concern is the articulation of the moral theological intentions that underpin engagement in disagreement. It is worth recalling the content of our proposed theology of disagreement: gracious, godly speech, seasoned with salt and inspired by the Spirit, undertaken in the pursuit of peace and in the context of the cultivation of the fruit of the Spirit. Such qualities do not, of themselves, resolve disagreement (nor do they determine whether a particular disagreement is of primary significance or *adiaphora*) but they offer a moral theological framework within which disagreement could be transformed. In this chapter, the visibility of these attributes in the public theological engagement of the church will be considered.

It is also necessary to acknowledge the complexity inherent in a Christian understanding of public speech. Acts of worship, and the sermons or homilies offered within them, are almost always public occasions, seldom restricted in terms of public access. Synodical discussions might vary in their openness, but tend to offer public statements about conclusions reached. Internal questions facing the church in relation to its policy on vexed doctrinal matters will often involve the public airing of disagreement and dispute through all forms of media as well as public meetings. Many aspects of the life of the church, including its moral and theological disagreements, are inescapably on public view.

Examining material from Anglican and ecumenical contexts, we will consider the extent to which the ethics of public speech are of concern to churches as they engage in public theological reflection. We will note that, rather too often, such engagement assumes (or optimistically implies) that Christians speak from a position of corporate coherence and unanimity; the damaging impact of disagreement, and indeed conflict, risks being ignored. Engagement with the fact of disagreement among Anglicans will show the inherent tensions that surround the honest facing of the presence and impact of disagreement; then, our engagement with some of the work of the Anglican–Roman Catholic International Commission offers unusually candid insights from an ecumenical encounter, not least concerning the dangers of mutual caricature. But before we consider the insights from these two examples in detail, it is necessary to outline the nature of the challenge being faced.

The problem of Christian public speech in the context of disagreement

The very title of Oliver O'Donovan's series of 'online sermons' concerning Anglican responses to homosexuality, later published as a book, is revealing: 'A Conversation Waiting to Begin'. In words of commendation, Rowan Williams praises the book, because it 'consistently takes us to the questions others are not asking and refuses the ready-made questions and answers that paralyse our thinking about the sexuality debates'.[1] And yet Williams' words point to the ease with which debates on controversial issues swiftly become paralysed – by mutual incomprehension and sometimes hostility. Public theological engagement must necessarily move beyond such paralysis, but such a move is not easily achieved. Perhaps most telling of all is the lack of theological reflection on this state of Christian communication. The presence of denominational divisions, as well as myriad groupings within denominations, can often simply be regarded as the context within which theological work is undertaken, rather than being seen as an example of the Body of Christ failing to live up to its calling to loving unity.

Nicholas Adams frankly laments the quality of public debate within his denomination, writing:

> church leaders in my own Anglican Church publish letters against each other, to the unedifying delight of the mass media, rather than debate patiently and charitably in synod: they impatiently try to bypass process … There need to be hospitable practices for coordinating rival narratives: the hospitality has to be bigger than the rivalry.[2]

It is worth noting that these comments are made in the context of engagement with the discourse ethics of Jürgen Habermas; it was a consideration of how Christians might engage with those of other faiths that prompted important observations concerning the impact of internal disagreement on the church's public witness.[3] But Adams notes that there is a moral question here that should not be ignored, concerning the ethics that inform church leaders as they choose to engage opponents intemperately rather than charitably. He asks, 'How do communities with different narratives meet peacefully in the public sphere in order to argue with, and not merely encounter, each other?'[4]

While Habermas considers this in relation to groups from different religions, it is a question that might well be posed in relation to different *Christian* communities. Adams then proposes a response characterized by a submission to divine judgement and a recognition of the significance of Jesus' love commands. If Christians are to begin to debate their inherited norms effectively, they must be prepared for the challenging nature of such work:

> There is every possibility that testing norms becomes very difficult and painful. Such problems are real and cannot be magicked away by clever theories but must be worked through patiently, with all participants mindful that even our most cherished beliefs stand under divine judgement, and that the first and second commandments are to love God with all one's heart and love one's neighbour as oneself.[5]

There is a clear resonance here with this book's proposed theology of disagreement – and its methodological prioritizing of the double love command. Adams roots the possibility of effective disagreement in explicitly theological references of a sort that would be rejected by Habermas, but tellingly Adams also acknowledges the limitations of such an approach: 'the problem is not that such resources cannot be grounded in the diverse public sphere, but that *they cannot even be grounded inside the traditions themselves*' (original italics).[6] The quality of public theological discourse is such that it is hard to resource a process of fruitful disagreement; Adams has conceded that the ability of Christians to engage with the wider world is profoundly undermined by the way in which their internal disagreements are approached.

Disagreement may well seem irresolvable, but that fact alone does not remove from the Christian engaged in disagreement a responsibility to act in ways that can generously be interpreted as recognizably Christian. The need for patience in the midst of division, and a recognition that disunity will remain unless or until God decisively intervenes, navigates a credible course between naive optimism and pragmatic despair – and it seems to this writer that they are insights as applicable to debates *among* Christians as they are to conversations across more clearly defined faith divides. Crucially, Christian hope should not be excluded from this picture. The question is how the picture might be transformed if both parties in an inter-Christian disagreement were to take these ethical calls seriously, engaging in public disagreement with a humility that appreciates that their own understanding of an opponent's position may be clouded and partial. The two examples that now follow consider what it is to take seriously the problem of divisive Christian public speech in the context of disagreement. Both offer instances of the lived experience of the church enriching our theological ethic rooted in the New Testament. By engaging with these contemporary examples, we begin to demonstrate how Richard Hays' model is impoverished if it fails to interact and engage with the voices of tradition, reason and experience.

Anglicans doing theology – and disagreement – in public

A desire by the leaders of the Anglican Communion to model a better way to face their disagreements can be seen in a document issued during Rowan Williams' archiepiscopate, which constitutes a particularly striking example of a call for a new ethic to underpin public engagement. When the Primates of the Communion met in Alexandria in 2009, their meeting concluded with a communiqué given the telling title 'Deeper Communion, Gracious Restraint'. It pleaded with the Communion's member provinces to refrain from further appointments of gay bishops, the development of services of gay blessing, and cross-border incursions across provincial boundaries:

> If a way forward is to be found and mutual trust to be re-established, it is imperative that further aggravation and acts which cause offence, misunderstanding or hostility cease … While we are aware of the depth

of conscientious conviction involved, the position of the Communion defined by the Lambeth 1998 Resolution 1.10 in its entirety remains, and gracious restraint on all three fronts is urgently needed to open the way for transforming conversation.[7]

This call for gracious restraint in both word and action fell rather spectacularly on deaf ears: more gay bishops, gay blessings and cross-border incursions within the life of the Communion have occurred since 2009. More recently, The Episcopal Church's decision in July 2015 to extend marriage to same-sex couples (voting just days after the United States Supreme Court ruled in favour of a legal right to such marriage throughout the Union) raises challenges to Anglican unity with implications that are yet fully to emerge. But in 2009, the Anglican Primates' call for gracious restraint was telling, in particular, for the candour with which the context of their meeting was recalled in the final communiqué:

> At the beginning of the meeting, the Archbishop of Canterbury invited five of us to speak about how the current situation in the Communion affected mission in our own contexts. We were able to talk honestly and openly about our experiences and perceptions. We were reminded powerfully of the sense of alienation and pain felt in many parts of the Communion, as many are tested by difficult theological tensions. Nevertheless, there was a discernible mood of graciousness among us in our engagements: a mood which assisted and sustained our conversation.[8]

Here an explicit link is made between personal ethical decisions made – in this case, to act graciously even towards those with whom one is in disagreement – and the well-being of the Body of Christ as a whole. Grace 'assisted and sustained' conversation: 'we were able to discuss and debate these issues in a spirit of open and respectful dialogue. There has been honest exchange and mutual challenge at a new and deeper level.'[9] For the Anglican Primates, attending to the quality of their relationships with one another bore fruit for their theological engagement in seemingly unanticipated ways; and while we might suggest that such a link should be unsurprising, we should also note that little scholarly attention is generally paid to the link between such gracious interaction and the way in which disagreements then proceed. Such a link is, however, crucial to the foundations of a theology of disagreement, which proposes that a re-examination of the *way* in which potentially fraught conversations are approached can, of itself, be transformative.

In the months following the Primates' meeting in Alexandria, the House of Bishops of The Episcopal Church in the United States commissioned a special issue of the *Anglican Theological Review*, devoted to the question of gay marriage, and which sought to 'offer a distinctively theological approach to the controversy'.[10] My task is not to reflect on the specific arguments raised in relation to gay marriage, but rather to consider this genuine attempt to promote theological conversation between those who disagree. So the opening words of 'The Traditionalist Response' to the initial 'liberal' paper is instructive when it notes that 'the conversation between the traditionalist and liberal teams on this panel has been charitable and constructive, and we affirm the sincere desire of our counterparts to be faithful and to build up the church'.[11] This is the sort of mutual recognition of sincere discipleship that is so often lacking in fraught debates about sexuality. As Sarah Coakley notes in her 'Response', the exchange 'raises the currently divisive discussion of same-sex desire in the Anglican Communion to a new level of theological clarity and mutual courtesy, and for those traits alone it deserves wide ecclesial attention and reflection'.[12]

In her 'Epilogue' that follows the liberal–traditionalist exchange, and the scholarly responses, Ellen T. Charry notes that the voice that emerges from the various perspectives on offer

> highlights several pneumatological loci. One is the role of the Spirit in bringing the church into all truth (John 16:13). Can we ever be certain that the witness of the Spirit that we perceive to be working among us is not our own voice writ large rather than the voice of the Holy Spirit?[13]

It is a question that now can only be heard in the context of the decision by the 2015 General Convention of The Episcopal Church to remove gender-specific language from its marriage liturgies and associated canons, opening the way for same-sex ceremonies.[14] Charry's question about the church being led into all truth highlights a real challenge for any church wishing to depart from an inherited norm: it remains unclear how the circumstances can be determined when such a break with tradition is theologically coherent and even a response to the Spirit's guiding. This question is, of course, complicated by the ecclesiology of the Anglican Communion, bringing together as it does a family of autonomous churches in sometimes uneasy relationship. Investigating how churches and communions can determine the legitimacy of divisive theological innovations is beyond the scope of a theology of disagreement – but we can usefully note that the *Anglican Theological Review* had sought to model a more constructive approach to disagreements about marriage.

Rowan Williams' successor as Archbishop, Justin Welby, has sought to continue to promote unity and interrogate the ethics that underpin how disagreeing Anglicans engage one another. Welby's foreword to a recent resource, *Living Reconciliation*, is of particular interest for us, because he uses it to outline a number of principles that underpin his approach and that are of direct relevance for our emerging theology of disagreement. Crucially, in a Communion where impersonal international use of social media foments damaging division, he asserts that 'getting to know one another is surely a prerequisite if we are to address the challenges of disagreement'.[15] Human interaction and fellowship are essential. So too is a recognition of a shared starting point, however limited that might be; the Anglican Marks of Mission[16] fulfil such a purpose:

> We agree on these marks. Yet in so many other things, we disagree. Given our transparent and open structures, we often do so loudly. But we do so as part of a family which, however much it falls out, remains linked. We have to deal with the reality that, no matter how strained the relationships may become at times, we belong to each other.[17]

The use of a family metaphor to describe relationships among Anglicans grounds disagreement in an acceptance that it exists and can be damaging, alongside a determination to sustain relationships even when they are strained. Welby thus asks, 'Where we disagree we need to ask ourselves: what is there of the gospel, of Jesus, in the view and life of those I disagree with?'[18] To focus on areas of shared agreement is, for Welby, to honour the interconnectedness that comes with being brothers and sisters in Christ.

> So we do not have the option, if we love one another in the way that Jesus instructs us, simply to ditch those with whom we disagree. You do not chuck out members of the family: you love them and seek their well-being, even when you argue. Good and loving disagreement is a potential gift to a world of bitter and divisive conflict. What can be more radical than to disagree well, not by abandoning principle and truth, but by affirming it with respect?[19]

There are two important points to note in response. First, Welby's words can be read as implying that a family should never divide, and by implication neither should a church. This book has already argued that a theology of disagreement retains space for fracture and even schism within the Body of Christ, as in certain circumstances this may be the only way forward in the face of not merely disagreement but teaching that marks a departure from orthodox Christianity. But just as our study urges a disposition towards the maintenance of loving unity, so too Welby is keen to emphasize a reorientation of Anglican discourse towards a celebration of that which is shared rather than a constant exploration of difference. Even if all tensions are not resolved, such an affirmation-focused process can be a gift to the wider world.

There is a second and broader criticism of the *Living Reconciliation* approach, which is about the way that its discussion of disagreement all too easily and swiftly leaps to a discussion of reconciliation. Our concern, quite deliberately, is to tackle disagreement – rather than conflict – because it is in the course of an initial disagreement that seeds of what might later descend into a protracted conflict are often sown. The reconciliation of parties in established conflicts may well require specialist mediation in addition to prayerful invocation of the Holy Spirit. In such conflicts, it is largely too late to learn the lessons of a theology of disagreement. For Justin Welby, there is a danger that a strong affirmation of 'good disagreement' hopes that simply by disagreeing more effectively, reconciliation can be found – whereas a much longer and painstaking process of mutual listening and dialogue may well be essential before even gestures towards reconciliation can be made. A call for good disagreement can, however, be of real value to those in *emerging* situations of conflict, encouraging participants in debates to speak and act Christianly for the good of the Body as a whole.

A final terminological observation concerns the quest for 'good disagreement'. It is a phrase that has been widely adopted.[20] In his presidential address to the General Synod in February 2014, Justin Welby said:

> Already I can hear the arguments being pushed back at me, about compromise, about the wishy-washiness of reconciliation, to quote something I read recently. But this sort of love, and the reconciliation between differing groups that it demands and implies, is not comfortable and soft and wishy-washy. Facilitated conversations may be a clumsy phrase, but it has at its heart a search for good disagreement.

Earlier I quoted Welby's reference to 'good and loving disagreement'. Interestingly, this appears to be his only written reference to *loving* disagreement, while *good* disagreement is widely discussed. For this author, that seems regrettable: the former phrase carries with it a sense of kingdom-shaped oxymoron, with the very concept of loving disagreement only making sense within a Christian anthropology. Good disagreement, meanwhile, risks sounding like the least worst option. Of course, better a good disagreement than a bad one, but there is a dangerous inference that good disagreement is the end in itself, rather than a means to a truthful and redeemed end in God.

When the church speaks in public, it cannot escape the fact that it bears witness to the wider world as it does so. As such, it needs to consider how it might speak in such a way that its voice is heard with credibility and authenticity. This book's repeated call is that individual Christians need to re-examine the ethic with which they approach such public speech, most particularly when engaged in instances of disagreement, such that they attempt to speak and act with reference to the framework of Jesus' double love command, always with a view to the well-being of the Body of Christ as a whole. As we have seen, there are instances of Anglicans articulating such a vision as offering a way forward in that Communion's fractious common life, but there is a reluctance to explore in detail the extent to which the *way* that disagreements are approached affects the pursuit of loving unity. We now turn to consider the same challenges in ecumenical perspective, and might begin by noting that ecumenism only exists because divided Christians recognize the value of mutual engagement to promote better understanding and even pursue greater unity. But as we shall see, ecumenical encounters also risk an idealized masking of the reality of disagreement, to the detriment of ecumenism itself.

Ecumenical disagreement and the myth of unity

Introductory remarks in a collection of essays by Protestant ethicists engaging Roman Catholic moral teaching offer an appropriate introduction to the challenge we face as we acknowledge the impact of unhelpful idealism on Christian public engagement in ecumenical context. Reinhard Hütter, writing in 1998, introduced his ecumenical ethical project by pointing out that there had been an abundance of Protestant–Catholic dialogue on matters of doctrine, whereas 'in comparison questions of ethics have only on rare occasions received similar attention'.[21] The collection, written with respectful mutual attentiveness by moral theologians of both Roman Catholic and Protestant backgrounds, carefully highlights perceived strengths and weaknesses in their ethical positions in a spirit of cooperation but also honest enquiry. However, for our purposes, it is one particular passage in Hütter's opening essay that is key:

we are highly aware of the fact that ethical conflicts and disagreements – as well as agreements – are not just phenomena occurring *between* churches but as well and at least as much *in* each church. Therefore this collection can by no means claim to be in any way representative of the variety of perspectives present in the respective church bodies. And while the framework of this project did not allow the contributors to address the diversity and complexity of moral debates in the respective church bodies, the authors hope to advance the mutual understanding *between* the various traditions in moral matters.[22] (italics all original)

We can hardly fail to note the significance of Hütter's comments in relation to a theology of disagreement. Not for him an optimistic assumption about unity among Protestants; rather, a strikingly honest acknowledgement of the scale of disagreement that exists 'at least as much' within churches as between them. Tellingly, this means that the collection he has edited is representative only of the individual views of its authors rather than the corporate ethical positions of the churches of which they are members: these scholarly experts cannot be assumed to reflect the official views of the denominations they represent. And even while we might well wish to defend the place of free-thinking, exploratory work among theological ethicists, Hütter's candid remarks underline the scale of the challenge that is faced. There has been a collapse in confidence concerning who speaks for whom, and disagreements among Christians are a primary contributing factor. Unless the quality of internal church debates, undertaken in public, can be improved, ecumenical dialogues can all too easily appear irrelevant if they are based upon an assumed foundation of internal doctrinal and ethical unity that is in fact illusory.

The 1994 report of the Anglican–Roman Catholic International Commission, ARCIC, provides some crucial material for this discussion because, in its surprising candour, it not only underlines the nature of the challenge we have articulated but also offers tentative, hopeful steps forward on the journey of Roman Catholics and Anglicans towards visible unity, with important lessons that can be applied to Christians from any denominational background engaged in dialogue between churches. The report, *Life in Christ: Morals, Communion and the Church*, was unusual for an ecumenical document in that it addressed moral rather than doctrinal questions, and in so doing offers us some important insights concerning how inevitable Christian disagreement can best be acknowledged and faced in public settings. We have already highlighted the danger of assumed corporate unanimity when Christians engage with those of other religions or with secular voices; in ecumenical dialogue, there is at least a recognition in the very act of ecumenism that difference exists and needs to be acknowledged, but this document is valuable for the way in which it considers such questions in detail. As such, it is worth quoting some sections at length:

There is a popular and widespread belief that the Anglican and Roman Catholic Communions are divided most sharply by their moral teaching. Careful consideration has persuaded the Commission that, despite existing disagreement in certain areas of practical and pastoral judgment, Anglicans and Roman Catholics derive from the Scriptures and Tradition the same controlling vision of the nature and destiny of humanity and share the same fundamental moral values. This substantial area of common conviction calls for shared witness, since both Communions proclaim the same Gospel and acknowledge the same injunction to mission and service. A disproportionate emphasis on particular disagreements blurs this important truth and can provoke a sense of alienation.[23]

Here a sense of moral priority is articulated in relation to disagreement. Differences between Anglicans and Roman Catholics are not to be ignored, but the report proposes that the damage that can be caused by a disproportionate focus on disagreement should be noted, not least in relation to its impact on shared missionary work for the good of the gospel. As such, a prior question becomes paramount: 'The fundamental moral question, therefore, is not "What ought we to do?", but "What kind of persons are we called to become?" For children of God, moral obedience is nourished by the hope of becoming like God (cf. 1 Jn 3:1–3).'[24]

The document calls on Christians to recognize the importance of that which is shared at a foundational level, while also acknowledging the greater likelihood of disagreement in relation to specific applied ethical areas: 'Christians of different Communions are more likely to agree on the character of the Christian life and the fundamental Christian virtues and values. They are more likely to disagree on the consequent rules of practice, particular moral judgments and pastoral counsel.'[25] Such a recognition enables the potential celebration of a shared ethos even when specific ethical teaching differs; a perspective which seeks to affirm common ground as much as it seeks to point out obstacles represents a strikingly different approach to Christian disagreement and opens the way for fruitful dialogue among one-time ecclesial enemies:

> In our conversations together we have made two discoveries: first, that many of the preconceptions that we brought with us concerning each other's understanding of moral teaching and discipline were often little more than caricatures; and secondly, that the differences which actually exist between us appear in a new light when we consider them in their origin and context.[26]

Perhaps most tellingly of all, the document includes a candid section where lingering untruths held by some in each denomination in relation to the other are robustly dismissed:

It is not true that the Roman Catholic Church has predetermined answers to every moral question, while the Anglican Church has no answers at all. It is not true that Roman Catholics always agree on moral issues, nor that Anglicans never agree. It is not true that Anglican ethics is pragmatic and unprincipled, while Roman Catholic moral theology is principled but abstract. It is not true that Roman Catholics are always more careful of the institution in their concern for the common good, while Anglicans disregard the common good in their concern for the individual. It is not true that Roman Catholic moral teaching is legalistic, while Anglican moral teaching is utilitarian. Caricature, we may grant, is never totally contrived; but caricature it remains.[27]

As we consider ways in which public church discourse can engage in disagreement without causing lasting damage to the Body of Christ as a whole, these reflections from the ARCIC process are of real value. In particular, they underline the corrosive impact of mutual suspicion and mistrust built on a caricatured view of the other; the document challenges its readers to recognize that a respectful but probing mutual interrogation of disagreement and opposing claims, undertaken as a shared pursuit of truth, is likely to result in a less hostile attitude towards a Christian neighbour, even as and when points of difference remain.

There are, however, aspects of the approach found in *Life in Christ: Morals, Communion and the Church* that demand further scrutiny. An unavoidable initial observation concerns the extent to which any group of Anglicans can hope to speak on behalf of the sheer diversity of their own Communion. So we should at least note that ARCIC is not immune from the danger of an optimistically assumed internal unity with which the respective ecumenical partners engage each other. But there is also a question that relates specifically to the moral questions in this report, raised by Michael Root in a careful analysis of the relationship between ecumenism and ecclesial disagreement. He argues that shared general convictions and underlying assumptions are not enough when considering questions of moral theology, especially when the scale of division and variation in pastoral practice is widely known:

> Ecclesial communion requires not only a common vision of the Christian life, but a common recognition that the rules and practices of the churches adequately embody that vision and sufficient unity in those rules and practices to permit a common pursuit of that life.[28]

Root calls for a robust honesty in ecumenical encounter, where the seduction of elegant generalities is resisted in favour of robust but respectful engagement with the reality of difference being faced:

That unity will be complex. It will be a differentiated consensus, but it will be a differentiated consensus with a variety of elements: basic values and specific rules, comprehensive visions and concrete practices. The dialogues have begun this work, but most of the task is still ahead of us, and it is not becoming easier.[29]

His is a call for precision in the description of difference and disagreement faced, and one can hardly criticize such a call. But we also need an approach that maintains gracious generosity in the face of disagreements that can easily become debilitating, and that may at times involve an approach that does not always address the presenting issue head-on, as if such an approach is the only credible option.[30] We are reminded once again that a theology of disagreement challenges those facing difference to consider the process as well as the stated end. In ecumenical dialogue, that end may seem so far off as to make the value of such dialogue questionable – but the picture is transformed if the value of shared loving relationship within the Body of Christ is prized, even as and when differences on certain issues remain. A theology of disagreement forces those who debate in public to consider that there might be value in improving the quality of encounter between divided Christians, even while the issues that divide them may remain seemingly intractable.

Conclusion

Joseph Monti has noted that 'moral questions are always also ecclesiological questions pertaining to the character integrity of the community of faith'.[31] There is clearly still more to be done in establishing the common ground where fruitful dialogue can occur, recognizing the challenges posed by competing ecclesiologies as well as ethical divergence – but as Monti acknowledges, the 'character integrity' of those who participate in ecclesial disagreement is a crucial factor. This is an observation that forces us to recognize that the manner of a disagreement is significant, alongside the matter under consideration. If disagreeing Christians can learn to speak more Christianly in public, the quality of their disagreement can improve. Nigel Biggar has affirmed that our concern needs to move beyond language:

> Content, however, is not all. The other part of what makes a theological argument behave in public is its manner. Certainly, the selection of content itself signifies respect or disrespect; but so does the manner of its delivery and, more broadly, the manner in which conversation as

a whole is conducted. Christians bear witness to what they believe at least as much in how they speak as in what they say.[32]

Biggar proposes several virtues that might guide this public theological witness: 'docility, tolerance-as care, charity-as-respect and charity-as-optimal-construal, critical candour ... these are among the virtues that should govern the manner of Christians' conversation and should cause them to *behave* in public.'[33] Christians should consider the ethical dimension of how they speak, rather than simply engaging in a relentless and merciless pursuit of their agenda at the expense of all others; this gracious and generous approach to discourse is at the heart of a theology of disagreement.

Writing in a resource produced for members of the Church of England General Synod as they faced discussions on sexuality, Phil Groves notes that the quest for good disagreement – championed by the Archbishop of Canterbury – is 'the radical opposite of defeating your enemy with clever debating tactics. Good disagreement is a painful and complex journey towards the fullness of truth.'[34] Thus public debate and disagreement is not about seeking expedient compromise, but it should entail the establishment of conditions for fruitful engagement. When differences are then aired in public, Christians should be mindful of the extent to which they are revealing the fruit of the Spirit in and through their deliberations. We might reasonably hope that they would seek to build consensus, act charitably, love and honour their neighbour, and promote unity, even and as they pursue with determination the truth that sets free.

Our consideration of the experience of Christians engaged in disagreement, both within denominations and across ecumenical divides, prompts an enlarged perspective on the New Testament's prioritizing of the pursuit of loving unity. While Richard Hays devotes only brief attention to extra-biblical sources of inspiration, this chapter has shown that the experience of the church in disagreement can, of itself, help shape the construction of a Christian ethic from New Testament origins. An acknowledgement of the damaging nature of ecclesial disagreement prompts a recognition that moral theological resources are required to assist these disagreements in proceeding in a more recognizably and authentically Christian manner – grounded, as this book proposes, in John 13.35's insistence that mutual love within the church sustains the public recognition of discipleship. This prioritizing of the pursuit of loving unity has the potential to influence the way in which disagreement is pursued, with protagonists mindful of the inescapably public context in which difference is routinely faced. But, as the next chapter argues, such disagreements will only proceed Christianly with a renewed appreciation for the place of the guidance of the Holy Spirit, and the possibility of its inspiration, in the midst of disagreement.

Notes

1 Oliver O'Donovan, 2009, *A Conversation Waiting to Begin: The Churches and the Gay Controversy*, London: SCM Press, quotation on front cover.

2 Nicholas Adams, 2006, *Habermas and Theology*, Cambridge: Cambridge University Press, p. 21.

3 Kathryn Tanner, also writing in relation to engagement with non-Christians, hopes that the threat of divisiveness is offset not by a futile search for agreement, but by 'the constraints of civility supported by the dispositions of modesty and toleration that follow from Christian beliefs about a sinful world. In a fallen world, Christian triumphalism has no place ... the fact of disagreement between Christians and non-Christians must be patiently born. Anything more awaits the intervention of God, who has sole responsibility to make up for the always inadequate efforts of Christians in public debate with others.' See Kathryn Tanner, 1996, 'Public Theology and the Character of Public Debate' in Harlan Beckley, ed., *The Annual of the Society of Christian Ethics*, Washington DC: Georgetown University Press, p. 86.

4 Adams, *Habermas*, p. 219.

5 Adams, *Habermas*, p. 229.

6 Adams, *Habermas*, p. 227.

7 Anglican Communion Office, 2009, 'Deeper Communion; Gracious Restraint. A Letter from Alexandria to the Churches of the Anglican Communion', www.anglicancommunion.org/media/68372/Pastoral-Letter.pdf, para. 12 (accessed 21 April 2014).

8 Anglican Communion Office, 'Deeper', para. 5.

9 Anglican Communion Office, 'Deeper', para. 8.

10 Ellen T. Charry, 2011, Preface, *Anglican Theological Review* 93,1, p. xiii.

11 John E. Goldingay, Grant R. LeMarquand, George R. Sumner and Daniel A. Westberg, *Anglican Theological Review* 93,1, p. 89.

12 Sarah Coakley, *Anglican Theological Review* 93,1 p. 111.

13 Ellen T. Charry, *Anglican Theological Review* 93,1 p. 141.

14 See the decision to amend Canon I.18 at the 2015 General Convention: www.generalconvention.org/gc/2015-resolutions/ (accessed 1 September 2015).

15 Justin Welby, 2014, 'Foreword: Reconciliation is the Heart of the Gospel' in Phil Groves and Angharad Parry Jones, *Living Reconciliation*, London: SPCK, p. ix.

16 They are:

    1 To proclaim the Good News of the Kingdom;

    2 To teach, baptise and nurture new believers;

    3 To respond to human need by loving service;

    4 To transform unjust structures of society, to challenge violence of every kind and pursue peace and reconciliation;

    5 To strive to safeguard the integrity of creation, and sustain and renew the life of the earth.

See www.anglicancommunion.org/mission/marks-of-mission.aspx (accessed 1 December 2020).

17 Welby in Groves and Parry Jones, *Reconciliation*, p. x.

18 Welby in Groves and Parry Jones, *Reconciliation*, p. xi.

19 Welby in Groves and Parry Jones, *Reconciliation*, p. xiii.

20 See the discussion in the Introduction of Andrew Atherstone and Andrew Goddard, eds, 2015, *Good Disagreement? Grace and Truth in a Divided Church*, Oxford: Lion Hudson. Another example is the way in which the pressure group Accepting Evangelicals has established a section of its website under the same title, featuring a commissioned essay by the Dean of St Paul's Cathedral, which includes the telling observation by the journalist Andrew Brown that for campaigning groups in Anglican sexuality debates 'what's good about disagreement is the moment when the enemy crumbles' – hardly the 'good disagreement' being sought by Archbishop Welby, but an honest depiction of the reality of some current discourse. See www.acceptingevangelicals.org/good-disagreement/ (accessed 1 August 2015). A recent volume of essays seeks to promote 'good disagreement' among evangelicals with varying views on sexuality: see Jayne Ozanne, ed., 2016, *Journeys in Grace and Truth: Revisiting Scripture and Sexuality*, London: Ekklesia.

21 Reinhard Hütter and Theodor Dieter, 1998, *Ecumenical Ventures in Ethics: Protestants Engage Pope John Paul II's Moral Encyclicals*, Grand Rapids: Eerdmans, p. 1.

22 Hütter and Dieter, *Ecumenical*, p. 3.

23 Anglican–Roman Catholic International Commission (ARCIC), 1994, *Life in Christ: Morals, Communion and the Church*. See www.anglicancommunion.org/media/105236/ARCIC_II_Life_in_Christ_Morals_Communion_and_the_Church.pdf, para. 1 (accessed 16 December 2020).

24 ARCIC, *Life in Christ*, para. 6.

25 ARCIC, *Life in Christ*, para. 34.

26 ARCIC, *Life in Christ*, para. 50.

27 ARCIC, *Life in Christ*, para. 51.

28 Michael Root, 2012, 'Ethics in Ecumenical Dialogues: A Survey and Analysis' in Michael Root and James Buckley, eds, *The Morally Divided Body: Ethical Disagreement and the Disunity of the Church*, Eugene: Cascade Books, p. 133.

29 Root, 'Ethics', p. 134.

30 We might usefully recall Jesus' response to the woman caught in adultery (John 8.1–11): enigmatically, he delays an answer to the Pharisees' question by writing in the sand, before asking those without sin to throw the first stone. Notwithstanding the disputed provenance of the particular text, it portrays Jesus as one who refuses to engage in a situation of disagreement on the terms presented to him by his opponents.

31 Joseph Monti, 1995, *Arguing about Sex: The Rhetoric of Christian Sexual Morality*, Albany: State University of New York Press, p. 261.

32 Nigel Biggar, 2011, *Behaving in Public: How to Do Christian Ethics*, Grand Rapids: Eerdmans, p. 71.

33 Biggar, *Behaving*, p. 75.

34 Church of England, 2014, *Grace and Disagreement: Shared Conversations on Scripture, Mission and Human Sexuality. A Reader: Writings to Resource Conversation*, London: The Archbishops' Council, p. 60. The church's Faith and Order Commission has also published a report for the General Synod, *Communion and Disagreement*, to assist Synod members in their reflection on disagreement: see www.churchofengland.org/sites/default/files/2017-10/communion_and_disagreement_faoc_report_gs_misc_1139.pdf (accessed 16 December 2016).

9

Pneumatology: Invoking the Holy Spirit in Christian Disagreement

My proposed theology of disagreement is rooted in one paradigmatic text – Paul's description of the fruit of the Spirit in Galatians 5:

> Now the works of the flesh are obvious: fornication, impurity, licentiousness, idolatry, sorcery, enmities, strife, jealousy, anger, quarrels, dissensions, factions, envy, drunkenness, carousing, and things like these. I am warning you, as I warned you before: those who do such things will not inherit the kingdom of God.
>
> By contrast, the fruit of the Spirit is love, joy, peace, patience, kindness, generosity, faithfulness, gentleness, and self-control. There is no law against such things. And those who belong to Christ Jesus have crucified the flesh with its passions and desires. If we live by the Spirit, let us also be guided by the Spirit. Let us not become conceited, competing against one another, envying one another. (Gal 5.19–26)

This chapter further interrogates the concept of the fruit of the Spirit and considers in more detail how a theology of disagreement can be rooted in this text, and what ecclesiological implications might follow from such a claim. I begin, however, by highlighting what might best be described as a Trinitarian deficit in contemporary Christian ethics – a general lack of rigorous engagement with the concept of the Holy Spirit at work in the life of both the individual Christian believer and the church. My proposal is that without a dynamic appreciation of the potential work of the Spirit in the midst of Christian ethical reflection in general, and in disagreement in particular, the church risks an impoverished understanding of the possibility and potential for God's work and inspiration as moral dilemmas are faced.

An assumed foundation for this work is the desirability of a church characterized by the fruit of the Spirit as described by Paul – not a church that suppresses or denies disagreement, but one which faces it in a context of the pursuit of a human virtue that seeks the well-being of the Body of Christ. In considering two examples from contemporary experience – psychological self-examination and scriptural reasoning – we will encounter two instances where our appreciation for the role of a theology of disagreement is enlarged as a result of interaction with extra-biblical theological writing. This represents an illustrative example of Richard Hays' 'pragmatic task' in action, where a New Testament ethic begins to engage with other sources of theological authority. For our limited purposes at this stage, such observations offer an example of how a scripturally-rooted ethic can be enriched through dialogue with other insights from living Christian tradition. Finally, such insights will be related back to the life of the church and the challenge it faces if, in its corporate life, it is to reflect the fruit of the Spirit even in and through its disagreements.

Examples of a Trinitarian deficit in contemporary Christian ethics

It would be wrong to imply that contemporary Christian ethical reflection ignores the work of the Spirit entirely, but we do have cause to reflect on why it is that Christian ethics, as a discipline that prizes autonomy and personal decision-making, nonetheless seldom seeks to identify or characterize the *means* by which Christians will draw inspiration as they make ethical decisions on issues small and great. Some initial contemporary examples serve to underline the ways in which appeals to the work or presence of the Holy Spirit are too often made somewhat in passing, if at all, raising more questions than answers. First, we consider a reference to the Holy Spirit by Brian Brock, written in the context of a consideration of the use of the Bible in ethical reflection:

> The use and inhabitation of Christian descriptions of reality happens in irreducibly particular circumstances and thus depends not only on a grasp of the systematic connections of theology but also on having been shaped into people who know how to ask for and discern the Spirit's appearance. This suggests a concept of the 'clarity of obedience,' which conceptually parallels the 'clarity of Scripture' in that both conceive human action as sustained by dependence in faith on the reliability of God's speaking. Faith in the clarity of Scripture is revealed as ethical in scope.[1]

Brock's observation that Christian ethical action occurs in 'irreducibly particular circumstances' recognizes that ethics needs to be able to speak cogently into the particularity of our lives; our moral reflection must have the capacity to make this leap from generalized teaching to inspiration in specific circumstances – including in relation to instances of disagreement. These particular circumstances require both an understanding of theology's 'systematic connections' and that we have become people 'sustained by dependence in faith on the reliability of God's speaking'. Here we find a rare appeal to the presence of the Spirit in the life of the Christian, held alongside an appeal to the authority of Scripture, within the context of ethical reflection. We might well wish to endorse the need for Christians to appreciate the systematic connections of theology, but my concern is that Christian ethics as a discipline *itself* too often fails to give a proper account of the work of the Spirit within its assumed Trinitarian framework. Brock suggests that authentic Christian ethical response depends on 'having been shaped into people who know how to ask for and discern the Spirit's appearance', but examining what this shaping, asking and discerning might mean in the Christian life is not explored further. Brock's emphasis on ethical particularity is important, but leaves questions hanging about how this role he identified for the Spirit is learnt and fostered within Christian community.

Michael Banner's work on ethical specificity echoes Brock's call for Christian wisdom to be applied to particular everyday circumstances. Banner suggests that 'what we currently lack and what we need is a coherent and perspicuous account of the practice of the Christian life, which would, in a space of cultural contestation, describe and sustain this form of life as a particular way of being human in the world'.[2] It should be noted, however, that Banner proposes a Christian ethics that engages with everyday specificity but without any sustained consideration of pneumatology. For Banner, the anchor points of the Christian life are assumed to be the Eucharist and historic creeds, but his lack of any specific appeal to the work or inspiration of the Holy Spirit in moments of ethical choice or deliberation risks impoverishing the scope of Christian ethics – and the extent to which the third person of the Trinity is understood to be engaged in the individual lives of Christian disciples.

This question of how the work of the Spirit relates to Christian moral action begins to find some consideration in Oliver O'Donovan's three volumes of 'Explorations in Christian Ethics', as he reflects upon how love becomes operative in the Christian life. He writes: 'that faith is "formed" through love is not in doubt – the formula goes back to Saint Paul himself (Gal. 5:6) – but that is not because faith is inactive, but because its active power is undetermined and unworldly until it is given an object to focus upon in love.'[3] This grounded appeal to love, rooted in the fifth chapter of Galatians, offers helpful ballast for our own observations concerning the foundational importance of this love that is a fruit of the Spirit in the Christian moral life. But O'Donovan seems less clear about the nature of the relationship of this morality to the work of the Holy Spirit: 'morality supposes life of a certain kind, life of intelligence, responsibility, and freedom which is, as Saint Paul has told us, the life of "Spirit." Even to pose a moral question is already to tread water, to trust our weight upon the element of Spirit.'[4] Exactly what this active trusting entails is the pneumatological question that would benefit from deeper examination.

Writing in relation to the Lord's Prayer, O'Donovan notes that 'it is for the Holy Spirit that we ask whenever we think what we are to do in full consciousness of the conditions of our agency. At the heart of moral thinking is a prayer for the coming of God to reshape our freedom from within.'[5] It does not seem unreasonable to suggest that a greater explanation of the relationship between the leading of the Spirit and the Christian's agency would considerably aid many readers. It is noteworthy that in the second part of his trilogy, O'Donovan does give some more detailed attention to the work of the Spirit, writing that it 'teaches us to reflect upon the moral instruction of Jesus, illuminating it for each successive attempt to understand, obey and communicate ... The essential note of an evangelical ethics will be missing if the freedom of the Gospel is not understood as life in the Spirit.'[6]

It can be suggested that a pattern we discern is not so much a total lack of consideration of the work of the Holy Spirit, but rather an assumed role that is seldom examined with a depth of scrutiny that is customary in relation, for example, to the authority and role of the Bible in the Christian moral life. Richard Hays is more straightforwardly explicit than some about his understanding of the centrality of the Spirit in the Christian life – but he too explores pneumatological questions with great brevity. We have already noted that Hays has a clear view of the contribution made by the Holy Spirit in the lived experience of the church: 'when the community suffers division, the temple of God is dishonoured. But the presence of the Spirit in the community should produce unity rather than conflict.'[7] For a theology of disagreement, it is the *should* of Hays' latter sentence that requires investigation. It is manifestly the case that churches that seek the presence of the Holy Spirit – or at least affirm its work in the words of their formal liturgies – nonetheless experience disagreement and division. One could suggest that Hays merely echoes Paul's warning that even those who recognize the fruit of the Spirit can become conceited and competitive. But the presence or absence of such fruit should not be seen in all-or-nothing terms; rather, the challenge of discipleship is, to use Paul's language, to minimize the impact of the works of the flesh and enjoy the fruit of the Spirit in return.

These instances of unsatisfyingly glancing engagement with pneumato-logical themes illustrate a wider trend – but it is also worth noting that, for their part, studies focused on pneumatology are often light on ethical reflection. Anthony Thiselton's magisterial *The Holy Spirit: In Biblical Teaching, through the Centuries, and Today* barely touches on morality or the ethical implications of life in the Spirit, save for a brief consider-ation of holiness as a theme in some revival movements.[8] For a theology of disagreement, this apparently mutual disciplinary antipathy may hint at why it is that disagreement retains such a damaging influence within the life of the church, notwithstanding a generally accepted sense that Christians should love their neighbour. If the Holy Spirit is as central to a fruitful Christian life as both Jesus[9] and Paul argue, then we should not be surprised if a lack of engagement with the life and work of that same Spirit results in a church that wearily accepts damaging disagreement as part of its common life. We will now consider Paul's conception of the fruit of the Spirit, and responses to it, in greater detail, before we then examine how the seeking of this fruit might best be understood both personally and corporately.

Fruit of the Spirit: ethical implications

Simeon Zahl notes the way in which Galatians 5 is 'an important locus for discussions of the complex relationship between divine and human agency'.[10] The ambiguity of the passage cannot be ignored, not least in relation to

> its curious combination of agencies … on the one hand, the Spirit as all-powerful ethical agent, whose presence renders gratification of the flesh impossible; yet on the other hand the appeal and exhortation to the Galatians not only to live by the Spirit but also to be guided by the Spirit (5:25), as if such things are at least to some extent in their power.[11]

Given the affective quality of many of the fruits, it is not as if their pres-ence can simply be willed in the life of a particular Christian – but neither can the Spirit override an individual's agency and transform them into a model of Christian love against their will. Zahl suggests:

> to transform a desire, as the Spirit does, is not to run roughshod over a person's agency: it is rather to engage and attract and reconstitute the very core of their agency. Our desires are not some separate force or entity, distinct from our true selves: they are a fundamental part of who we are as agents.[12]

These are important observations, for they begin to sketch how it is that the individual Christian, open to the power and possibility of the work of the Spirit, might cooperate with God in order that they might become more Christlike. It is worth pausing for a moment to consider how this might relate to a theology of disagreement. When faced with an instance of a fellow Christian taking a view different from our own, we may well easily slide into jealousy, anger, dissension or a quarrel. Meanwhile we know that a simple act of will alone cannot transform our response into a patient, kind, generous, loving one – particularly if we continue to disagree. The promise of the Holy Spirit is that it can engender trans-formation in those who seek to live by it (through a life committed to a deepening engagement with Christian faith, in prayer and worship, and in the fellowship of a church community). Invoking the Spirit generates change – in us, and even in those with whom we disagree. The substance of a disagreement can remain between two parties, but if that disagree-ment is approached with patience, kindness, generosity and love, even by just one party, it will be transformed. It is the work of the Holy Spirit that makes such disagreement possible.

Paul's notion of the fruit of the Spirit thus places pneumatology centre stage in the living out of Christian ethical commitments. As Frank Matera observes, for the Galatians, 'in light of the Christ event, the ethical life has been redefined for them. If they walk by the Spirit and are guided by the Spirit, the Spirit will produce its fruit within them, allowing them to fulfil the law.'[13] Seeking the Spirit becomes central to the realization of a recognizably Christian life. But the Galatians are also warned that life in the Spirit does not mean a life free of temptation – not least those temptations which would undermine the very fruit that is being enjoyed. As James Dunn notes in relation to the warning against conceit and competition in verse 26,

> Paul exhibits a shrewd insight into human psychology, as confirmed repeatedly in spiritual awakenings in the history of Christianity: those who claim to have been spiritually graced by the Spirit often assume an importance and authority well beyond even their Spirit-enhanced abilities, encouraging a spirit of competitiveness in charismatic mani-festations and provoking schism within the larger community.[14]

For Paul, it seems that any recognition of the power of the Spirit to enhance the life of the church must be held alongside a sober appreci-ation of the threats to unity that might accompany such intentions. In the striking immediacy of his contrast between flesh and Spirit, we encounter a close association of opposing forces that has long been of interest to both preachers and theologians concerned to locate a pithy summary of the unique challenge at the heart of the Christian ethical life.[15] Our contention is that it is possible to do something more specific: rooting the practical ethical outworking of a theology of disagreement in a paradigmatic appeal to the importance of the fruit of the Spirit. Specific questions about how the Spirit operates, and associated controversies, of course lie beyond the scope of this study, but our concern is to prompt reflection about the extent to which ecclesial disagreement can be transformed if those engaging in such disagreement do so with deliberate reference to the pursuit of the fruit of the Spirit.

Reason and experience informing approaches to disagreement

The fruit of psychological self-examination

Our consideration of how the fruit of the Spirit might be sought in the context of disagreement now takes a more personal turn, engaging with the work of the psychologist, priest and theologian Joanna Collicutt. She, like Simeon Zahl – though using insights from contemporary psychological studies rather than biblical exegesis – recognizes that the Christian seeking to live faithfully inhabits a tension between their own agency and the presence and inspiration of God. For those who recognize that they wish to live in ways more consonant with Christian tradition, the decision to embrace certain virtues, and foster certain habits, needs to be met with determination to sustain the new practices, alongside a recognition that the grace of God is an essential part of this picture. For Collicutt,

> the tension between allowing an organic and ultimately mysterious process to do its work and taking some responsibility for helping it along seems to me to be well summed up in the phrase "cultivating the fruit of the Spirit". This paints a picture of formation as a kind of horticultural or perhaps agricultural pursuit in which, like the flourishing plant, we bear fruit, but also, like the fit body, actively participate in the enterprise.[16]

Our earlier consideration of the interdependence of the vine in John 15 might resonate here; if our desire is to be a flourishing part of the plant, we have to develop the means by which we can appreciate whether or not our own actions are at least an attempt at something recognizably Christian. One of the spiritual gifts that a Christian engaged in disagreement might well desire is that of discernment. One of the key challenges

presented by instances of disagreement is the repeated inability of different parties to appreciate the ways in which their wounds might wound
others on the vine. From a psychological perspective, Collicutt urges
the development of self-awareness, but cautions that such work 'should
never turn into an exercise in navel-gazing. Its purpose is to enable us to
place our properly identified resources at the disposal of God, and to pay
attention to aspects of our individual and corporate personalities that
habitually get in the way of God.'[17] In relation to disagreement, we might
ask whether our own belief that we are right, or our apparent need for
our voice to be heard, leads to our engagement in disagreement in ways
that undermine the health of the Body – whether or not our arguments
turn out to be correct.

Collicutt also reminds her reader that joy can be an overlooked fruit
– but that a clear lack of joy can lie behind the ways in which some
Christians engage with others. We might consider whether such occasions
of joylessness can lead to unloving, tetchy, needling disagreement. She
recalls the joy of abiding on the vine: 'the first Christian communities,
secure in their identity as children of God, were marked by strong affec-
tional bonds consolidated through the intentional taking of delight in
others.'[18] Here, the pursuit of loving unity takes on a new dimension. I
am encouraged not merely to try and love those with whom I disagree,
but to seek out occasions of joy that might be shared, recognizing that the
pursuit of delight in the context of community results in infectious joy.
The shadow side of this observation is her recognition that the intense
sense of corporate identity among members of communities of faith can
provoke hostility to the outsider:

> We need to be aware of who 'the other' is for us, and bear in mind the
> research findings indicating that religious folk are *more* not less prone
> to out-group suspicion and hostility. Perhaps our other is the secular
> world; perhaps it is other religions; most likely of all it is Christian
> traditions that differ from our own.[19]

It may not be particularly encouraging to read that our hostility towards
the Christian neighbour with whom we disagree may be felt more
keenly even than any hostility towards violent fanatics in other faiths
or aggressive secularists; but this insight does further help us appreciate
why disagreement within the church can turn so toxic. In this regard,
Collicutt's appeal to the cultivation of peacemaking is of considerable
relevance in relation to a theology of disagreement rooted in the work of
the Spirit:

the spiritual fruit of peace and its making can be expressed in stillness and waiting; in holding a situation and calming conflict; in holding one's tongue for the greater good; in speaking out to name what is wrong or to challenge a lie; in adopting a way of life that silently but powerfully and influentially subverts what is wrong; in exhorting others to address an issue; in making a stand on something that has the potential to divide a community and, as in healthy cell division, enables that community to grow. What it can never be is putting a lid on conflict and hoping it will go away.[20]

This is a deeply insightful description of the range of responses to disagreement that could be made, none of which result in it being ignored, and all of which demonstrate the spiritual fruit of peace at work. Collicutt offers a window on various scenarios where the well-being of the Body is maintained – and even grown – while disagreement is faced. It is a vision of a church that can mature even through its instances of debate and disagreement.

Collicutt also considers the themes of compassion and reconciliation – though, for our purposes, it would have been helpful to read more consideration of the anatomy of a disagreement before her engagement with themes of forgiveness and repentance. As has already been noted within our own discussion, there is a wealth of theological resource available to Christians and churches needing to respond to entrenched conflict, but much less attention has been paid to the ways in which initial disagreements might be faced fruitfully. For Collicutt, a compassionate attentiveness towards others – including, from our perspective, fellow Christians with whom we disagree – is crucially important. It is only with compassion that non-retaliation can be practised. But embracing an attitude of non-retaliation means embracing 'the most difficult and counter-cultural of all the principles of Christian discipleship',[21] recognizing that it is not 'a minor quirky detail' of Jesus' ethics; rather, it is 'absolutely central to his identity and his understanding of what God was doing in reconciling all things to himself; and it sent him to the cross'.[22]

The fruit of scriptural reasoning

As we continue to seek to enlarge our perspective on a theology of disagreement, rooted in a consideration of the fruit of the Spirit, we have – through a consideration of Joanna Collicutt's psychological reflections – engaged with an instance of contemporary theological reason enriching an ethical enquiry rooted in the New Testament. We now consider an example drawn from human experience, as we engage with David Ford's reflections on the facing of disagreement in the course of scriptural reasoning.[23]

In *The Drama of Living: Becoming Wise in the Spirit*,[24] Ford reflects on what it is for Christians to seek wisdom in multifaith societies where they are forced to recognize that their own claims of religious wisdom or insight can be matched or contradicted by other faith voices in the public square. The emergence of scriptural reasoning has sought to promote mutual understanding and friendship across religious divides. For our purposes, it is David Ford's candid engagement with the disagreements that have also arisen as part of this process, and the ethical response such disagreement has demanded, that is fascinating. He describes the roots of scriptural reasoning being in his observation of a Jewish group of textual scholars and philosophers meeting together to engage in 'textual reasoning' of their own tradition: 'The intensity, the range, and the seriousness of disagreement – together with bursts of laughter – were an intoxicating mixture. It soon dawned on us Christian fringe members that we were witnessing something remarkable.'[25]

It is worth noting Ford's description of a context where members of a single religion were engaged in sharp disagreement but also laughed together in the course of the same meeting. We might infer that the quality of relationships among members of the group meant that both laughter and disagreement could be experienced together, without fear emerging about whether the group could remain intact. Ford emphasizes that the emergence of scriptural reasoning, bringing together representatives from different faiths in textual study, has particular value because it begins by recognizing the inherent human worth of all participants. The cultivation of relationships across what might in other contexts be considerable divides provides an important ethic of human relationship upon which the dialogue can be built. For a theology of disagreement, it is the way that Ford links human relationship and disagreement that is of particular interest:

> Learning of other traditions, beliefs, and practices from the inside, through face-to-face sharing, can give a quality of understanding that not only allows for recognizing similarities and agreements but also for improving the quality of irresolvable disagreement about dissimilarities, divisions and conflicts.[26]

Ford is candid about the presence of 'irresolvable disagreement' – and it is worth noting that he assumes the inevitability of such disagreement in an interreligious gathering. For Christians disagreeing together, a mutual call to pursue truth does not afford the luxury of accepting that disagreement is irresolvable. But even when Christians are prepared to work hard to face difference together, too often another of the qualities of scriptural reasoning identified by Ford is absent: a commitment to *improving the quality* of those disagreements. It may, ironically, be the case that a charitable disposition towards those of other faiths enables a quality of disagreement among those engaged in scriptural reasoning that can be absent among disagreeing Christians, who may have long developed a sense of frustration and resentment about the theological views of their Christian neighbour with whom they disagree.

For a theology of disagreement, it is the fifth of five 'emerging principles', described by Ford as maxims to guide the process of scriptural reasoning, that is of particular interest – not least because of its inescapable resonance with the fruit of the Spirit:

> *Go deeper into your disagreements as well as your agreements.* It is good when there are agreements across differences and these can be deepened. But there are always likely to be disagreements too; it matters greatly how they are handled, whether they lead to violence, hatred, bitterness, fear, prejudice, or alienation, or whether we find ways to improve the quality of our disagreements by patient understanding, respectful argument, and generous judgement – it is possible both to be good friends and to disagree on much.[27]

An initial observation is that these words can apply as compellingly to Christians disagreeing with one another as they do in their original, multi-faith context. It is an indication of how poisoned some inter-Christian interactions have become that it is from an interfaith method that wisdom for disagreement is found. On a foundation of friendship and an affirmation of the inherent worth of shared relationship, Ford emphasizes that there is a personal ethical choice to be faced when it comes to each individual's decision about how to respond to the fact of disagreement in the group. Each may well feel justified to speak in ways that deepen the disagreement and lead to it becoming more polarized and damaging; but it is also possible to apply qualities that recall some of the fruit of the Spirit: 'patient understanding, respectful argument, and generous judgement'. Friendship and disagreement can and should be mutually sustained.

David Ford's reflections on scriptural reasoning enlarge the scope of our vision as we consider disagreement among Christians. Among his concluding words on the topic, there is a slight danger of a utilitarian concern for practical outcomes: 'Alliances across deep divisions for the sake of the common good are probably the single most important element in enabling the realization of practical answers.'[28] But from our perspective, we should hardly ignore how the notion of the common good might be applied to the common life and witness of the church. It is, we might say, for the *common good* of the church that disagreements are faced more effectively; and from a Christian perspective, the 'practical answer' might be greater effectiveness in mission. Ford's consideration of the ethics of interreligious engagement thus resources reflection on Christian disagreement; it is work that further underlines the value of casting a wide net, beyond the Bible, in pursuit of wisdom that can inform moral theology – even moral theology firmly rooted in the words of the New Testament.

Seeking the Spirit, and its fruit, in ecclesial disagreement

Our consideration of the text of the New Testament in relation to disagreement led us to conclude, in Richard Hays' terms, that the discussion of fruit of the Spirit in Galatians 5 should have the status of a *paradigm* in a theology of disagreement. In seeking to undertake Hays' 'pragmatic task', we have brought this biblical paradigm into contact with insights from the reason and experience of the contemporary church. Having already proposed that Christian ethical reflection too often exists with insufficient reference to the potential work of the Holy Spirit, we now seek to ground this observation in further reflection on the way in which the pursuit of the fruit of the Spirit can offer a new paradigmatic foundation for approaches to disagreement within the church.

We begin with a final insight from David Ford, which grounds Christian discipleship in a context of the pursuit of love, within community, while resonating with Paul's fruit of the Spirit:

The Gospels make it clear that for Jesus and for his followers the point of living is loving. This is not primarily about introspection or self-cultivation but about long-term committed relationships in community, accompanied by other relationships (even with enemies) marked by love, justice, compassion, forgiveness and generosity.[29]

Our question is how the articulation of such aspirations moves beyond optimistic idealism and translates into lived communal reality – and the argument of this chapter is that a determined appeal to the relevance of the fruit of the Spirit can open the way to see disagreement always in relation to this spiritual seeking. Christian ethical reflection needs to find the vocabulary to reintegrate spiritual questions into the heart of the discipline; to do Christian ethics is not merely to seek after theologically plausible answers to moral conundrums, but to enable Christians engaged in moral reflection to do so in a way that is not divorced from the ecclesial and communal practice of their life in faith. If David Ford's assertion that 'the point of living is loving' is to move beyond generalized hope, an ethical framework for such living is required; an emerging theology of disagreement proposes that such a framework depends, for its efficacy, on a recognition of the place for pneumatology in Christian ethical reflection.

Writing in relation to questions about the future of ecumenical theology, Paul Avis cites Galatians 5 when he argues that a longing for Christian unity 'is undoubtedly inspired by the Holy Spirit and will be fulfilled by the Spirit, provided we allow ourselves to be led by the same Spirit, as the Apostle Paul urges'.[30] For Avis, it is crucial that Christians engaged in ecumenical dialogue recognize that the Spirit is present in both parties – and this insight is surely of equal significance even when disagreement or division exists within the same local church or national denomination:

> The Spirit who resides in us, in our expression of the Church, reaches out to embrace the same Spirit who resides in our fellow Christians and in the expression of the Church to which they belong. Just as Christ cannot be divided, his Spirit cannot be divided.[31]

The presence of God in both parties in a Christian disagreement subverts many of the strategies that might ordinarily be found in adversarial debate: if both parties take seriously the mutual presence of the Spirit, that theological reality must surely have a bearing on the ethical approach to disagreement that follows.

For Avis, this demands an honest appraisal of the ease with which Christians are content to see their mutual relationships undermined, not least as a result of suspicious caricature of one another. The challenge is for the church to begin to find an ethical framework upon which repaired relationships may be built:

> communion cannot come about until there is mutual understanding, rapport and trust. The Church, in which misunderstandings, distorted perceptions and competitive power struggles are endemic, is called to be a community of authentic interpretation, a community of understanding, a community of personal knowledge.[32]

As we have already seen in our thick description of Anglican sexuality debates, it is all too easy – even for those committed to the improvement of the quality of disagreement – to lapse into ways of arguing that are much more easily identifiable with the Pauline notion of flesh than with the fruit of the Spirit. A theology of disagreement needs to be able to resource the church in its determination to live with greater affinity to the latter.

The challenge, as so often in Christian ethical reflection, is to discern how it might be possible to move confidently towards an agreed aspiration. This book's very focus on disagreement seeks to highlight the moment of opportunity that often exists in the emerging stages of what might easily become a conflict – when it is possible, although testing and some-times self-sacrificing, to speak with patience and grace in pursuit of the flourishing of the Body of Christ as a whole. In his response to the chal-lenge presented by the fruit of the Spirit, Jürgen Moltmann emphasizes that any realization of the fruit of the Spirit in the life of the church must be received as gift:

> It is obvious that no one can 'make' this life, either through asceticism or through discipline. But one can *let it be* and let it come. The fruit of the Spirit ripens by itself. It ripens in us, and we ripen in it. The source of life wells up and flows of itself.[33]

The pneumatological reality at the heart of this ethical quest is asserted: for the fruit to become visible, Christians must open themselves to the work of God within them.[34]

Moltmann is clear about the impact that this work of the Spirit should have on the church: 'the community's life and actions are to correspond to the peace of God in this world of conflict (1 Cor. 7.15) and antici-pate them (Eph. 4.3) because the community lives from the peace of God through the Lordship of Christ.'[35] A focus on the call of the church to live in ways that correspond to the peace at the heart of God offers a help-ful reminder for this book's focus on disagreement among Christians, not least when faced in public settings. But Moltmann does also use the fruit of the Spirit to open the possibility for less peaceful engagement by Christians in the wider world:

> life in the Spirit is always discipleship of Jesus, and discipleship leads to conflict with the powers and the powerful of 'this world', and to the bearing of the cross. Separation from the powers and compulsions of 'this world' necessarily conduces to solidarity with the victims of these powers and compulsions, and to intervention on their behalf.[36]

Questions concerning how Christians seek to disagree in public with those *beyond* the church lie beyond the specific focus of this book. But just as in our consideration of the Synoptic Gospels, we drew a distinction between the actions and teaching of Jesus, here in Moltmann's words we are reminded that as the Christian engages with the world, occasions of injustice will need to be faced. The extent to which the Christian can justify departing from the pursuit of the fruit of the Spirit as regards the nature of their response in such contexts is a complex question beyond our remit, but it is worth noting that even when Moltmann envisages the possibility of conflict with the wider world, and intervention on behalf of victims, he does not expect that potential lack of peaceful engagement also to be found within the church. We are reminded once again of the Johannine emphasis that it is the loving unity visible within the church that makes it attractive to outsiders; and we cannot also fail to note that alongside his opening of the possibility of robust response, Moltmann also expects the church to bear its cross when engaging with the wider world.

Conclusion

At the beginning of this chapter I highlighted a Trinitarian deficit in Christian ethical reflection, and it is to this theme that we return as we prepare to consider, in the next chapter, how the liturgical life of the church offers a platform for the development of ethical life in the Spirit. David Cunningham proposes that a recovery of an appropriately Trinitarian theological outlook would involve three specific moves that would mean it is possible to: 'release the doctrine from its imprisonment within the dusty confines of the history of dogma'; 'render it more intelligible, to both Christians and non-Christians'; and 'testify to its profound significance for the shape of Christian life'.[37] For Cunningham, such a project would have inescapable ethical implications. He proposes that thought is given to the notion of 'Trinitarian virtues', which hold together a dynamic appeal to the work of the Spirit with appeals to Father and Son that might more ordinarily feature on a mainstream theological radar. For the purposes of this book, it is his reflection on violence and peace that is of inescapable relevance:

> Our sinful condition does not naturally incline us away from violence; indeed, it inclines us toward revenge. If we had retained the fullness of the image of God, as described in the creation account, we would also have retained God's peaceableness; but we have fallen to violence (a fall not only enshrined in the primeval histories of Genesis, but re-enacted daily among human beings). Peace can only be restored by God's gracious act of self-giving, through which we come to participate in the peace of God. In this process, God's Trinity plays a key role: in their polyphony, mutual participation, and non-individualistic particularity,

the Three form us – through specific communal practices – into a peaceable and peacemaking people.[38]

The damaging disagreement so often seen in the life of the church might
well be described as the beginnings of the violence that too easily infects
Christian common life. Too often, such violence is justified as being a
necessary element in the pursuit of truth – not least in contexts where
the truth at the heart of Christian faith is feared to be threatened. But
an engagement in damaging disagreement in such instances points to a
lack of response to the call of peace that is central to the communal
practice of Christian life. As we shall explore in the following chapter,
the challenge is how a celebration of peace in the Eucharist becomes
visible in the lived experience of the church. This chapter has argued
that without a refreshed pneumatological perspective, moral theological
reflection within the church risks being undertaken without reference to
the Spirit which inspires unity and invites disciples on a journey towards
peace. How that call to loving unity can be lived out in the messy particularity of human existence remains a challenge at the heart of Christian
ethics. With the fruit of the Spirit as the paradigmatic foundation of our
emerging theology of disagreement, we now move to consider the place
of liturgy within the life of the church, as the virtue-forming practice that
has the potential to reassert the importance of the pursuit of loving unity
in churches where such an ethical ambition is all too easily abandoned.

Notes

1 Brian Brock, 2007, *Singing the Ethos of God: On the Place of Christian
Ethics in Scripture*, Grand Rapids: Eerdmans, p. 259.

2 Michael Banner, 2014, *The Ethics of Everyday Life: Moral Theology, Social
Anthropology, and the Imagination of the Human*, Oxford: Oxford University
Press, p. 28.

3 Oliver O'Donovan, 2013, *Self, World and Time: Ethics as Theology*, vol. 1,
Grand Rapids: Eerdmans, p. 108.

4 O'Donovan, *Self*, p. 4.

5 O'Donovan, *Self*, p. 42.

6 Oliver O'Donovan, 2014, *Finding and Seeking: Ethics as Theology*, vol. 2,
Grand Rapids: Eerdmans, p. 2. For an extended discussion of what she calls O'Donovan's 'much more accentuated account of the foundational and transforming
role of the Spirit in the moral life (in and through prayer) than he had provided
heretofore', see Sarah Coakley, 2019, 'A Response to Oliver O'Donovan's Ethics
as Theology Trilogy', *Modern Theology* 36,1, pp. 186–92.

7 Richard B. Hays, 1996, *The Moral Vision of the New Testament*, New York:
HarperCollins, p. 34.

8 Anthony C. Thiselton, 2013, *The Holy Spirit: In Biblical Teaching, through
the Centuries, and Today*, London: SPCK, pp. 74–5, 329–30.

9 See our earlier discussion of John's Gospel, and in particular 16.13 and 14.17.

10 Simeon Zahl, 2014, 'The Drama of Agency: Affective Augustinianism and Galatians' in Mark Elliott, Scott Hafemann, Tom Wright and John Frederick, eds, *Galatians and Christian Theology: Justification, the Gospel, and Ethics in Paul's Letter*, Grand Rapids: Baker Academic, p. 335.

11 Zahl, 'Drama', p. 337.

12 Zahl, 'Drama', p. 343. Simeon Zahl has expanded this discussion of affection and the Holy Spirit, and the need for theological reflection on distinctively Christian spiritual experience (and the role this plays in moral formation) in 2020, *The Holy Spirit and Christian Experience*, Oxford: Oxford University Press.

13 Frank Matera, 1996, *New Testament Ethics: The Legacies of Jesus and Paul*, Louisville: Westminster John Knox Press, p. 172.

14 James D. G. Dunn, 1993, *The Epistle to the Galatians*, Grand Rapids: Baker Academic, p.318.

15 See John Riches, 2008, *Galatians through the Centuries*, Oxford: Blackwell, where the responses of Augustine, Chrysostom, Aquinas, Luther and others to the 'fruit of the Spirit' are considered.

16 Joanna Collicutt, 2015, *The Psychology of Christian Character Formation*, London: SCM Press, p. 95. This book's use of a 'cultivation' metaphor, in relation to the fruit of the Spirit, is thanks to Joanna Collicutt's observation here.

17 Collicutt, *Psychology*, p. 95.

18 Collicutt, *Psychology*, p. 105.

19 Collicutt, *Psychology*, p. 166.

20 Collicutt, *Psychology*, p. 154.

21 Collicutt, *Psychology*, p. 194.

22 Collicutt, *Psychology*, p. 198.

23 The process whereby members of different religious groups meet to study together their respective sacred texts, with the aim of deepening their understanding of their own tradition and growing in understanding of other faiths.

24 David Ford, 2014, *The Drama of Living: Becoming Wise in the Spirit*, Norwich: Canterbury Press.

25 Ford, *Drama*, p. 39.

26 Ford, *Drama*, pp. 100–1.

27 Ford, *Drama*, p. 46.

28 Ford, *Drama*, p. 162.

29 Ford, *Drama*, p. 57.

30 Paul Avis, 2010, *Reshaping Ecumenical Theology: The Church Made Whole?*, London: T&T Clark, p. 64.

31 Avis, 2010, *Reshaping*, p. 63.

32 Avis, 2010, *Reshaping*, p. 64.

33 Jürgen Moltmann, 1992, *The Spirit of Life: A Universal Affirmation*, London: SCM Press, p. 177.

34 The role of prayer and worship in enabling such responsiveness to the work of the Spirit is considered in the following chapter.

35 Moltmann, *Spirit*, p. 291.

36 Moltmann, *Spirit*, p. 154.

37 David S. Cunningham, 1998, *These Three are One: The Practice of Trinitarian Theology*, Oxford: Blackwell, p. ix.

38 Cunningham, *Trinitarian*, p. 248.

IO

Liturgy: The Place of Worship in the Pursuit of Loving Disagreement

My consideration of Richard Hays' approach to New Testament ethics has led me to affirm the value of moral theology that is rooted in particular scriptural texts; but I have also had cause to question the quality and scope of Hays' engagement with sources beyond the Bible. In this next chapter assessing illustrative examples of the ecclesiological implications of an emerging theology of disagreement, rooted in the New Testament but open to wisdom from tradition, reason and experience, I consider the particular role of liturgy in shaping moral response. Here my concern is to underline the need for a Christian ethic to be alive to the means of its adoption, as well as its teaching. Hays not only risks overlooking the importance of sources beyond the Bible to inform ethical teaching in the contemporary church; he also shows little concern for how it is that the ethics he proposes might be affirmed in and through certain practices of the Christian life – not least in the context of collective worship. As we shall see, through a reintegration of Christian ethics and liturgy, which remains open to the pneumatological insights of the previous chapter, it is possible to identify the practice of worship as having a key role in the moral formation that enables Christians to approach disagreement more fruitfully.

In the latter stages of this chapter we will examine the place of the Eucharist in Christian life, through the specific instance of the (often physically expressed) exchange of 'the Peace' in Anglican eucharistic worship. Exploring this as an opportunity, within a liturgical context, for disagreement to be faced and reconciliation found, we will also encounter some candid critiques of current shortcomings in this liturgical practice. Then, reflecting on the recent enthusiasm for 'improvisation' as a metaphor for Christian ethical living, we will affirm its place within liturgy as a means to enable the life of communal loving unity that grounds a theology of disagreement. First, however, it is important to establish how a New Testament ethic, rooted in a methodology similar to that proposed by Richard Hays, can begin to engage fruitfully with liturgical practice.

This is considered initially through an examination of narrative as the substance that finds meaning in communal acts of worship.

Liturgy as embodiment of shared narrative

Our concern here is to note that while narrative theology usefully offers an overarching coherence to Christian theological endeavour, enthusiasm for the significance of narrative in theology can also easily be accompanied by the same lack of attention to apparently irritating detail that we earlier identified in Richard Hays' desire to synthesize the New Testament and deliberately overlook seemingly inconvenient minority voices. For narrative theology, a considerable potential shortcoming is that a generalized appeal to a narrative shape in Christian life risks implying a rather tidier narrative context for the life of the church than might be strictly accurate. We might thus consider Alexander Lucie-Smith's conclusion about the relationship between narrative and morality:

> A narrative presents us with a coherent and accessible story, through which we as a community and as individuals come to understand truths about ourselves and our communities and the rules through which we live. It constitutes our identity to a greater or lesser degree and enshrines that which we believe about the world.[1]

The challenge for the church, and not least for those committed to moral theological reflection within it, is to affirm the significance of such a statement in relation to the overall narrative scope of the Christian story, without overlooking the importance of specific moments of unexpected detail and intrigue within that same story. A narrative can easily be transformed by a small detail. In the context of our study, an apparently marginal instance such as Jesus' engagement with the Syrophoenician woman turns out to have substantial significance in the construction of a theology of disagreement. If narrative is to provide a robust link between an emerging ethic and the liturgical life of the church, it needs to be able to maintain space for complexity as well as generality. But, as Gerard Loughlin argues persuasively, it is not as if we can abandon the Christian story. Rather, our task is to learn how to live effectively within it, complexity included:

> Christian faith rests not upon universal reason or human self-consciousness, but is sustained through and as commitment to a story. The story is not supported by anything else, by another story, theory or argument.

The story is simply told, and faith is a certain way of telling it, a way of living and embodying it; a habit of the heart.[2]

It is through engagement with the liturgical life of the church that this process of habituation occurs, and so if moral theology is to seep into the lived experience of Christians, rather than simply existing within a scholarly framework, it needs to widen its vocabulary so that it can engage as much in the context of worship as it does in academic debate. In our emerging theology of disagreement, the importance of an openness to the potential work of the Holy Spirit needs to be located not in theological abstraction but in the life of the church. As Loughlin observes, 'The Church is the community that tells Christ's story by being itself the continuing story of Christ; embodying the story of Christ in the circumstances of its day. As Christ is his story, so the Church is its story.'[3] For Christians to really *be* the continuing story of Christ, an openness to the Spirit is the means by which that continuation occurs – and will be guided and framed in acts of worship.

It remains notable, however, that narrative theology seldom considers the role of liturgy as a means by which the Christian narrative is both communicated and adopted. George Stroup offers a mere six-page consideration of liturgical context in *The Promise of Narrative Theology*, noting that 'apart from the recital of Christian narrative the sacraments are vulnerable to distortion and misinterpretation'.[4] His emphasis on the *recital* of narrative risks a narrow view of how narrative might be experienced within the context of liturgy; and his fear of 'distortion and misinterpretation' implies a concern for sacramental fragility. As we shall see later in this chapter, a call to improvisation in the Spirit can enliven liturgy rooted in sacraments without downplaying the importance of narrative. But it is through an appeal to virtue, as a bridge between narrative intent and liturgical practice, that we can now examine the potential for Christian worship to host the effective facing of disagreement.

Liturgy and the formation of virtuous response to disagreement

Questions concerning narrative and its relationship with liturgy cannot be divorced from this associated consideration of the place of virtue in ethical reasoning. If the inhabitation of the Christian narrative is deemed important, then the practice of virtue can help guide the Christian, enabling the faithful living out of an authentic narrative of discipleship. Our argument is that liturgy provides a crucial vehicle for such processes of virtuous habituation: an affirmation of the significance of liturgical context is essential if Christians are to be resourced to approach inevitable disagreements with the grace, peace and patience that we have already identified as key markers of authentic Christian response to the facing of debate in the church. Colin Gunton emphasizes the acknowledgement that needs to be given to the adoption of virtue, indicative of a striving for holiness which is crucial to the life of discipleship:

> Human virtue provides one of the central ways by which God the Spirit may enable anticipations of the end to be realised in course of the human journey, because it refers to the way settled dispositions to 'good works' are shaped ... it is the christological orientation which turns the moral agent outwards, away from self-development, to being conformed to the image of God which is Jesus Christ.[5]

This double insistence that virtue is a vehicle for the work of the Spirit, and should be seen in a clearly eschatological context, usefully demonstrates that a distinctively Christian appeal to virtue does not bring with it a self-sufficiency that calls into question the need for divine presence. Indeed, Gunton sees virtue as a way of moving towards conformity with Christ, with each virtuous act itself being a move of the Spirit. The important point for our purposes is the confident bringing together of virtue and Christian theology, and the recognition that the human decision to pursue virtue need not stand apart from the activity of the Spirit in the life of the individual believer. But Gunton, rather like Hays in his context, makes these observations without exploring the potential of worship as a space in which a life of virtue can be incubated. He does, however, emphasize the communal value of such a pursuit, underlining that the process involved in seeking after virtue should not become inward-looking or self-indulgent: 'virtues are not for self-realisation, but for the sake of the world. The Fourth Gospel teaches that the love within the community is to serve – its ulterior motive – the divine purpose of bringing all nations into the fold.'[6]

Although, frustratingly, Gunton does not elaborate on this nod in John's direction, we might usefully recall our earlier consideration of Jesus' call to his disciples to abide in a loving unity which, of itself, proves attractive to the world. It is the missionary imperative at the heart of John 13.35 that enables Gunton to remind us that John's concern for mutual love among the disciples is grounded in a desire to see the growth of the kingdom. For a theology of disagreement, it is a call that urges Christians engaged in debate with one another to consider the impact that such public disagreement can have on the visibility of the indwelling mutual love that should be characteristic of the church. We will shortly consider how liturgy can, in specific ways, enable the striving towards such a goal; but first we must consider two potential objections to our consideration of this sort of role for liturgy as moral formation.

The first challenge concerns what Gilbert Meilander has referred to as an 'unbridgeable chasm' – that gap between virtuous intention and fulfilment: 'the slow, laborious achievement of virtue requires imitation of those already virtuous, but imitation alone will never make one virtuous. We must imitate the exemplar by doing the deed in a virtuous manner. We can get to virtue only by first being virtuous!'[7] The implication here is that liturgy can facilitate and even celebrate mere imitation, rather than have an impact on the moral character of those involved. In engaging in a liturgical act, we might be seen to set our own personal morality on one side, suspended while we become part of a communal enactment. Such concerns are certainly part of the critique of virtue ethics considered in detail by Jennifer Herdt.[8] She examines the extent to which 'putting on virtue' is hypocritical, and is anxious, in the process, to avoid too sharp a distinction between Christian and pagan virtue.

Our argument is that to locate the pursuit of virtue within worship is profoundly to change the context within which virtuous formation occurs. An act of will was required to engage in the worship at all, but the presence and engagement of the Holy Spirit places the pursuit of virtue well beyond any notion of (merely) human endeavour; instead, the disagreeing Christian comes before God in worship, open to the possibility of divine inspiration that might transform their approach to the disagreement they face. The notion of sanctification can be helpful here, as we seek to root our appreciation of virtue in liturgical ground. Joseph J. Kotva writes that sanctification is 'a process through time, one's lifetime. It is a process (begun in conversion, justification, and faith) where one moves from the kind-of-person-one-is to the kind-of-person-one-is-called-by-God-to-be.'[9] An attempt to grow in virtue is not devoid of context for the Christian who makes such an attempt within the liturgy. Acts of worship constitute particular moments of intentional engagement with the God who can transform even a seemingly intractable disagreement.

The second specific challenge facing my assertion that liturgy inspires moral response concerns whether such an argument inappropriately instrumentalizes worship. Vigen Guroian maintains that *'the liturgy is not a tool for conscientization or moral formation. Moral formation is neither the raison d'être of the liturgy nor the final criterion by which the efficacy and integrity of Christian worship will be judged, nor the faithfulness of the church measured.'*[10] Guroian is concerned to stress that while moral conclusions may be drawn as a result of engaging with liturgy, the purpose of worship remains the honing of attention towards

God. It is not a time to be noted for its efficacy in imparting moral truths; its success comes when Christians are able to exist more fully within their baptismal covenant. For Guroian, this means that the eschatogical dimension of worship must always be given primacy, and it is only when Christians embrace the totality of what it is to worship God that they might also then see their lives being formed morally in response.

> The liturgy is not just one among a variety of authorities and sources for Christian ethics: *it is its ontological condition.* It is the principal dialogic encounter where God and human beings meet and the ecclesial body is knit together to form a single cloth of narrative, teaching, repentance and forgiveness, confession and proclamation, prophecy and doxology. This cloth is woven on the extensive frame of an eschatological vision.[11]

Although Guroian rightly emphasizes that moral formation is not the primary purpose of liturgy, his subsequent emphasis on liturgy being Christian ethics' 'ontological condition' does affirm, rather than undermine, the core significance of worship as moral formation. But we should also not lose sight of the way in which worship that is not intended to achieve moral ends nonetheless, in inspiring Christians in their lives as disciples, sees consequences flow from it that include practical moral responses to individual situations. Daniel Hardy and David Ford regard the relationship between worship and moral formation as one that is best understood as the response in praise of an individual believer, made in gratitude as a result of the graciousness of God. Having acknowledged God's power and love in acts of praise, moral formation is then seen in a context of awe – as the frail human attempts to live up to their divine calling.

For Hardy and Ford, ethical response is thus couched in terms of a realistic appraisal of the difficulty of living up to Christian moral ideals, but accompanied by a desire to find God in praise:

> Christianity of course has an ethic, but it is so all-involving and extraordinary that it can never be followed by setting it up as a duty to be carried out. The only way is to be filled with the Spirit, to be so taken up with the love of God that one can live with joyful discipline, extravagantly drawing on his grace and risking the shame of constant failure and repentance.[12]

Worship is seen as the way that the church reminds itself of the mystery of God in which its life is grounded; inspiration that follows – whether moral or otherwise – needs to be received in humility and gratitude. It is the Spirit, as promised to the woman of Samaria in John 4.24, that enables 'worship in spirit and truth', and it is this that energizes and enables the Christian to form moral convictions that resonate harmoniously with the traditions of the church.

Even if we are content that the two potential objections to our bringing together of liturgy and moral formation have been answered, we need to remain cautious about an attendant danger – that of an idealization of worship itself. The particularity and complexity of worship, including its being at times distinctly underwhelming, needs to be acknowledged; at the same time, any suggestion that worship constitutes (or justifies) a retreat from engagement in the wider world should be resisted. This is, after all, surely how Jesus intends his disciples' engagement with the world to proceed: resourced by the Spirit and sustained by their mutual love, disciples are to show this love practically to the wider world and not merely retreat into the practices of their own piety. The eucharistic and other habits of worship that emerge within the life of the church have value in their power to orient the worshipper's gaze heavenwards, but also to motivate them to play their part in realizing the kingdom on earth. Worship thus becomes a concrete way of expressing the narrative that Christians inhabit.

Eucharistic problems and the pursuit of meaningful peace

If such observations are to be applied fruitfully to a theology of disagreement, a specific context is needed. Within this chapter, that context is the occasion whereby 'the Peace' is exchanged during Anglican eucharistic worship. As Harmon L. Smith has observed,

> we are not naturally friends of God and people of peace. We have to learn to be the people whom God has destined us to be; we have to learn to be lovers of God; we have to be trained in the ways of friendship. And this, in part, is what a salutation with the peace of Christ intends to express and accomplish.[13]

Situated within the liturgical framework at the point after which sins have been absolved, but before holy communion is received, the Peace, 'borrowed from the Church of South India where it was introduced to overcome caste divisions, reflects the importance of the Church as the whole body of Christ'.[14] Our task, in the context of a theology of disagreement, is to ask whether it represents an example of the sort of moral formation that can, at best, be found in liturgical context.

This task begins by reflecting on a blunt assessment of the limitations of the Eucharist as a bearer of moral formation, within a collection of essays that consciously affirms a creative integration of ethics and liturgy. Michael Northcott argues that the role of the Spirit in worship demands greater attention:

> This recognition is an important corrective to the overemphasis in Catholic theology, at least since Thomas Aquinas, on the outward performance of the sacrament, as if the performance of the sacrament alone can act as a guarantee of grace and as source of the moral life. There is plenty of evidence from the history of the Church that this is not the case; nor does anything in the New Testament justify this over-objectification of the graced action of the Holy Spirit in the sacraments. The Eucharist was celebrated in churches whose patrons burnt crofting communities out of their homes at the time of the Clearances in Scotland, and among the communities of settlers in North America who oversaw the genocide of Native American communities and the violent expropriation of their lands.[15]

His list continues, with examples of German Lutherans celebrating the Eucharist next door to Nazi concentration camps, and army chaplains doing so on aircraft carriers bearing the atomic bomb. Northcott is not alone in wishing to highlight the seeming mismatch between the sheer power and centrality of the Eucharist as described by many Christian traditions, and its apparent failure to effect change in various circumstances where this power might usefully have been demonstrated. Matthew Myer Boulton argues that 'our participation in these proceedings, far from demonstrating our admirable devotion, in fact showcases our Christian hypocrisy, our only too eager efforts to pass off our thin commitments as fidelity and adoration'.[16] His concern, echoing Northcott, is that for all the seriousness with which Christians might participate in the Eucharist, and for all the interior spiritual benefit it might offer, any suggestion that it engenders moral formation seems questionable, as do those perspectives that afford the Eucharist an inherent power to shape moral response.

These concerns about the Eucharist as a whole find particular expression in relation to the Peace. David Cunningham points out that the way in which this particular ritual has developed risks undermining the clarity of the message that it sends to participants:

> Unfortunately, this practice has often been minimised. What was once a 'kiss of peace,' uniting bodies in an almost frighteningly intimate way, now often consists only of a tentative handshake and a mumbled

greeting ... even when these handshakes become hugs and the 'peace' becomes a fairly lively affair, it rarely brings us into contact with anyone other than those who are seated closest to us; and this is unfortunate, for often these are not the people with whom we most need to be reconciled.[17]

The problem with the Peace is that it routinely fails to represent meaningfully its moral purpose. Of course we must resist a temptation to generalize and instead acknowledge that this practice will be adapted and 'owned' by individual worshipping communities in varied ways, responding to circumstances and context, not least when public health considerations necessitate a cessation of physical touch. But Cunningham's concern is that in its essence, whether experienced physically or not, the Peace is too weak to function in the way that it should. He argues that 'the Church will function as the "school for peace" only if it tells stories and habituates practices that allow peaceableness to shape our lives'.[18] The concern here is that this particular practice fails to make an impact in the way that its liturgical form might hope. We are left to respond to a candid question: 'for how long (after the end of the worship service) does that peace really take hold of our lives, and become our "first principle"?'[19]

Cunningham's question is a striking one to consider, not least in relation to a theology of disagreement. The implication of the question is that the Eucharist might not be as effective in shaping moral response as either we might expect or the church might ordinarily claim; but if we are to avoid a rather blunt assessment of the efficacy of worship, it is worth us considering some of the context to such a discussion offered by Sam Wells. His work in this area is engaging not least for its determination to relate reflection on liturgy and Christian ethics to the life of unremarkable English parishes. He reflects theologically on ordinary and imaginatively accessible scenarios; his eucharistic context is not one of idealized order, but rather a frank consideration of the sheer variety of people, each representing different approaches to discipleship, who converge on their local church for this Body-constituting act:

> It takes all these kinds of people to make a Eucharist. Their gathering into an assembly is seldom an ordered, tidy process. Some will be early and others late, some will be noisy and others silent. But this gathering, more than anything else besides Baptism, gives the Church its identity.[20]

Wells suggests three 'gifts' whereby this shared, communal identity is construed: time, space, and action. It is this third 'gift' that is helpful for our purposes:

This specific action, eating together, bestows on the Church its identity, because it gives it a definitive practice. Learning to perform this action well informs and educates Christians in their performance of all other actions. If the Eucharist is the definitive practice of the Church, it is the first place Christians should look to guide their own practice.[21]

The rituals undertaken in church become paradigmatic for the ways that Christians then approach the rest of life. Even amid the near-chaos of a parish family service, the communal taking of bread and wine offers a transcendent glimpse of order which is intended to nourish the believer long after they leave the church building. In and through the habit of being part of a community that gathers in this way, Christians open themselves to the possibility of the Spirit's work through this intentional space where the normal concerns of life are temporarily placed on hold.

It is in Wells' reflection on an occasion of the sharing of the Peace that we find material of particular interest to our discussion:

One local congregation had a parish away day during which a litany of complaints, anxious frustrations, and a sense of helplessness about one aspect of the church's ministry rained down upon those responsible. That day, when the time came for the Holy Communion, the peace was shared without words – the simple handshake and holding of eye contact were a statement of trust and commitment and reconciliation after perhaps too many words had been said. In being able to share the peace after such a traumatic day the congregation rediscovered that it was possible to name the truth without fear.[22]

Although Wells presents this incident as an example of the efficacy of the Peace, some reflection on this anecdote is worthwhile. It is regrettable that the decision to exchange handshakes in silence is not explained; we are left uncertain as to whether this was a spontaneous corporate response to a wounding day, or a silence encouraged by the leader of the service. We might also note that although Wells asserts that the silent gestures of this exchange 'were a statement of trust and commitment and reconciliation', it is by no means clear that all participants would have agreed with this reading. We can at least ask, with some justification, whether here we find a ritual that can carry the full range of meaning it purports to communicate.

For Wells, it is important that the focus remains not on internal division but on the possibility that those present might have affirmed something that can then be shared more widely: 'The members of the congregation seek peace with one another in order to embody the peace they have found with God.'[23] It is a peace that, at best, is carried out from the gathered Christian community at worship and offered as a blessing in much broader contexts: 'The practice of sharing peace embodied and learned in the liturgy is to be extended into a whole range of relationships, near and far. Each member of the congregation asks how they can be a reconciling presence in the life of their neighbour.'[24] But in relation to a theology of disagreement, a simple question remains about whether we are fully convinced that the Peace as witnessed here really does have the reconciling potential of which Wells writes. If not, it risks being a ritual element within the Eucharist that enacts aspiration rather than celebrating spiritual reality – and as such, its impact is weakened. Elsewhere I propose that footwashing may be affirmed as a liturgical act that is able to convey moral theological content, and shape communal approaches to disagreement.[25]

Improvisation as liturgical response to disagreement

Our discussion of disagreement has highlighted the challenge facing Christian ethics concerning how it is that moral theology is lived out within the church, and also how it might be that liturgy can inform and enrich the shaping of moral theology in a way largely unimagined by Richard Hays. It is also worth us giving some consideration at this stage to the frequency with which contemporary theological reflection on liturgy's role affirms the place of improvisation. In particular, we will explore how David Ford's notion of 'becoming wise in the Spirit', in the context of improvisation, resonates with this book's concern that Christians should be resourced to face the particularity of individual disagreements, without excluding the possibility of the work of the Spirit and while remaining faithful to the moral priorities of the New Testament.

We should first note Tom Wright's now famous analogy of the Christian life as a Shakespeare play with a lost fifth act. He suggests that in response to this problem of missing material, rather than commissioning a fifth act, which would 'commit Shakespeare as it were to being prospectively responsible for work not in fact his own', highly trained actors would 'immerse themselves in the first four acts, and in the language and culture of Shakespeare and his time, *and ... then be told to work out a fifth act for themselves*'.[26] Wright's appeal to the importance of Christian disciples entering into the story of God, and using their own powers of discernment to decide freely how to act, is attractive. But given the prevalence of disagreement within the church, one can hardly imagine – however scripturally literate Wright's actors were – that they might be unanimous in their view as to how the drama should develop. His model captures the need for faithful improvisation, but without offering a worked model that can be developed and honed.

This chapter proposes that, at best, liturgy does offer such a model, and particularly when it is seen as moving beyond mere ritual re-enactment and viewed in the context of a lively pneumatology. This distinction needs to be made with clarity: it is not to suggest that ritual liturgy is inherently lacking an appeal to the presence of God, but rather that acts of worship in all their forms depend for their efficacy on an openness to the transformative presence of God. This requires an interior commitment of those engaged in worship; the Spirit that inspires moral action needs to be sought as the Christian community gathers together in praise. It is this distinction that is made by Gerard Loughlin when he encourages a move beyond both liturgical enactment and improvisation:

> Living the Christian life within the ecclesial community involves more than just liturgical enactments; it involves radically reimagining and resituating one's entire life within the story of Jesus, seeking to remove once and for all the line between acting and play-acting. This is why even the figure of play-acting, of performance, fails to grasp the risk and radical contingency, the open-endedness, of the play being enacted, the performance being given.[27]

The potential of liturgy in moral formation should not, however, be dismissed too easily. We might well ask *how* Loughlin intends this situation in the story of Jesus to happen if not through acts of worship. Although there may be a role for personal prayer or reflection, it seems unlikely that he wishes to commend a removal of corporate worship from the Christian life. Here we can usefully recall our previous discussion of the importance of a pneumatological perspective in Christian ethics, which can be seen as foundational both in and beyond occasions of worship. David Ford asserts both the importance of an engagement with the Spirit *and* the value of improvisation, locating this argument in his reading of the Gospel of John: 'not only is it thoroughly dramatic, but it also daringly improvises on its own sources; in addition, it encouraged further improvisation by readers as part of being led *into all the truth* (16.13) – what my subtitle calls "becoming wise in the Spirit".'[28]

Ford offers a framing for this improvisatory process: it is to be seen as undertaken 'in the Spirit' and with the intention of being led into all truth. Of course, neither of these two guidelines for Christian improvisation remove the possibility of disagreement, but they do offer a foundation for improvisation that moves beyond an assumed agreement on reading the

Bible that weakened Tom Wright's Shakespeare analogy. In relation to a theology of disagreement, Ford is particularly striking when he notes the way in which this sort of appeal to the Spirit, in the midst of the improvisatory nature of Christian existence, recognizes the particularity of each situation and the need for divine inspiration in the moment: 'Because both understanding and situations change, wisdom needs to improvise continually.'[29] This is not to propose a theological free-for-all; but rather to recognize that the Gospel of John, in particular, asserts the role of the Spirit as the guide for the life of discipleship: 'the Spirit both looks back to remind disciples of Jesus and inspires them in what they say and do in the continuing drama.'[30]

The point to note here is that anxiety about the authenticity of 'putting on virtue' can become exaggerated; the nature of the church from its outset seems to have pointed more in the direction of a fellowship marked by clearly articulated ideals but accompanied by a certain degree of pastoral tolerance – an aspect of ecclesial life that has, of course, varied substantially throughout the Christian landscape. But it is in this sense of committing the whole of life, including life's moral misjudgements, into God's hands that represents authentic discipleship. In this context, virtue is a means towards a holy end. In Colin Gunton's words, 'we become virtuous not by imitating God – though there is an element of imitation – but by being brought into a particular relation to God the Father through the Son and by the Spirit.'[31] This pursuit of virtuous imitation is given life and possibility in the context of improvisation in the Spirit, guided by an awareness of narrative that seeks to prompt theologically authentic action. The Christian facing damaging disagreement can glimpse a way forward in this improvisatory liturgical context.

Conclusion

Christian ethics, as a discipline, is interested not merely to identify moral theological teaching on specific questions but also to consider how such responses might be lived out by individual Christians and corporate church communities. In this chapter's consideration of liturgy as a tool for moral formation, we have explored some of the ways in which the liturgical tradition of the church can enrich a theology of disagreement hitherto shaped by the Bible. In so doing, we cannot avoid noting the lack of enthusiasm that Richard Hays' model of New Testament ethics displays for such a process. The proposal of this book is that a theology of disagreement can be built on New Testament foundations, but also needs to recognize the value of tradition, reason and experience in forming a theological response to the challenge of disagreement in the church. Our engagement to this point with liturgical themes serves to highlight that the creation of liturgical spaces, where Christians who disagree are reminded of the spiritual context in which those disagreements must be viewed, opens up specific settings within which the possibility emerges for disagreement to be transformed.

We cannot ignore the wider challenge implicit in such consideration, namely that sometimes clearly defined barriers between the practice of academic theology and the life of the church are removed – or, at least, partially dismantled. If our appeals to pneumatology and liturgy inform-ing moral response are to be taken seriously, then the place of spiritual practices cannot be seen as separate from the task of moral theology. Sam Wells captures something of this challenge:

> I am asking the Christians to take seriously the place of the imagin-ation in ethics and the need to train that imagination through corporate practices ... And I am asking theologians not to justify their work to the world as responsible but to offer it to the church as constructive play, play that perhaps comes closer to the reign of God than the earnest striving for ethical solutions ever can.[32]

Notwithstanding an unhelpful inference that church and academy are entirely distinct entities that seldom influence one another, Wells use-fully affirms that Christian disciples need to reflect on the practices of the church that might enable moral formation to occur, and that theologians should not be afraid to enter into such ecclesial and liturgical territory. This is precisely the sort of reflection almost entirely absent from Richard Hays' approach to theological ethics, even in the context of his 'prag-matic task'. But our argument remains that the worshipping life of the church, defining much about its common identity, can be regarded as a crucible for the theological exploration of ethical questions, and – in the power of the Spirit – as a vital location of moral formation. The practice of liturgy thus shapes the development of Christian ethics. And if our particular question of disagreement among Christians is to be addressed fruitfully in ways that engage with sources beyond the Bible, the role of liturgy cannot be ignored.

Notes

1 Alexander Lucie-Smith, 2007, *Narrative Theology and Moral Theology: The Infinite Horizon*, Aldershot: Ashgate, p. 11.

2 Gerard Loughlin, 1996, *Telling God's Story: Bible, Church and Narrative Theology*, Cambridge: Cambridge University Press, p. 33.

3 Loughlin, *Telling God's Story*, p. 84.

4 George W. Stroup, 1984, *The Promise of Narrative Theology*, London: SCM Press, p. 258. Stanley Hauerwas and L. Gregory Jones, 1989, *Why Narrative? Readings in Narrative Theology*, Grand Rapids: Eerdmans, also avoids any consideration of worship contexts. Most recently, Jacob L. Goodson discusses narrative theology alongside Christian ethics, but reflects on his academic context rather than considering the liturgy of the church as a vehicle for moral formation. See his 2015, *Narrative Theology and the Hermeneutical Virtues*, Lanham: Lexington Books.

5 Colin Gunton, 2000, 'The Church as a School of Virtue? Human Formation in Trinitarian Framework' in Mark Thiessen Nation and Samuel Wells, eds, *Faithfulness and Fortitude: In Conversation with the Theological Ethics of Stanley Hauerwas*, Edinburgh: T&T Clark, p. 228.

6 Gunton, 'Church', p. 229.

7 Gilbert Meilander, 1986, 'Virtue in Contemporary Religious Thought' in Richard Neuhaus, ed., *Virtue: Public and Private*, Grand Rapids: Eerdmans, p. 26.

8 See Jennifer Herdt, 2008, *Putting on Virtue: The Legacy of the Splendid Vices*, Chicago: Chicago University Press.

9 Joseph J. Kotva, 1996, *The Christian Case for Virtue Ethics*, Washington DC: Georgetown University Press, p. 74.

10 Vigen Guroian, 1997, 'Moral Formation and Christian Worship', *The Ecumenical Review* 49,3, p. 373.

11 Guroian, 'Moral', p. 372.

12 Daniel Hardy and David Ford, 1984, *Jubilate: Theology in Praise*, London: Darton, Longman and Todd, p. 143.

13 Harmon L. Smith, 1995, *Where Two or Three are Gathered: Liturgy and the Moral Life*, Cleveland: The Pilgrim Press, p. 101.

14 Gordon Jeanes, 2013, 'Eucharist' in Juliette Day and Benjamin Gordon-Taylor, eds, *The Study of Liturgy and Worship*, London: SPCK, p. 141. The biblical source for the tradition is in Jesus' words at Matthew 5.23–24: 'if you remember that your brother or sister has something against you, leave your gift there before the altar and go; first be reconciled to your brother or sister, and then come and offer your gift.'

15 Michael S. Northcott, 2011, 'Being Silent: Time in the Spirit' in Stanley Hauerwas and Samuel Wells, eds, *The Blackwell Companion to Christian Ethics*, 2nd edn, Oxford: Blackwell Publishing, p. 475.

16 Matthew Myer Boulton, 2008, *God Against Religion: Rethinking Christian Theology through Worship*, Grand Rapids: Eerdmans, pp. 217–18.

17 David Cunningham, 1998, *These Three are One: The Practice of Trinitarian Theology*, Oxford: Blackwell, p. 254.

18 Cunningham, *These Three*, p. 268.

19 Cunningham, *These Three*, p. 268.

20 Samuel Wells, 2006, *God's Companions: Reimagining Christian Ethics*, Oxford: Blackwell, p. 128.

21 Wells, *God's Companions*, pp. 129–30.

22 Wells, *God's Companions*, p.184.

23 Wells, *God's Companions*, p.188.

24 Wells, *God's Companions*, p.188.

25 Christopher Landau, 'News Media for Just Peace? Footwashing Making Headlines' in Jolyon Mitchell, Lesley Orr, Martyn Percy and Francesca Po, eds, *Wiley Blackwell Companion to Religion and Peace*, Oxford: Wiley Blackwell, 2021.

26 Tom Wright, 1991, 'How Can the Bible be Authoritative?', *Vox Angelica* 21, p. 18.

27 Gerard Loughlin, 1995, 'Following to the Letter: The Literal Use of Scripture', *Literature and Theology* 9,4, pp. 379–80.

28 David Ford, 2014, *The Drama of Living: Becoming Wise in the Spirit*, Norwich: Canterbury Press, p. xvi.

29 Ford, *Drama*, p. 25.

30 Ford, *Drama*, p. 22.

31 Gunton, 'Church', p. 227.

32 Samuel Wells, 2004, *Improvisation: The Drama of Christian Ethics*, London: SPCK, p. 219.

Conclusion

Movements that have drifted away from crucial elements in their founding narrative can – sometimes dramatically – experience a convulsion that prompts reassessment. The opening paragraphs of this book considered an argument that Britain's Labour Party risked, in government in the late 1990s, abandoning its foundational commitment to socialism. The events of summer 2015, with a once isolated left-winger winning the leadership after a general election defeat, underlined that profound change is possible (though it proved not to be politically sustainable). The church, through its own processes of theological self-examination, also has the potential to recognize moral failure and change its approach.

This book is unique in offering a sustained consideration of disagreement as a theme across the text of the New Testament. In response to the inevitable and continuing presence of disagreement among Christians, our argument is that a theology of disagreement, rooted in the text of the New Testament, has the capacity to remind the church that its often damaging ways of engaging in disagreement need not represent an ongoing and irreversible departure from the clear thrust of its founding narrative. In the New Testament, even though varied responses to occasions of disagreement are present, there is a constant urging of Christians to seek a loving unity through which others might then view the love of God – and this has inescapable implications for the ways Christians speak and act during times of disagreement, not least in the initial stages when a slide into dispute, conflict or even schism is not yet inevitable.

In this Conclusion I will review my approach to discerning a theology of disagreement from the text of the New Testament, showing how my proposed modifications to Richard Hays' methodology for discerning moral vision enable a robust theology of disagreement to emerge from those biblical texts. My consideration of the pragmatic task of engaging these texts with the contemporary experience of the church is described as a move 'towards loving disagreement'. This claim is viewed, finally, in relation to mission: unless disagreement is seen in such a context, it will be difficult for individual Christians to appreciate why it is that disagreeing Christianly is important.

Richard Hays' interaction with the New Testament, and the discernment of a theology of disagreement

Our engagement with the work of Richard Hays has affirmed the architecture of his scheme for engaging with the text of the New Testament, while at the same time proposing some modifications. We have, with Hays, affirmed the central place that reflection on the text of the New Testament should have in the formulation of a Christian ethic; but we also wish to see such reflection placed in a wider context that is fully open to extra-biblical theological inspiration and interested not merely in moral theological conclusions but in the ways in which the life and practice of the church might both enable and shape the adoption of such conclusions.

This interaction with Richard Hays has been centred on his fourfold task of scriptural engagement. His descriptive task remains uncontroversial, and we have carefully engaged with the text of the New Testament to mine it for material relevant to a theology of disagreement. At the next stage of the process, however, Hays' desire to synthesize – and, notably, to exclude minority accounts – risks denying the rich complexity of scriptural witnesses with which any faithful Christian must engage. His 'focal images' can become a methodological distraction, seeking to justify particular theological frameworks rather than enabling the narrative to speak for itself. For that reason, this book has proposed that Jesus' own summary of his ethical concerns, made clear in his articulation of the double love command, offers a more appropriate foundation on which to build a consideration of New Testament ethics.

Hays' third, hermeneutical task also risks an overemphasis on an attempted control of the multiple voices of the New Testament. His 'modes of appeal' to the text create overly complicated divisions, including one between principles and paradigms that seems difficult to sustain; but more significantly, Hays is determined that hermeneutics is a process that happens with a synthesized text *before* it engages with theological sources beyond the Bible – and with the tradition, reason and experience of the church. Our proposal, that such hermeneutical engagement with extra-biblical sources should form part of Hays' fourth, 'pragmatic' task, enables an appropriate arena for fruitful interaction between varied sources of authority in the life of the church.

Perhaps my most significant departure from Hays concerns the facing of internal complexity within the New Testament. Of course, such complexity will vary from issue to issue – but in relation to disagreement, any synthetic approach that implied a New Testament univocality would do so setting aside too many legitimate examples. Instead, my concern has been to recognize the consistency with which the pursuit of loving unity is articulated, and to consider how the pursuit of such unity might have an impact on the way that disagreements are faced, not least in their earliest stages. Hays' desire to synthesize leads him to varied conclusions – as we have highlighted in relation to homosexuality and divorce – that are fragile in the face of critique. Modelling love of God, neighbour and self at times of disagreement is not easy, but to apply a theology of disagreement to moments of emerging conflict has the potential to see loving unity maintained when a descent into acrimonious dispute might otherwise seem inevitable.

None of this is possible, however, without a dynamic appeal to the presence and inspiration of the Holy Spirit – a dimension of Trinitarian theology neglected not merely by Richard Hays but all too easily within Christian ethics as a disciplinary whole. While Hays is a strong advocate of moral theology crossing disciplinary boundaries within theology, he participates too willingly in what we have described as a Trinitarian deficit in Christian ethics, whereby the potential work of the Holy Spirit in prompting the moral decision-making of the individual Christian is routinely overlooked. While our assessment of the text of the New Testament did not enable us to arrive at a clear conclusion concerning how those who disagree might be disciplined within a Christian community, we were able to affirm the discussion of fruit of the Spirit in Galatians 5 as a paradigmatic text for a theology of disagreement, articulating a moral framework within which Christian disagreement should be approached within the Body of Christ.

This framing of a theology of disagreement with the pursuit of the fruit of the Spirit is complemented by the three rules that, following Hays' procedural guidelines, we have established as key to a theology of disagreement: *Let your speech always be gracious, seasoned with salt, so that you may know how you ought to answer everyone; pursue Godly speech, inspired by the Spirit; if it is possible, so far as it depends on you, live peaceably with all.*[1] In the midst of disagreement, when they risk caricaturing an opponent and seeking to exclude them from fellowship, disagreeing Christians are called to pursue peace with grace, open to the Spirit's prompting. This is not about Christian ethics delivering a right answer to the presenting question; rather, it is about Christian ethics informing the way in which a moral response proceeds, urging that such discourse happens in a way that is recognizably resonant with the core concern for loving unity found consistently within the text of the New Testament.

As we have seen, critics of Richard Hays have exposed a fragility in the application of his model, particularly in relation to its ability to deliver convincingly consistent answers to applied moral dilemmas. But such fragility should not lead to a dismissal of Hays' approach. Instead, greater care is needed about the extent to which conclusions can confidently be drawn about a unity of New Testament moral teaching on any given issue. In relation to disagreement, we have identified unanimity in relation to the *way* that disagreements might be approached, open to the work of a God who calls his people to live in a peaceable community that models something attractive to those outside it. Richard Hays continues to offer the most rigorous contemporary framework for careful engagement with the New Testament on moral issues. For a theology of disagreement, it is an approach that challenges the church to consider the quality of its internal relationships, and calls individual Christians to engage in disagreement with due regard to the well-being of the Body as a whole.

Towards loving disagreement

While Parts 1 and 2 of this book engaged exclusively with the text of the New Testament, Part 3 used illustrative examples to demonstrate the importance of Christian ethical reflection moving beyond critical engagement with the Bible in pursuit of a fully rounded moral theological approach to disagreement. The scope of our study necessitated a focus in specific areas, which responded to key subjects of relevance as articulated by the New Testament material. So, in discussing the church's public theological witness, its pneumatology, and its liturgy, we explored examples where insights reliant on more than the biblical text alone contribute to the maturing of a theology of disagreement that is able to engage with contemporary ecclesial life.

Crucial to these discussions was a close consideration of the quality of public speech undertaken in the midst of disagreement: the challenge of speaking Christianly was made clear. The unusual candour of the ARCIC report, *Life in Christ: Morals, Communion and the Church*, shed sometimes amusingly clear light on the danger of mutual caricature in disagreement. The ongoing challenge is whether Christians are willing to consider the value of gracious restraint when a dogged pursuit of their understanding of truth, whatever the impact on an opponent, seems irresistible. The public theological witness of the church will surely only gain credibility if and when Christians are seen to disagree in a way that does not equate with an abandonment of their mutual love; all too easily, Christian public discourse models the worst of mutual suspicion and rancour, as if the quality of internal ecclesial relationships were of negligible value.

The role of the Holy Spirit in such contexts, already affirmed in our engagement with the New Testament, was restated in a way designed to point out the value of extra-biblical engagement as a core element in moral reflection. Insights from the diverse settings of psychological self-examination and interfaith scriptural reasoning point to the important ways in which wisdom of value to the church can be found in perhaps unexpected places; such appeals to reason and experience have the potential to enhance the credibility of any Christian ethic that seeks to engage fruitfully in public. To deepen confidence in the Holy Spirit that inspires disciples to live in peaceful loving unity is to begin to believe that the norms of damaging disagreement can be transformed; this book has repeatedly emphasized that such transformation must begin in the decisions of individual Christians as they approach moments of disagreement.

It is in our consideration of the role of liturgy as moral formation that our emphasis on a canvas wider than that envisaged by Richard Hays is made most explicit. His biblical focus makes little room for any consideration of the virtue-forming practices that might enable a Christian to move forward in relation to any particular moral goal. It is, in the view of this book, essential that Christian ethics gives serious consideration not merely to the articulation of ethical norms or ideals, but also how they might be pursued within the context of the Body of Christ. In exploring the limitations of 'the Peace', we have affirmed the importance of reflection on the role of liturgy in giving concrete and even bodily expression to the aspirations contained within a theology of disagreement.

These explorations of the ways in which the lived tradition, reason and experience of the church can inform a Christian ethic serve as examples of the fruitful interplay between Scripture and other sources of authority in the pursuit of moral theological wisdom. Our explorations have begun to consider the sorts of new perspectives on disagreement that might emerge – if the church were to approach such disagreements in a way more clearly resonant with the foundations of Christian morality as expressed in the New Testament. But a question remains about the status afforded to disagreement, and here it is worth returning to our consideration of Justin Welby's commendation of 'good disagreement'. We might well wish to concur that good disagreement is better than bad, but a church that aims at good disagreement risks settling at a staging post well short of its intended destination. For as long as the church continues to assert that it is being led into all truth, disagreement should only ever be a means to that truth-filled end; the risk of an overly enthusiastic adoption of the term 'good disagreement' is the implication that so long as Christians can learn to disagree well, all will be well.

This is not to say that disagreement is unavoidable, or should be minimized; rather, it is to assert that disagreement should always be seen as part of the creative tension inherent in the life of the church. It is for this reason that the pursuit of *loving disagreement* is commended within these pages. It is a phrase that stands as a kingdom-shaped oxymoron. The world beyond the church might well understand the importance of 'good disagreement' – and our early noting of discussions in contemporary philosophy exposed the somewhat wearily limited hopes of Christopher McMahon's championing of secular 'reasonable disagreement'. But 'loving disagreement' makes little sense in a world where the maintenance of loving unity among those who disagree can seem largely irrelevant. It is within a Christian anthropology that loving disagreement has purpose, in a way that returns us to our foundation in John 13.35: 'By this everyone will know that you are my disciples, if you have love for one another.'

This appeal to loving disagreement is one that also relies on the importance of our appeal to the work of the Holy Spirit. It is the Spirit that enlivens this love in the heart of Christian believers; and it is this same Spirit that urges a focus on fruit rather than flesh, that offers the possibility that inevitable disagreement can move beyond factional infighting and the risk of mutually assured destruction. It is worth, at this point, noting the observations made by Stephen Sykes in relation to the presence of disagreement in the early church:

> The disagreements which the writers of the New Testament had to encounter are not accidental. Even if all these disagreements were resolved by identical solutions (which, in the light of the data seems implausible), it would still be the case that it was the very nature of Christian profession itself which provoked these disagreements. Internal conflict inheres in the Christian tradition, even in its earliest forms.[2]

Sykes' underlining that internal disagreement is part of the fabric of Christianity only enhances the need for Christian moral reflection to inform how such inevitable disagreement proceeds, and his comments also hint at the need for spiritual guidance at such times: 'authentic Christian discipleship, which is achieved out of the midst of ambiguity and with necessary attendant controversy, thrusts believers into a position of difficulty and danger where there is need both of guidance and of a power of discrimination.'[3] Perhaps tellingly, Sykes later refers to 'the extraordinarily elusive concept of religious experience'.[4] This book's contention remains that an impoverished view of the potential work of the Spirit, in relation to Christian disagreement, all too easily leads to the church neglecting a resource at its heart that could enable the transformation of approaches to the facing of difference. Loving disagreement, inspired by the Spirit, contains the potential to increase the church's ability to address controversial issues without inevitable associated damage.

Disagreement as mission in the contemporary church

Our final task is to reassert the context for this work. In John 13.35, we read Jesus' own assessment of how it is that disciples are recognizable. Through their mutual love, followers of Jesus can be identified, and in this love the attractive heart of the Body of Christ is revealed. In contemporary Western contexts, where the role of the church is marginal in many places where once it thrived, questions must surely be asked about the impact that damaging public disagreement has on the attractiveness of the church to those beyond it. The sentiments of John 13.35 can seem remote. And yet, as this book has shown, disagreement that involves point-scoring, mutual caricature and the denunciation of the Christian neighbour with whom one disagrees represents little that is consonant with the New Testament's concern for the maintenance of loving unity. Such loving unity matters because it is the way that others might see something of the truth of God's transforming presence. If a church disagrees as damagingly as any other actor in society, little wonder if it appears to have precious little that is distinctive to offer.

There is a certain irony that some of the most compelling articulation of loving disagreement has been found in ecumenical encounters that themselves seek to repair damage done by previous Christian disputes. The Anglican–Roman Catholic International Commission has been particularly instructive for our purposes, and it is worth us noting some final observations from the ARCIC process:

> In the course of history Anglicans and Roman Catholics have disagreed on certain specific matters of moral teaching and practice, but they continue to hold to the same vision of human nature and destiny fulfilled in Christ. Furthermore, their deep desire to find an honest and faithful resolution of their disagreements is itself evidence of a continuing communion at a more profound level than that on which disagreement has occurred.[5]

This assertion of a deep unity that transcends moments of difference offers an important foundation for the sort of bridge-building potential contained within a theology of disagreement. As the ARCIC authors note:

the disagreements on moral matters, which at present exist between us, need not constitute an insuperable barrier to progress towards fuller communion. Painful and perplexing as they are, they do not reveal a fundamental divergence in our understanding of the moral implications of the Gospel.[6]

Paul Avis, considering disagreement in ecumenical perspective, observes that 'in our reaching out to communion with each other as Christians of separated traditions we are actually being caught up into the transcendent dynamics of the trinitarian nature of God'.[7] To seek loving unity is to model something at the very heart of a God who exists in three persons; to give due account to the work of the Holy Spirit within this model is to regard ethical disagreement not as a challenge merely to be faced in human terms but as an opportunity to invite God's inspiration in the midst of the challenging reality of church life. Avis candidly concedes that optimistic aspirations towards ecumenical unity 'may seem a far cry from the actual behaviour of most Christians, in church history and today', and he refers to the debilitating presence of disagreement and dispute as 'a humbling paradox at the centre of anything we may want to say about the power of the Spirit in the Church'.[8]

The implied question at the heart of this study is whether disagreeing Christians are willing to open themselves to the possibility that God might wish to see his church disagreeing in a way that is more straightforwardly consonant with the New Testament's consistent call for disciples to seek to live in loving unity, responding to the moral force of Jesus' own articulation of the double love command. This theology of disagreement, rooted in the text of the New Testament, and shaped by my critique of Richard Hays' methodology, sets this question in a Trinitarian context, where the work of the Holy Spirit in prompting and guiding ethical response demands attention. The fruit of the Spirit offers a paradigmatic setting within which disagreeing Christians might face their differences, but without automatically undermining the unity of the church. Inescapably, public Christian disagreement has an impact on the church's mission. This book's emerging theology of disagreement is offered as a contribution towards the development of improved ethical approaches to the facing of difference within the church: an integral part of its mission, however ugly the expression, is to disagree Christianly.

Notes

1 Colossians 4.6; Matthew 10.19–20; Luke 12.12; Acts 4.31; Romans 12.18.

2 Stephen Sykes, 1984, *The Identity of Christianity*, London: SPCK, p. 21.

3 Sykes, *Identity*, pp. 25–6.

4 Sykes, *Identity*, p. 32.

5 Anglican–Roman Catholic International Commission (ARCIC), 1994, *Life in Christ: Morals, Communion and the Church*. See www.anglicancommunion.org/media/105236/ARCIC_II_Life_in_Christ_Morals_Communion_and_the_Church.pdf, para. 96 (accessed 16 December 2020).

6 ARCIC, *Life in Christ*, para. 101.

7 Paul Avis, 1990, *Christians in Communion*, London: Geoffrey Chapman Mowbray, p. 128.

8 Avis, *Christians*, p. 133.

Bibliography

Achtemeier, Paul J., 1987, *The Quest for Unity in the New Testament Church*, Philadelphia: Fortress Press.

Adams, Nicholas, 2006, *Habermas and Theology*, Cambridge: Cambridge University Press.

Adamson, James B., 1976, *The Epistle of James*, Grand Rapids: Eerdmans.

Althaus-Reid, Marcella, 2003, *The Queer God*, London: Routledge.

Anglican–Roman Catholic International Commission (ARCIC), 1994, *Life in Christ: Morals, Communion and the Church*. See www.anglicancommunion. org/media/105236/ARCIC_II_Life_in_Christ_Morals_Communion_and_the_ Church.pdf, para. 1 (accessed 16 December 2020).

Aran Murphy, Francesca, 2007, *God is Not a Story: Realism Revisited*, Oxford: Oxford University Press.

Archbishops' Council of the Church of England, 2014, *Grace and Disagreement: Shared Conversations on Scripture, Mission and Human Sexuality. A Reader: Writings to Resource Conversation*, London: The Archbishops' Council.

Ashton, John, ed., 1986, *The Interpretation of John*, London: SPCK.

——, 1998, 'John and the Johannine Literature: The Woman at the Well' in John Barton, ed., *Cambridge Companion to Biblical Interpretation*, Cambridge: Cambridge University Press.

——, 2007, *Understanding the Fourth Gospel*, Oxford: Oxford University Press.

Atherstone, Andrew and Goddard, Andrew, 2015, *Good Disagreement? Grace and Truth in a Divided Church*, Oxford: Lion Hudson.

Atherton, John, 2000, *Public Theology for Changing Times*, London: SPCK.

Augustine, St, 1995, 'Homilies on John' (59.5) in Philip Schaff, ed., *Nicene and Post-Nicene Fathers*, vol. 7, Peabody: Hendrickson.

Avis, Paul, 1990, *Christians in Communion*, London: Geoffrey Chapman Mowbray.

——, 2010, *Reshaping Ecumenical Theology: The Church Made Whole?* London: T&T Clark.

Banner, Michael, 2014, *The Ethics of Everyday Life: Moral Theology, Social Anthropology, and the Imagination of the Human*, Oxford: Oxford University Press.

Barrett, C. K., 1974, 'Pauline Controversies in the Post-Pauline Period', *New Testament Studies* 20,3 (April).

——, 1978, *The Gospel According to St John*, London: SPCK.

——, 2002, *Commentary on Acts*, London: T&T Clark.

Barton, S. C., 2001, *Life Together: Family, Sexuality and Community in the New Testament and Today*, Edinburgh: T&T Clark.

Bauckham, Richard, ed., 1998, *The Gospel for All Christians: Rethinking the Gospel Audiences*, Edinburgh: T&T Clark.

——, 1999, *James: Wisdom of James, Disciple of Jesus the Sage*, London: Routledge.

——, 2007, *The Testimony of the Beloved Disciple: Narrative, History, and Theology in the Gospel of John*, Grand Rapids: Baker Academic.

——, 2007, 'Historiographical Characteristics of the Gospel of John', *New Testament Studies* 53,1.

Bauckham, Richard and Mosser, Carl, eds, 2008, *The Gospel of John and Christian Theology*, Grand Rapids: Eerdmans.

Bauerschmidt, Frederick Christian, 2004, 'Being Baptized: Bodies and Abortion' in Stanley Hauerwas and Samuel Wells, eds, *The Blackwell Companion to Christian Ethics*, Oxford: Blackwell.

Berkman, John and Cartwright, Michael, eds, 2001, *The Hauerwas Reader*, Durham: Duke University Press.

Biggar, Nigel, 2009, 'Specify and Distinguish! Interpreting the New Testament on "Non-Violence"', *Studies in Christian Ethics* 22,2.

——, 2011, *Behaving in Public: How to Do Christian Ethics*, Grand Rapids: Eerdmans.

Biggar, Nigel and Hogan, Linda, eds, 2009, *Religious Voices in Public Places*, Oxford: Oxford University Press.

Bock, Darrell L., 2007, *Acts: Baker Exegetical Commentary on the New Testament*, Grand Rapids: Baker Academic.

Bockmuehl, Markus, 1998, '"To Be or Not to Be": The Possible Futures of New Testament Scholarship', *Scottish Journal of Theology* 51,3.

——, 2008, 'Ruminative Overlay: Matthew's Hauerwas', *Pro Ecclesia* 17,1.

Bockmuehl, Markus and Thompson, Michael B., eds, 1977, *A Vision for the Church: Studies in Early Christian Ecclesiology*, Edinburgh: T&T Clark.

Boersma, Hans, 2003, 'A New Age Love Story: Worldview and Ethics in the Gospel of John', *Calvin Theological Journal* 38,1.

Bolyki, J., 2003, 'Ethics in the Gospel of John', *Communio Viatorum* 45,3.

Bradshaw, Paul, 1992, *The Search for the Origins of Early Christian Worship: Sources and Methods for the Study of Early Liturgy*, London: SPCK.

——, 2004, *Eucharistic Origins*, London: SPCK.

——, 2009, *Reconstructing Early Christian Worship*, London: SPCK.

——, ed., 2013, *The New SCM Dictionary of Liturgy and Worship*, London: SCM Press.

Bradshaw, Tim, ed., 2003, *The Way Forward? Christian Voices on Homosexuality and the Church*, London: SCM Press.

Bradstock, Andrew, 2012, 'Using God-Talk in a Secular Society: Time for a New Conversation on Public Issues?', *International Journal of Public Theology* 6.

Breitenberg, E. H., 2003, 'To Tell the Truth: Will the Real Public Theology Please Stand Up?', *Journal of the Society of Christian Ethics* 23,2.

Bretherton, Luke, 2006, *Hospitality as Holiness: Christian Witness amid Moral Diversity*, Aldershot: Ashgate.

Brierley, Michael, ed., 2006, *Public Life and the Place of the Church*, Aldershot: Ashgate.

Brock, Brian, 2007, *Singing the Ethos of God: On the Place of Christian Ethics in Scripture*, Grand Rapids: Eerdmans.

Brown, Raymond, 1970, *The Gospel According to John*, New York: Doubleday.
———, 1979, *The Community of the Beloved Disciple*, New York: Paulist Press.
Bruce, F. F., 1984, *The Epistles to the Colossians, to Philemon, and to the Ephesians*, Grand Rapids: Eerdmans.
Bruner, Frederick Dale, 2012, *The Gospel of John: A Commentary*, Grand Rapids: Eerdmans.
Bultmann, Rudolf, 1971, *The Gospel of John*, Oxford: Blackwell.
Burridge, Richard, 2007, *Imitating Jesus: An Inclusive Approach to New Testament Ethics*, Grand Rapids: Eerdmans.
Cahill, L. S., 1990, 'The New Testament and Ethics: Communities of Social Change', *Interpretation* 44,4.
Camosy, Charles C., 2012, *Peter Singer and Christian Ethics: Beyond Polarization*, Cambridge: Cambridge University Press.
Cane, Anthony, 2005, *The Place of Judas Iscariot in Christology*, Aldershot: Ashgate.
Carson, D. A., 1991, *The Gospel According to John*, Grand Rapids: Eerdmans.
Charry, Ellen T., 2011, Preface, *Anglican Theological Review* 93,1.
Chennattu, Rekha, 2006, *Johannine Discipleship as a Covenant Relationship*, Peabody: Hendrickson.
Christensen, David and Lackey, Jennifer, eds, 2013, *The Epistemology of Disagreement: New Essays*, Oxford: Oxford University Press.
Cockerill, Gareth Lee, 2012, *The Epistle to the Hebrews*, Grand Rapids: Eerdmans.
Collicutt, Joanna, 2015, *The Psychology of Christian Character Formation*, London: SCM Press.
Collins, Raymond F., 2002, *I and II Timothy and Titus: A Commentary*, Louisville: Westminster John Knox Press.
Constantineanu, Corneliu, 2010, *The Social Significance of Reconciliation in Paul's Theology: Narrative Readings in Romans*, Edinburgh: T&T Clark.
Countryman, L. William, 1987, *The Mystical Way in the Fourth Gospel*, Philadelphia: Fortress Press.
Culpepper, R. A., 1991, 'The Johannine Hypodeigma: A Reading of John 13', *Semeia* 53.
Cunningham, David, 1998, *These Three are One: The Practice of Trinitarian Theology*, Oxford: Blackwell.
Davies, W. D. and Allison, Dale C., 2004, *Matthew: A Shorter Commentary*, London: T&T Clark.
Davis, Ellen F. and Hays, Richard B., 2003, *The Art of Reading Scripture*, Grand Rapids: Eerdmans.
Dodd, C. H., 1963, *Historical Tradition in the Fourth Gospel*, Cambridge: Cambridge University Press.
———, 1968, *The Interpretation of the Fourth Gospel*, Cambridge: Cambridge University Press.
Dunn, James D. G., 1993, *The Epistle to the Galatians*, Grand Rapids: Baker Academic.
———, 1993, '"The Law of Faith," "the Law of the Spirit" and "the Law of Christ"' in Eugene H. Lovering and Jerry L. Sumney, eds, 1996, *Theology and Ethics in Paul*, Nashville: Abingdon Press.
———, 2006, *Unity and Diversity in the New Testament: An Inquiry into the Character of Earliest Christianity*, London: SCM Press.

Edwards, Mark, 2004, *John: Blackwell Bible Commentaries*, Oxford: Blackwell.

Edwards, Ruth, 1996, *The Johannine Epistles*, Sheffield: Sheffield Academic Press.

——, 2003, *Discovering John*, London: SPCK.

Esler, Philip, 2003, *Conflict and Identity in Romans: The Social Setting of Paul's Letter*, Minneapolis: Fortress Press.

Evans, Craig, 2012, *Matthew*, Cambridge: Cambridge University Press.

Fee, Gordon D., 1988, *New International Biblical Commentary: 1 and 2 Timothy, Titus*, Peabody: Hendrickson.

Fitzmyer, Joseph A., 1998, *The Acts of the Apostles: A New Translation with Introduction and Commentary*, New Haven: Yale University Press.

——, 2008, *First Corinthians: A New Translation with Introduction and Commentary*, New Haven: Yale University Press.

Fletcher, Joseph, 1966, *Situation Ethics: The New Morality*, Louisville: Westminster John Knox Press.

Ford, David, 2007, *Christian Wisdom: Desiring God and Learning in Love*, Cambridge: Cambridge University Press.

——, 2014, *The Drama of Living: Becoming Wise in the Spirit*, Norwich: Canterbury Press.

Ford, David and Stamps, Dennis L., 1996, *Essentials of Christian Community*, Edinburgh: T&T Clark.

Forrester, Duncan, 2000, *Truthful Action: Explorations in Practical Theology*, Edinburgh: T&T Clark.

Forster, Greg, 2003, *The Ethics of the Johannine Epistles*, Cambridge: Grove Books.

Fortna, Robert and Thatcher, Tom, eds, 2001, *Jesus in Johannine Tradition*, Louisville: Westminster John Knox Press.

France, R. T., 2002, *The Gospel of Mark: A Commentary on the Greek Text*, Grand Rapids: Eerdmans.

——, 2007, *The Gospel of Matthew*, Grand Rapids: Eerdmans.

Frances, Bryan, 2014, *Disagreement*, Cambridge: Polity Press.

Frei, Hans, 1993, *Theology and Narrative: Selected Essays*, Oxford: Oxford University Press.

Furnish, Victor Paul, 1968, *Theology and Ethics in Paul*, Nashville: Abingdon Press.

——, 1972, *The Love Command in the New Testament*, Nashville: Abingdon Press.

——, 2005, 'Foreword' in Michael Cullinan, *Victor Paul Furnish's Theology of Ethics in Saint Paul: An Ethic of Transforming Grace*, Rome: Editiones Academiae Alfonsianae.

Gagnon, Robert, 2001, *The Bible and Homosexual Practice*, Nashville: Abingdon Press.

Gaillardetz, Richard, 2008, *Ecclesiology for a Global Church*, New York: Orbis Books.

Goodson, Jacob L., 2015, *Narrative Theology and the Hermeneutical Virtues*, Lanham: Lexington Books.

Green, Garrett, ed., 1987, *Scriptural Authority and Narrative Interpretation*, Philadelphia: Fortress Press.

Grisez, Germain, 1983, *The Way of the Lord Jesus*, Chicago: Franciscan Herald Press.

Groves, Phil and Parry Jones, Angharad, 2014, *Living Reconciliation*, London: SPCK.

Gunton, Colin, 2000, 'The Church as a School of Virtue? Human Formation in Trinitarian Framework' in Mark Thiessen Nation and Samuel Wells, eds, *Faithfulness and Fortitude: In Conversation with the Theological Ethics of Stanley Hauerwas*, Edinburgh: T&T Clark.

Gunton, Colin and Hardy, Daniel, eds, 1989, *On Being the Church: Essays on the Christian Community*, Edinburgh: T&T Clark.

Guroian, Vigen, 1997, 'Moral Formation and Christian Worship', *The Ecumenical Review* 49,3 (July).

Gustafson, J. M., 1970, 'The Place of Scripture in Christian Ethics: A Methodological Study', *Interpretation* 24,4.

Hardy, Daniel and Ford, David, 1984, *Jubilate: Theology in Praise*, London: Darton, Longman and Todd.

Harries, Richard, 2004, 'Article Review', *Scottish Journal of Theology* 51,1.

Hart, Trevor and Guthrie, Steven, eds, 2007, *Faithful Performances: Enacting Christian Tradition*, Aldershot: Ashgate.

Hauerwas, Stanley, 1981, *A Community of Character: Toward a Constructive Christian Social Ethic*, Notre Dame: University of Notre Dame Press.

——, 1981, *Vision and Virtue: Essays in Christian Ethical Reflection*, Notre Dame: University of Notre Dame Press.

——, 1984, *The Peaceable Kingdom*, London: SCM Press.

——, 1994, *Character and the Christian Life: A Study in Theological Ethics*, Notre Dame: University of Notre Dame Press.

——, 2002, *With the Grain of the Universe: the Church's Witness and Natural Theology*, London: SCM Press.

——, 2006, *Matthew*, London: SCM Press.

——, 2011, *Learning to Speak Christian*, London: SCM Press.

Hauerwas, Stanley and Burrell, David, 1989, 'From System to Story: An Alternative Pattern for Rationality in Ethics' in Stanley Hauerwas and L. Gregory Jones, eds, *Why Narrative? Readings in Narrative Theology*, Grand Rapids: Eerdmans.

Hauerwas, Stanley and Jones, L. Gregory, 1989, *Why Narrative? Readings in Narrative Theology*, Grand Rapids: Eerdmans.

Hauerwas, Stanley and Wells, Samuel, eds, 2011 [2004], *The Blackwell Companion to Christian Ethics*, 2nd edn, Oxford: Blackwell.

Hays, Richard B., 1996, *The Moral Vision of the New Testament*, New York: HarperCollins.

——, 2009, 'Introduction to Victor Paul Furnish, *Theology and Ethics in Paul*' in Victor Paul Furnish, *Theology and Ethics in Paul*, Louisville: Westminster John Knox Press.

——, 2010, 'Response to Richard Burridge, *Imitating Jesus*', *Scottish Journal of Theology* 63,3.

Herdt, Jennifer, 2008, *Putting on Virtue: The Legacy of the Splendid Vices*, Chicago: Chicago University Press.

Holmes, Stephen, 2008, *Public Theology in Cultural Engagement*, Milton Keynes: Paternoster Press.

Hooker, Morna, 1991, *The Gospel According to Mark*, London: Continuum.

Horrell, David G., 1998, *The Epistles of Peter and Jude*, Peterborough: Epworth Press.

——, 2005, *Solidarity and Difference: A Contemporary Reading of Paul's Ethics*, London: T&T Clark.

Hultgren, Arland, 2011, *Paul's Letter to the Romans: A Commentary*, Grand Rapids: Eerdmans.

Hütter, Reinhard and Dieter, Theodor, 1998, *Ecumenical Ventures in Ethics: Protestants Engage Pope John Paul II's Moral Encyclicals*, Grand Rapids: Eerdmans.

Isaacs, Marie E., 2002, *Reading Hebrews and James: A Literary and Theological Commentary*, Macon: Smyth & Helwys.

Isherwood, Lisa and Cornwall, Susannah, eds, 2009, *Controversies in Queer Theology*, London: SCM Press.

Iverson, Kelly, 2007, *Gentiles in the Gospel of Mark*, London: T&T Clark.

Jeanes, Gordon, 2013, 'Eucharist' in Juliette Day and Benjamin Gordon-Taylor, eds, *The Study of Liturgy and Worship*, London: SPCK.

John, Jeffrey, 2012 [2000], *'Permanent, Faithful, Stable': Christian Same-sex Partnerships*, rev. edn, London: Darton, Longman and Todd.

John Paul II, 1995, *Ut Unum Sint*, London: Catholic Truth Society.

Kallenberg, B. J., 2004, 'The Strange New World in the Church', *Journal of Religious Ethics* 32,1.

Kaye, B., 2008, 'Communication, Argument and Conversation for Anglicans', *Journal of Anglican Studies* 6,2.

Keener, Craig S., 2005, *1–2 Corinthians*, Cambridge: Cambridge University Press.

Kim, Sebastian, 2011, Editorial, *International Journal of Public Theology* 1,1–4.

——, 2011, *Theology in the Public Sphere: Public Theology as a Catalyst for Open Debate*, London: SCM Press.

Kirkpatrick, Frank G., 2001, *The Ethics of Community*, Oxford: Blackwell.

Kotva, Joseph J., 1996, *The Christian Case for Virtue Ethics*, Washington DC: Georgetown University Press.

Kruse, Colin, 2012, *Paul's Letter to the Romans*, Nottingham: Apollos.

Lane, William L., 1974, *The Gospel According to Mark*, London: Marshall, Morgan & Scott.

Lieu, Judith, 1991, *The Theology of the Johannine Epistles*, Cambridge: Cambridge University Press.

——, 2008, *I, II & III John: A Commentary*, Louisville : Westminster John Knox Press.

Lindars, Barnabas, Edwards, Ruth B. and Court, John M., 2000, *The Johannine Literature*, Sheffield: Sheffield Academic Press.

Linzey Andrew, and Kirker, Richard, eds, 2005, *Gays and the Future of Anglicanism*, Winchester: O Books.

Lohse, Eduard, 1991, *Theological Ethics of the New Testament*, Minneapolis: Fortress Press.

Longenecker, Richard, 1995, *The Expositor's Bible Commentary: Acts*, Grand Rapids: Zondervan.

Loughlin, Gerard, 1995, 'Following to the Letter: The Literal Use of Scripture', *Literature and Theology* 9,4 (December).

——, 1996, *Telling God's Story: Bible, Church and Narrative Theology*, Cambridge: Cambridge University Press.

——, ed., 2007, *Queer Theology: Rethinking the Western Body*, Oxford: Blackwell.

Lucie-Smith, Alexander, 2007, *Narrative Theology and Moral Theology: The Infinite Horizon*, Aldershot: Ashgate.

Luther, Susanne, Van der Watt, Jan Gabriël and Zimmermann, Ruben, eds, 2010, *Moral Language in the New Testament: The Interrelatedness of Language and Ethics in Early Christian Writings*, Tübingen: Mohr Siebeck.

MacIntyre, Alastair, 2007, *After Virtue*, 3rd edn, London: Duckworth.

Macquarrie, John, 1975, *Christian Unity and Christian Diversity*, London: SCM Press.

Martin, Dale, 1998, 'Review of Hays, *The Moral Vision of the New Testament*', *Journal of Biblical Literature* 117,2.

Martyn, J. Louis, 2003, *History and Theology in the Fourth Gospel*, 3rd edn, Louisville: Westminster John Knox.

Matera, Frank J., 1996, *New Testament Ethics: The Legacies of Jesus and Paul*, Louisville: Westminster John Knox Press.

——, 2003, *II Corinthians: A Commentary* (Louisville: Westminster John Knox Press.

Matheson, Jonathan, 2015, *The Epistemic Significance of Disagreement*, Basingstoke: Palgrave Macmillan.

McCall, Richard D., 2007, *Do This: Liturgy as Performance*, Notre Dame: University of Notre Dame Press.

McIntosh, Mark, 2010, 'Review of *God Is Not a Story: Realism Revisited* by Francesca Aran Murphy', *The Journal of Religion* 90,1 (January).

McMahon, Christopher, 2009, *Reasonable Disagreement: A Theory of Political Morality*, Cambridge: Cambridge University Press.

Meeks, Wayne A., 1993, *The Origins of Christian Morality: The First Two Centuries*, New Haven and London: Yale University Press.

Meilander, Gilbert, 1986, 'Virtue in Contemporary Religious Thought' in Richard Neuhaus, ed., *Virtue: Public and Private*, Grand Rapids: Eerdmans.

——, 2010, 'Review of Jennifer Herdt, *Putting on Virtue: The Legacy of the Splendid Vices* in Studies', *Christian Ethics* 23,1.

Mendieta, Eduardo and Vanantwerpen, Jonathan, eds, 2011, *The Power of Religion in the Public* Sphere, New York: Columbia University Press.

Meye Thompson, Marianne, 2001, *The God of the Gospel of John*, Grand Rapids: Eerdmans.

——, 2003, '"His Own Received Him Not": Jesus Washes the Feet of His Disciples' in Ellen David and Richard Hays, eds, *The Art of Reading Scripture*, Grand Rapids: Eerdmans.

Moltmann, Jürgen, 1992, *The Spirit of Life: A Universal Affirmation*, London: SCM Press.

Monti, Joseph, 1995, *Arguing about Sex: The Rhetoric of Christian Sexual Morality*, Albany: State University of New York Press.

Moo, Douglas J., 2000, *The Letter of James*, Leicester: Apollos.

Moody Smith, D., 1987, *Johannine Christianity: Essays on its Setting, Sources and Theology*, London: Continuum.

——, 1995, *The Theology of the Gospel of John*, Cambridge: Cambridge University Press.

Mott, S. C., 1987, 'The Use of the New Testament for Social Ethics', *Journal of Religious Ethics* 15,2.

Mudge, Lewis, 1998, *The Church as Moral Community*, New York: Continuum.

Muers, Rachel, 2004, *Keeping God's Silence: Towards a Theological Ethics of Communication*, Oxford: Blackwell.

Myer Boulton, Matthew, 2008, *God against Religion: Rethinking Christian Theology through Worship*, Grand Rapids: Eerdmans.

Neyrey, Jerome, 2009, *The Gospel of John in Cultural and Rhetorical Perspective*, Grand Rapids: Eerdmans.

Niebuhr, Reinhold, 1936, *An Interpretation of Christian Ethics*, London: SCM Press.

——, 1957, *Love and Justice*, Louisville: Westminster John Knox Press.

Northcott, Michael S., 2011, 'Being Silent: Time in the Spirit' in Stanley Hauerwas and Samuel Wells, eds, *The Blackwell Companion to Christian Ethics*, 2nd edn, Oxford: Blackwell.

Nygren, Anders, 1953, *Agape and Eros*, London: SPCK.

O'Donovan, Oliver, 1996, *The Desire of the Nations*, Cambridge: Cambridge University Press.

——, 2002, 'Homosexuality in the Church: Can there be a Fruitful Theological Debate?' in Eugene Rogers, ed., *Theology and Sexuality*, Oxford: Blackwell.

——, 2005, *The Ways of Judgement*, Grand Rapids: Eerdmans.

——, 2013, *Self, World and Time: Ethics as Theology*, vol. 1, Grand Rapids: Eerdmans.

——, 2014, *Finding and Seeking: Ethics as Theology*, vol. 2, Grand Rapids: Eerdmans.

O'Loughlin, Thomas, 2010, *The Didache: A Window on the Earliest Christians*, London: SPCK.

——, 2015, *Washing Feet: Imitating the Example of Jesus in the Liturgy Today*, Collegeville: Liturgical Press.

Ozanne, Jayne, ed., 2016, *Journeys in Grace and Truth: Revisiting Scripture and Sexuality*, London: Ekklesia.

Pelikan, Jaroslav, 2006, *Acts*, London: SCM Press.

——, 2009, *A Conversation Waiting to Begin: The Churches and the Gay Controversy*, London: SCM Press.

Percy, Martyn, 1998, *Power and the Church: Ecclesiology in an Age of Transition*, London: Cassell.

——, 1999, *Introducing Richard Hooker and the laws of Ecclesiastical Polity*, London: Darton, Longman and Todd.

Perry, John, 2010, 'Gentiles and Homosexuals: A Brief History of an Analogy', *Journal of Religious Ethics* 38,2 (June).

——, 2012, 'Vocation and Creation: Beyond the Gentile-Homosexual Analogy', *Journal of Religious Ethics* 40,2 (June).

Porter, Jean, 1995, *Moral Action and Christian Ethics*, Cambridge: Cambridge University Press.

——, 1997, 'Mere History: The Place of Historical Studies in Theological Ethics', *Journal of Religious Ethics* 25,3.

Pryor, John W., 1992, *John, Evangelist of the Covenant People: the Narrative and Themes of the Fourth Gospel*, London: Darton, Longman and Todd.

Puglisi, James F., 2005, *Liturgical Renewal as a Way to Christian Unity*, Collegeville: Liturgical Press.

Quinn, Jerome D., 1990, *The Letter to Titus*, New Haven and London: Yale University Press.

Ramsey, Paul, 1965, *Deeds and Rules in Christian Ethics*, Edinburgh: Oliver & Boyd.

Riches, John, 2008, *Galatians through the Centuries*, Oxford: Blackwell.

Root, Michael, 2012, 'Ethics in Ecumenical Dialogues: A Survey and Analysis' in Michael Root and James Buckley, eds, *The Morally Divided Body: Ethical Disagreement and the Disunity of the Church*, Eugene: Cascade Books.

Ross, Melanie and Jones, Simon, 2010, *The Serious Business of Worship: Essays in Honour of Bryan D. Spinks*, London: T&T Clark.

Sanders, Jack T., 1986, *Ethics in the New Testament*, London: SCM Press.

Schnackenburg, Rudolf, 1965, *The Moral Teaching of the New Testament*, Freiburg: Herder.

——, 1982, *The Gospel According to St John*, Tunbridge Wells: Burns & Oates.

Schrage, Wolfgang, 1988, *The Ethics of the New Testament*, Edinburgh: T&T Clark.

Scroggs, Robin, 1996, 'Paul and the Eschatological Body' in Eugene H. Lovering and Jerry L. Sumney, eds, *Theology and Ethics in Paul and His Interpreters*, Nashville: Abingdon Press.

Smalley, Stephen, 1998, *John – Evangelist and Interpreter*, Carlisle: Paternoster Press.

Smith, Harmon L., 1995, *Where Two or Three are Gathered: Liturgy and the Moral Life*, Cleveland: The Pilgrim Press.

Song, Robert, 2014, *Covenant and Calling: Towards a Theology of Same-Sex Relationships*, London: SCM Press.

Stevenson, Kenneth, ed., 1982, *Liturgy Reshaped*, London: SPCK.

Stibbe, Mark, 1992, *John as Storyteller: Narrative Criticism and the Fourth Gospel*, Cambridge: Cambridge University Press.

Stroup, George W., 1981, *The Promise of Narrative Theology*, London: SCM Press.

Struthers Malborn, Elizabeth, 2000, *In the Company of Jesus: Characters in Mark's Gospel*, London: Westminster John Knox Press.

Sumney, Jerry L., 2008, *Colossians*, Louisville: Presbyterian Publishing Corporation.

Swartley, Willard, 2006, *Covenant of Peace: The Missing Peace in New Testament Theology and Ethics*, Grand Rapids: Eerdmans.

Sykes, Stephen, 1984, *The Identity of Christianity*, London: SPCK.

Tanner, Kathryn, 1987, 'Theology and the Plain Sense' in Garrett Green, ed., *Scriptural Authority and Narrative Interpretation*, Philadelphia: Fortress Press.

——, 1996, 'Public Theology and the Character of Public Debate' in Harlan Beckley, ed., *The Annual of the Society of Christian Ethics*, Washington DC: Georgetown University Press.

Thatcher, Tom, 2007, *What We Have Heard from the Beginning: The Past, Present, and Future of Johannine Studies*, Waco: Baylor University Press.

Thiselton, Anthony C., 2013, *The Holy Spirit: In Biblical Teaching, through the Centuries, and Today*, London: SPCK.

Thomas, John Christopher, 1991, *Footwashing in John 13 and the Johannine Community*, Sheffield: Sheffield Academic Press.

Towner, Philip H., 2006, *The Letters to Timothy and Titus*, Grand Rapids: Eerdmans.

Trible, Phyllis, 1984, *The Texts of Terror: Literary-Feminist Readings of Biblical Narratives*, Philadelphia: Fortress Press.

Tuckett, Christopher, 1987, *Reading the New Testament: Methods of Interpretation*, London: SPCK.

van der Watt, Jan, 2010, *Thou Shalt ... Do the Will of God: Do New Testament Ethics have Anything to Say Today?*, Nijmegen: Radboud University Nijmegen Press.

Vanier, Jean, 2004, *Drawn into the Mystery of Jesus through the Gospel of John*, London: Darton, Longman and Todd.

Verhey, Alan, 1984, *The* Great Reversal: Ethics and the New Testament, Grand Rapids: Eerdmans.

Volf, Miroslav, 2011, *A Public Faith: How Followers of Christ Should Serve the Common Good*, Grand Rapids: Brazos Press.

Von Wahlde, Urban C., 2010, *The Gospel and Letters of John*, Grand Rapids: Eerdmans.

Wagner, J. Ross, Rowe, C. Kavin and Grieb, A. Katherine, eds, 2008, *The Word Leaps the Gap: Essays on Scripture and Theology in Honor of Richard B. Hays*, Grand Rapids: Eerdmans.

Wall, Robert W. and Steele, Richard B., 2012, *1 & 2 Timothy and Titus*, Grand Rapids: Eerdmans.

Wannenwetsch, Bernd, 2004, *Political Worship: Ethics for Christian Citizens*, trans. Margaret Kohl, Oxford: Oxford University Press.

Ward, Graham, 2006, 'Narrative and Ethics: The Structures of Believing and the Practices of Hope', *Literature and Theology* 20,4 (December).

Wells, Samuel, 1998, *Transforming Fate into Destiny: The Theological Ethics of Stanley Hauerwas*, Carlisle: Paternoster Press.

——, 2004, *Improvisation: The Drama of Christian Ethics*, London: SPCK.

——, 2005, 'Review of Bernd Wannenwetsch, *Political Worship: Ethics for Christian Citizens*', *Studies in Christian Ethics* 18,2.

——, 2006, *God's Companions: Reimagining Christian Ethics*, Oxford: Blackwell.

Williams, Rowan, 2000, 'Making Moral Decisions' in Robin Gill, ed., *The Cambridge Companion to Christian Ethics*, Cambridge: Cambridge University Press.

——, 2008, 'Secularism, Faith and Freedom' in Graham Ward and Michael Hoelzl, eds, *The New Visibility of Religion: Studies in Religion and Cultural Hermeneutics*, London: Continuum.

——, 2012, *Faith in the Public Square*, London: Bloomsbury.

Witherington III, Ben, 1998, *Grace in Galatia: A Commentary on St Paul's Letter to the Galatians*, Edinburgh: T&T Clark.

Witherington III, Ben with Hyatt, Darlene, 2004, *Paul's Letter to the Romans: A Socio-Rhetorical Commentary*, Grand Rapids: Eerdmans.

Wright, Tom, 1986, *Colossians and Philemon*, Nottingham: InterVarsity Press.

——, 1991, 'How Can the Bible be Authoritative?', *Vox Angelica* 21.

——, 1996, *Jesus and the Victory of God*, London: SPCK.

——, 2009, 'A Scripture-formed Communion?', *Journal of Anglican Studies* 7,4.

Yoder, John Howard, 1984, *The Priestly Kingdom: Social Ethics as Gospel*, Notre Dame: University of Notre Dame Press.

Zahl, Simeon, 2014, 'The Drama of Agency: Affective Augustinianism and Galatians' in Mark Elliott, Scott Hafemann, Tom Wright and John Frederick, eds, *Galatians and Christian Theology: Justification, the Gospel, and Ethics in Paul's Letter*, Grand Rapids: Baker Academic.

——, 2020, *The Holy Spirit and Christian Experience*, Oxford: Oxford University Press.

Zimmerman, Aaron, 2010, *Moral Epistemology*, London: Routledge.

Index of Bible References

Index of Names and Subjects